VOICES of LOVE

Through ROSEANN CERVELLI

Coleman Publishing
99 Milbar Boulevard
Farmingdale, New York 11735

Copyright © 1986 by Roseann Cervelli

Coleman Publishing
99 Milbar Blvd.
Farmingdale, N.Y. 11735

No part of this book may be reproduced by any mechanical, photographic, or electronic process, or in the form of a phonographic recording, nor may it be stored in a retrieval system, transmitted, or otherwise be copies for public or private use — other than for "fair use" — without written permission of the publisher.

First printing February, 1986
Manufactured in the United States of America
Cover design by Coleman Publishing

ISBN 0-87418-024-4

A Loving Message of Purpose

June 21, 1985

For you to know this day is a special meeting of the Soul, for here will Saul very much be touched by you and the good father, and he will have tremendous Love and Respect for this project. The money is not a problem, and he will help you. Tell Saul that he is the maker of idyllic dreams, that he who dreams is the one who knows how to create Realities. And so is this, we feel, your theme, for to Dream is to create the Reality of the Dream. The good father here will be the Wisdom, and you, the Love, and Saul, the Dream, and the three of you together will bring this project to Life. We ask this book to be the Experience of the Soul, as the book is the Living Cry of the Soul to be Itself. It was the cry of Noelle, Greg and the rest of the group, and so is it now the cry of any who read it.

*We feel the first section of the book is the introduction of each to the other. We ask, Roseann, for you to tell the story, and so make the group alive with their presences, feelings and energies. Place the Reader there with the group, and then, help the Reader to let his presence be known. Invite him to mingle his energies with the group. Then, with that group of people near him, he can live these lessons with his own Loved Ones. We feel there can be a part in each section in which one can write or reflect and so on. We feel it is important for the book to be **Alive**, an Intimate Friend to share the Secrets of the Soul.*

Dear Child, tell Saul of these things, and the three of you exchange these Ideas and Visions, and so will we help you, and continue to guide you. You are Beautiful Energies... You have worked together for a long time to come to this meeting place. So now, good father, let it be the Fruit of your Wisdom, Roseann, of your Love, and Saul, of the Dream... And so will it come to Life and bring Life to Many.

A Loving Message For All Children

June 22, 1985

For you, Dear Readers, Dear Living Children of Your Souls, we ask you to know this book is a compilation of material that was spoken as Word, heard as Word, and yes, is in the process of Becoming Flesh, of Becoming the Life Substance, the Life Energies of Many. For are you so very important to these Words, for they cannot Become Flesh in the Reality of Man until they become Flesh in you, until you too can smile with the Joy of Knowing that Your Soul walks with you and you are never alone . . . that you are ever Creating and being Created . . . that you are the Life Force Itself, and are here choosing to truly Live this Life from the Soul that Knows — to the Human Consciousness that is ever seeking to be its Whole and Loving Self. As you read these Words, do we ask you not only to read them, but to hear them as that part of You which Speaks. You who know your own Inner Voice, who understand your own Inner Language and its Words, we ask that you do not get caught or trapped or confused in any of the Words of these writings. Rather, pay attention to, listen to the energies stirred within you, and the Voice that speaks from **Your Own Inner Heart, Your Own Soul** *. . .*

Dear Children, we are asking you to become an Intimate Friend with Your Own Soul. These writings will help you to think as the Soul Thinks, to see as Your Soul Sees, to dream as Your Soul Dreams. Your Soul, Dear Children, is your Healing Friend. Know it walks with you as you go through these pages. Know that these writings will stir your own Inner Voice. It is your Inner Experience that is important, Dear Children. There are no lessons to learn or memorize, only a coming to Know and Love Yourself and Every Other . . . We ask you to Know, Dear Children, Your Soul is with You and Speaks to You. The Souls of Your Dear Ones also are with You and Speak with You. So now will you Listen, for these **Voices of Love** *are Your Own Holy Self, Speaking and Listening . . . Your Words Will Become Flesh, and Your Reality, the Reality of God and the Kingdom that has ever been promised to each of You, Beloved Children . . . And so, do we Love and Bless You Ever, Dear Children, with the Beauty and Power of Your Own Creative Love and Healing Light.*

The Story of the Voices of Love

So do we wish here to give you the background Vision as well as the ever expanding foresight Vision of this Book. And of the Process of the Becoming of the Child Roseann, who was finding Self filled with an Awareness of Love, but Love which had no expression in the context of the Life she was then living. For she was then married and the mother of two beautiful children, Christine and Jessica, and she was very much learning of the Love within Self through the Love and Learnings of her Beloved Friend, the good Father. This sense of Life and Love was becoming tremendously frustrated for her — for you see, she was looking for something great and noticeable to do and be, and she did not yet fully know the tremendous sense of Healing Love and Power that one could give even to a phone call to a friend or the preparing of a meal for the children. For her then was needed two things — one, was the sense of Beauty and Givingness of her own Loving Self, a Self to which she was totally blinded — and the other, for her to learn it was in the Simplicity of Self, in this Lovingness of Self, that the Power of Universal Love Lives and Moves and has its Being. She was then filled with a sense of mission, but could find no means of expression. She had opened her Life to the Loving of all Peoples and to the Caring of the Inner Heart of each. For through several painful experiences did she learn that one could care for the Inner Heart of another, but that caring would be felt only in as much as the person cared of themselves. And so did we then feel, this Child Roseann, needed to come in touch with her own Inner Heart; so did we have to teach her of her own Caring Self before she could begin to lead others to care for Selves, to Love Selves. Then could all be opened to the Caring Heart of One Another. So do you see then, this Child with a Caring Heart, needed to care for its Self . . . and in that, in that process, did others come to care for themselves. What she learned, she shared with others, and she in turn, learned from them. When others asked for Forgiveness, so did she, for she knew her own need to Forgive Self; when one did not Trust, so did she not Trust. When one despaired, so did she, as more than once, do we know in despair and anguish, did she throw her book of writings across a room in anger and confusion at what the eyes saw in front of her, at what the Inner Eyes could not see. The group grew because each Child saw their own search for Self in the Other.

We chose this Child to write because of her need for a mission in the context of her Life. This Child who always loved to write, and was writing poetry and often letters to many, was also keeping her own Journal of Thought, as she was growing into a new Consciousness. And so you see, one day did she offer to do a prayer teaching for a prayer group on the power of words — for did she witness an argument of friends where words were so hurtful to one . . . yet their power lost on another . . . And so did she think of the tremendous Power of the Word, and so did we, who were her Guides from before Birth and Friends Forever, so did we feel with this teaching will she begin her work . . . And so did the first thrust of writings burst forth the next morning — a huge funneling of thoughts — so that the next thought was there before the last one left — the thought beyond thought, the rapid flowing of the energy of Feelingness and Universal Knowing which is so vast, it caused the hand to tremble and shake as she wrote, for was it an energy so unknown to her physical body and thought patterns. Now do you see, however, the opening for new energy is ever widening — but the initial breakthrough, so is it as the initial thrust of the Child from the Mother's Womb, as both Child and Mother are born into a new Dimension of Life . . . So was this the opening for the Child Roseann. The world for her was never the same, for there was a new Child . . . And this new Child was the Birth of a new Awareness, an Awareness so new, she did not know what to do with it except to share its initial confusion with the Beloved good Father, and seek to understand its Mystery. As the time passed, it was seen there was nothing to fear and then, One by One, did Souls — whose cry was as her own — come to this Home, for they could here find a sense of Home.

We ask you all here now to know this same process is in you or you would not now be holding this book in your hands. Your Soul has brought you here to this Home. May you find within these pages, the sense of Home, the Loving Place where you can **Be You** and not be afraid. You can know others have read these words, argued of them, laughed of them, trusted them, forgiven them. These words have not only met a written book or a typed page . . . They have met Souls . . . And you see, the surprise, the Loving Surprise for you, Dear Children, is that they were written for **You** . . . **For You are the Words** . . . The Universal Knowingness and Feelingness that poured forth was of You . . . And now through the pen of this Child, it comes back to You so that You may hear it in the precious Silence of Your Own Loving Heart . . .

A Prayer of Angel Teachings
"To Live From My Soul"

To be truly and deeply and sincerely Compassionate to myself, so that I can be truly, deeply and sincerely Compassionate to Every Other.

To know that there is a Place of Lovingness inside of me where I can Live with the Angels, with All Life. To Know that in this Place of Lovingness, I can place all my fears and worries and dreams. All of Myself lives in this Place ... So do All Others ... So that there are no dualities, but only Oneness with All Life.

To know that I can expand and deepen everything, that Wants and Needs are but signals from my Soul to my earthly Self, that what I truly want and long for is something much greater than that which is in front of me, and I Will Listen to My Soul and follow its Voice and Wisdom.

That the God Essence flows through me as Creator, and that My Reality is Created as I so Choose to Create and Use His Power. If I choose to use His Power for Loving and Forgiveness, so then am I in touch with that vibration in the Universe, and I will attract to myself the Lovingness and Forgiveness of Jesus, the Angels, of wondrous Saints and Holy People. I will know that I am made of Loving Essence, and I seek to meet and connect to the Loving Essence in all People, in Jesus, the Angels, the Sun and the Clouds ... You see, All becomes Blessed and Holy.

That I am Holy, that All Life is Holy, and I seek to Live and Experience the Holiness of All Life ... that I may Know the Holiness of All I Do Not Understand.

That the Known and Unknown are parts of the Mystery of Me, that they are not separate. That there are realms of unknowns in that which I know about myself; that I Know in Essence much more about the Unknowns than I give myself credit for because My Soul Knows, and My Soul is Wise and Loving to me, and leads me to the path where Known and Unknown are One, an ever expanding Mystery, the Spirit that stirs me on and on.

That I seek to Live in the Isness of Myself and the Isness of all People and the Isness of this Holy Moment. That I seek no longer to mold myself into something I am not. Rather, that I can Bless Who I Am and then let the layers and layers of wax around me melt away, and that I can be in form, the true Expression of my Inner Light. That I also know I have no right to own or possess anyone or mold them into what I would like. So I Bless and Love Everyone for Who They Are this Moment . . . For I see their Light, I seek their Light, and I Know That Everyone Lives far beyond what their personality seems to show.

That I seek to live in Timelessness, so that I do not judge things in sequence or think in terms of cause and effect, but rather, I seek to live in Eternity — which is now unknown to me — but I can touch it here and there, when I touch an Eternal Moment . . . when I experience a Moment of Life that remains with me always, that colors my whole Past and is my stirring to the Future. When I can live in Timelessness and feel I have forgiven that which my body or emotional Self does not have the strength to forgive. When I can go to a past moment when I've hurt someone, and now Resurrect that moment to a new Consciousness, and fill it, consciously now, with Blessings of which before I was unaware . . . and leave the moment yet open to more Growth and Blessings.

That I Live with a Healing Consciousness and know that I can empower every kind word or deed or thought with my Love. That I can empower my Love with the Love of Jesus, and so bring Healing Life to all the moments of my day. To Know that All Life is Healing Me — that every person I meet is my Healer and my Friend, and Lives in My Soul to Heal Me.

To Know that every sorrow I feel is shared and understood by the Angels, that their Compassion for me is their Love and more expanded Vision of Myself, that I am never alone. To know that my every Joy also is shared and deepened in me, as is every pain . . . And I seek to bring this Joy to all, not by anything in particular, but just in the Living of it. That I know my Intentional Heart truly counts, that it too is a Life and a Vibration, and that when I do something that hurts another, that they may also feel the Intentional Heart which never wanted to hurt, but acted in Innocent Ignorance. And so for me, that I can Bless the Intentional Heart of every Other, and know that no one really wants to hurt me, that they would not hurt me if they knew better at this time . . . just as Jesus said, "Forgive them, for they know not what they do."

That Life is Holy, and every experience is Holy. That my Life is the Gift of God to me, and so I am in humble awe of my Self, of my feelings and dreams, for it is all God, expressing Himself through me. And knowing this then, I seek to give Glory to Him by being the most Beautiful Me I can Be. Yes, as a beautiful painting hangs humbly on a wall, testifying to the Skill and Imagination and Wonder of the Artist and the intricacies of his Mind and Vision, both his Soul and Artistic Self, so am I... That I can know it is God Who Lives and Dreams and Acts through me, and as Jesus, say, "I have come to give Glory to my Father." That I do not Honor my Father by telling Him what a terrible job He did in Creating me, and now can He please do me over. But no, that I am a Wonderful Creation... I just don't know it yet... But by purifying myself of my expectations, of what I think I should be, I let God express His Vision through me.

That as I Love myself, I cannot help but Love every Other, for they are in me as I in them and we in one another. That I may not experience this, but I Trust Jesus, his Love and Compassion — this Personhood as Someone I'd like to be. And I trust if I follow the Inner Light, if I go to my Inner Kingdom, I will find all the Peace and Joy he has promised.

That Giving and Receiving are One and the Same... That my Giving is the Joy I Receive. And so, I look for nothing, but I just Give, in quiet, where only the Heavenly Father Knows... And I Know that I am Being taken care of by my God and by the Energies that Love Me.

That I am in the midst of a wondrous process, that all I Know and Understand will grow — perhaps become even more unknown and mysterious as it does so — but I am in touch with my Inner Knowingness which tells me that this is okay, because I am Alive here and Peaceful here in this place.

That my own Energy is so important to my Life, that my energy strengthens and receives strength from the Angels, from Life itself. That my power, in all its Gentleness and Lovingness, is God's power. That others may use God's power for hatred and violence, but I see where that only brings sadness and pain. And God's power, as shown in the Lovingness and Compassion of Jesus, brings Healing and Peace. That it is my Choice to use the Power of God for the Love of Him and His Whole Creation, and that I bless His Name When I Bless the Name of His Creation — and yes, that includes me, When I Bless my Name as Well.

Reflections

Reflections

The Healing Awareness of Loving You

*The First Writings
December, 1982*

Voices of Love
MATTHEW, ELIOT AND JOHN

The First Writings
"Words"

December 3, 1982

The essence of God is in the words we speak and the words we hear — that is how we experience God. We may not be experiencing God correctly because of words themselves that get in the way.

We are so used to having everything described, defined, and we limit things that way. By attributing the Word of God as the Words of Life, we open Him up to all our experiences, especially the wordless ones, where there is so much love, or so much compassion, or intimacy or sorrow. God is especially there when we cannot speak. And so, to get in touch with God, we shouldn't use words — as when someone is so sorrowful, a touch is better than words; to show someone we love them, a kiss or a hug says it all.

Words are stumbling blocks; words change the meaning of what we are feeling. Because so often, the one who is listening hears what he needs to hear, so often our words don't communicate what we mean to communicate. And as we watch the reaction of the listener, we get caught up in the response, and then lose what we are saying.

Words reveal us on a human level; when we leave out the words, we touch the Divine. So Jesus said to *Live* by the Word — not necessarily to speak his words — but to keep them, live them.

By our words — "I know mine and mine know me" — we know who we are and where we belong. We do not go to a place where words do not welcome us. Signs and billboards and so on, tell us by their words where we can go to experience, to be *ourselves* And so, we follow the Word of God to Be Ourselves, to Become One with God, with His Word, His Reality. The words we hear and give power to are the words that shape our life.

Speak words of kindness and they will be spoken back to you and we can cover the earth with the good feelings that come from Living the Word of God. A glass can be empty or full, and so our words can be empty or full, depending on the content, depending on the context in which we live these words.

Words are rich or poor; we are wealthy or in poverty according to the words we speak and hear. And we can *choose* the words we want to hear. We can hang up a telephone if what is coming on the other end is not the Word of God. We can choose not to hear, and that's OK. Jesus spoke words, and tried in so many different ways to get the people to understand his message. We have the duty, if we want to get the message across, and it's not sinking in, to try it another way, to make it touch the experience of the listener, to come to the person where he's at. If he's hungry and warm, don't give him a coat or a house or a bed, for he wants food. Reach him where he's at.

Speak kindly, lovingly, richly. Speak with the Soul of Jesus on your lips, and your Life will be full of His Peace, and you will give that Peace to everyone around you.

* * *

Words themselves are God speaking to us . . . Let our hearts hear what He wants to say. Words are like a growing vine, intertwining itself in the Consciousness of our Minds. The vine can be channeled neatly onto trellises so that there is an order, a growing to them; the fruits of the words can be picked easily, clearly, in easy reach of all to taste and gather. Or, if we do not order it, the vine grows madly, gets caught in weeds, and the fruits are left for the birds, who in their freedom, see the fruits for what they are — the Gift of God to feed them. So the Words of God, of Jesus, of helpers, friends, are meant to feed us and nurture us, to grow and bear new fruit.

Words guarantee us a particular lifestyle. In choosing your words, you choose your life, and you have the power to make your life whatever you want it, need it, wish it to become.

Through the Power of God's Spirit, the words will heal, make you whole. Healing is the Wholeness of Living the deepest meaning of every Word we experience in our Life . . . the Word of God, the Word that brings us back Home to the Father, that brings us back to the Wholeness, the complete Perfection of His ever-creating Mind. Let God's Word flow through you and touch you. Give it space to become, give it the room it needs to breathe and live so that it becomes part of every fibre, every cell, every atom, every spark of Life within you. The God Essence is the Word of You . . . *You are the Word* . . . Each of us is the Word of God. Let us think about the responsibility we have to be the Living Word of God in the world today.

Praise God with your Words, praise the Life that you are, praise every word you speak, for you are speaking for, with and through the God of Life and Wholeness that breathes in you. Use words with your love. Handle them with care, for we are all so fragile, and we need all to be handled with love and care. As Jesus cares, so we care for one another and we care for ourselves. We care for Jesus and all that He is, and all that we will be because of Him.

* * *

Words are the picture of your Soul. Think of a painting... The artist paints and he wants to mix just the right colors, in just the right amounts, to create the feeling, the reality of the painting that he wishes his viewer to experience. He chooses his colors very carefully, his brushes carefully — everything that goes into the process of making the picture the wonderful creation it is. So we must choose our words carefully, place them in the right places, knowing always, that our words not only reach the ears of our listeners, but are touching their Hearts as well, their Souls. We have no conception how deeply a word may touch another, for there are worlds within people, worlds that they have not yet explored themselves. Often, a word may touch one of the worlds and elicit a reaction that even the person does not fully understand the intensity of. "Why do I feel this way? Why did that word make me cry? I'm stronger than this, I know better. Why did I let that remark bother me so?" It is because it touched a world within us that we ourselves, with our conscious minds, have yet to touch. The word is like a foreigner, a stranger in our Beingness, and it takes time for it to become a part of our Soul.

Words guarantee us of who and what we are. We need the words now, but when we touch the Divine, we do not need words to know who we are, for we *Become the Word Itself*. We don't need words to describe us when we Know that we are in Essence, the Word Itself, the Word made Flesh. And when we have lifted ourselves up to the Divine, the Word becomes Divine; no longer enfleshed, we experience the Heavenly Reality.

Do not speak words that are hard for you to say, do not say them aloud to another, for the falseness of it will show through. Rather, speak the words you wish to transform within yourself, to yourself, as if you are rehearsing the good words and the good feelings that you wish to give to others. Then like fruit that is richly ripened, the fruit of your words will taste their sweetest to the ears of the listener, it will touch their Hearts, ring with sincerity, and the power behind the word will really touch the person. If you speak words that you really do not mean, though the words themselves sound right, negative energy will reach the person. So when you cannot speak to another what you want to say, don't — rather, speak it in your Heart where it will grow stronger and stronger. Then, when it finally comes forth, it will convey all the Good and Loving Power that you want it to have.

* * *

The Word of God is like freshly fallen snow — white, pure, covering everything with a blanket of its softness. Even the trees, weighed down with the snow on their limbs, they just bow to the snow and let it rest on their branches till it melts into the core of their beingness, into the branches, into the earth from whence they come and grow. So the Word of God rests on each one of us — let us let that Word *BeCome* — *Be,* and then, *Come* into us, pore into us as melting snow pores into the ground, and nourishes the very plant from whence it fell.

The Word of God is Everyone of Us Becoming God, the Word of God is His Spirit Alive, Active, Loving, Caressing each of us. The Word of God is the Caress we give to Life, to One Another, to the Flowers, to the Earth, to All of Creation.

Words are ripe for us to hear at certain times of our life and not at others. We cannot rush the process for a true understanding of words, just as we cannot rush a child to speak for the first time. We can expose him to all the words in the world, but it is the child who chooses when he will speak his first word. So too — in the living of the real meaning of Living the Word, the process cannot be rushed, and we must be patient with ourselves and each other. We will come to Live the Word when we are ready to *choose* to do so, just as the child chooses, from the vast vocabulary stored in his mind, he chooses what his first word will be when he is ready. Living the Word is truly difficult, yet once we know it, once we are aware, it is easy, it becomes our way of Life. Even Jesus grew to a Realization of Self as the *Living Word* — it took him time too. So Jesus is ever patient and understanding of us. He watches us as we struggle with our misconceptions and our longings for Truth. As a gentle parent, who knows that their young child, who is in kindergarten, does not belong in sixth grade, so too, Jesus knows that the best place for us to be spiritually is where we are right now, to be hearing the words we are hearing right now, to open ourselves to an Awareness of their meaning and then to Live the Word, Live as God within us, to the best of what we can do — which is, exactly what we are doing now. We are all special people, we all know words and what they mean. Now it is time for us to stop thinking about words so much, and *Become the Word, Become the Christ* — *Be* the Christ as You *Come* to the Christhood. It is a Becoming Process that is Infinite, that goes on and on, until we are in Oneness with Christ, Oneness with God and all His Creation.

Listen well to the words of your brothers, but more, listen to his *Wordlessness* — listen well to the words he does not say. Try to capture the unspoken words in his eyes, try to sense the unspoken words in his Heart. Feel the wordlessness, love it, for what you are loving is the Essence of that person. *All that we cannot say is so often who we are.* Be attuned to those closest to you first, your closest family members and friends. Later, you will hear so many things that go unspoken. And then when you speak, asking the Spirit of Jesus to speak with you, you can say the loving words that that person needs to hear. Somehow you will know the right things to say for you will know that you are talking with Christ, for Christ, as you speak to that person. The smile on their face, or a light in their eyes will tell you that a certain word that had been the foreigner, has been transformed, and is now a comfortable word, a comfortable presence in their Beingness.

Appreciation of Beauty of Others Without Belittling Self

December 3, 1982

Each Soul is unique and special and a blessing to everyone around them. Each Soul gives forth the goodness and wonder of God to the empty spot inside of us. We see what we lack, and we fill it with the presence of another, drawing from them the energy, the beauty we feel we are lacking. We fill up the empty spot. The mistake is in thinking we don't have the same qualities just because we are filling ourselves up with an *Awareness* of what we are missing. We become aware of what we are missing through our contact with others — they give us the energy to stir up those qualities that are *already* in us. We take from these the Awareness — we do not diminish them or ourselves by admiring — we only raise ourselves higher to the Perfection we want to Be. "I need to grow in Awareness of who I am and who I want to be." Give God His Glory by Being this Perfection He Is.

Helping others is helping ourselves. In admiring others, we admire ourselves, for the same potential for Godness lives in us all. So yes, someone is wonderful, well so am I, and someone can sing, well so can I . . . maybe not as well yet, but I'm singing just the same and my melody fills the air just as anyone else's.

Be happy for the Beauty of your friends, for they see the same Beauty in you. You are all one circle, filling each other up, setting up fields of energy, of Light — all of you — complementary, glowing and brightening. There is no meeting of coincidence, no chance meetings. Remember you are all one human family and you are all the cells of each other. As the body needs all the parts functioning together, so too, the Reality you are creating and living in needs everyone there, present, with all their beauty, with all their empty spots. You are a Beautiful Child, and so are your friends. You are all part of each other, and you will all grow from knowing one another.

Be happy and know that you are in your right place, and Dear Child, do not cry, for you are a Loving Channel and God is waking you up to the Beauty that is within you. So be peaceful . . . You know me . . . You will be a beautiful Channel of help and healing to many. Now rest, and have a good night . . .

Joy

December 4, 1982

There is a need in all people to be free and easy, to be the joy for themselves that they are searching for. They go here and there, looking for joy, but they must come to learn that they will not experience joy until they see themselves as joy, as giving joy to others, as *Being Joy* themselves. The world is chaotic today because people are so busy finding joy. They go all over, to wrong places, good places, places of temporary joy... but they have not sought to look within, for the joy that is within, in the Christ, in the Fullness of Being, the Fullness of Joy.

Always we search for the meaning of happiness — parents look for it in their children and then are disappointed when their children show themselves to be human, when their children elicit feelings in them that they were not looking for, were not hoping for. Man seeks it in his job and gets disappointed when he knows he's reached success, but never touched it. So joy is within, in the realization that we are not meant to find joy in the outer, material things. Joy is the quality of the Soul where we meet God and Know we are Him, where we are so One with Him that everything else in our Reality becomes One with Him, all the tributaries of a river going to one big ocean of Self, of God. Joy is the result of Souls' recognizing their Godness — that is what a real smile is, a real contact of the eyes, the deepest sense of *I see, feel, touch, taste God in Me*. And so we are One, and we are joyful in our sameness and in our uniqueness. We are joyful in our mission to live and fill the world with God's Love. Joy is the cornerstone of the Soul, the place where we recognize God as the Breath of every cell of our Being, the Whisper behind every word we speak, the total rapture of Loving and Being Loved. We are a Joyful People and now it is up to us to give this Joy to others.

Healing Consciousness

December 4, 1982

The energy that you are feeling is flowing throughout the Mind and Consciousness of the whole human family. The energy is sleeping in so many and needs to be tapped through the love and caring of one for each other. Love is the only source that will awaken the energy, the healing energy that is flowing in us all. Sickness comes because the energy that comes from Oneness is sleeping inside of everyone. That is the real sickness of the human condition, and it manifests itself as cancer and all other diseases. Deep inside, we so want to be who we truly are, that we cannot help but become sick because we are so far away from our true identity. So to heal, the God energy must awaken in everyone. Everyone must come to see who they really are, and they will come to see who they really are, as they come in contact with people who have touched the energy — they want to be like that person, they want to experience the peacefulness, the laughter of that person and so, they will imitate and pattern themselves and feel the energy within. They will spread it all over the earth — the earth is going to surprise itself with the Joy and Beauty it will cover itself with. The energy is never ending, for it flows forever in every cell of everybody. It flows sleeping, waiting to wake up from the dream of sickness, waiting, waiting, and then, suddenly, it's there, and it all makes sense, and everyone knows why we're here — to love each other with the fullness of the Universe, the vastness, infinity, growing and growing. It cannot stop ever, for God's energy can never stop flowing — it touches one and another and another — the very earth and flowers need to feel the energy too — all of Creation needs to awaken itself to the God Power, the Life Force within. And you are doing it, and so are so many others, and it will be. The earth is in for such a surprise. It will learn, we all will learn, happiness is for Real and can be a permanent state, for the energy of God will be permanent within each one of us. We will feel the prayer of everyone, we will all be touched and we will all be One with the rest of the Universe, as we were so long ago in the very Beginning, in the very Beginning of *Isness.*

Prayer

December 7, 1982

    Prayer is the Whisper of the Soul's needs to oneself, that is really prayer. When we pray, we pray to ourselves that we will know our needs and know that the Healing is within us. Prayer brings us closer to ourselves — it is getting to know the Divine part of Self. The little Christ Child in each of us prays to know itself, so that one day, it will blossom into the Christ Consciousness of Adulthood. Look upon prayer as the cry, the gentle sigh of wishing to be a grown-up. Like the little girl with her mother's make-up — the child does the things of adulthood, and imagines and becomes. But to the child, she is not really imagining; she doesn't know the word for imagining. She believes she really *is;* for those moments of play, she becomes exactly what she wants to be. In her mind, there is no distinction — no sense of, "Now I am a Child and for a few minutes, I will be a grown-up." We are talking here about two, three year olds, before they become aware of the difference between imagination and reality as it is.
    And so now with us, in our prayer life... We pray as babes, we are unaware that we are not quite there yet. We think our prayer is true and touching God, and then we wonder why we're not heard. We create God into all sorts of shapes and sizes, so that He will fit our conception of what we want Him to be. And that is OK ... We keep praying, especially by being silent. Slowly, it will dawn on us, that when we pray, we are truly praying to ourselves, to the Power of God and Life that is locked and waiting in each one of us. Then we will no longer be the little child who is playing grown-up — we will touch the maturity of our Soul, we will know through prayer who we really are.
    Our words are our prayer, they are one's discovery of oneself. So the way we pray, the words we say, bring about what we experience. We answer our own prayer according to our beliefs, according to the words we say. That is why we must be careful with our words and really try to practice *Wordless Prayer,* where we just listen in the silence, and feel our life, and just try to feel who we are ... If we had never met ourselves, if we knew nothing about ourselves, no past, no future, no ties, no place — just

ourselves as Life — what would we know, sense, feel, touch, about the *Life* that flows through our Bodies, our Minds, our Souls? What do our eyes tell us, our hands, our feet? Each portion of us reveals Life to us. This is a good way to begin to learn how to pray — to strip ourselves of everything we think we are and meet ourselves for the first time. Much of the good we know of ourselves will come to mind. Any negatives, if we trace them back to their source, we will find, are man-made, and if man-made, then we can erase them with a stroke of the Will. We are going to learn to pray to the Christ Child in us; then we will eventually learn to pray to the Christ-Consciousness, the Resurrected Christ.

In our prayer efforts, each Christ Child will meet one another, and we will all help each other to see how when we pray the old way, we are as the little child who doesn't know she's imagining she's a grown-up. She believes she is, yet she isn't. As we pray to the Christ Child in us, we will Know the Truth about prayer and about God, and that prayer will make us Free.

A Healing Life

December 7, 1982

    The Universe is so happy when everyone is Healed — that is the real purpose of life, of our relationships with one another. We are constantly involved in a healing process for, everything we say and do is meant eventually to guide us back to our Healing, to bring us to the Truth of our Being. We are surrounded by the people who are our best doctors — our husbands, wives, children, closest friends and so on, they are our best doctors, for subconsciously, we act out the roles, the jobs, that help to awaken all the sleeping energies in those we love the most. We know a great deal more about each other than we think we know, otherwise we could not be so skillful in performing our roles that help spark the energy in others. So we know when to be there and when not to be there for a person, even though we do not know that we know. Then what happens to that person as a result of our absence or presence can serve as a catalyst for him. It is up to the person to use his life situation, his every life experience, to see all as his action in God, and so to use every event in his life as an opportunity to see God for himself and others.

    Healing for ourselves and others is a matter of listening to the God Power, the Healing Energies inside of you, and acting on them. Whether it is a thought to call a friend you haven't seen in a long time, or to buy someone a gift, or to bake a cake for a friend — whatever it is — all these things are part of the ongoing healing process for ourselves and others. So what we are saying is to use every event in your life, every person in your life as opportunities for healing — to awaken the energies within them as well as within yourself. In this kind of healing, doctors and patient both have medical degrees, both are always healing one another through their very involvement, existence in each other's lives. Praise God, asking for the Awareness to see where the sicknesses lie, for the Grace to say the right words at the right time, so that each person can be involved in a continual healing process the whole day long, constantly having experiences that are slowly evolving him into what he is searching for, and which he is already. He is only waking up. When you are physically asleep and you desire to get up in the morning, you don't have to do anything except wake up. You don't have to go outside or eat anything to realize you are no longer sleeping. You even remain in bed, but with the difference, you are now awake into a new experience, the experience of being awake. And so with healing, you don't have to do anything, but to wake up to the fact that you are a Child of God, you are Perfection, therefore, you are Healed. And oh yes, the Universe is so happy for you and for itself when one more Soul wakes up to the Beauty and Perfection inherent within! You know the Parable about the Prodigal Son — that's why such a great feast, a great celebration — he came Home to his Father and in so doing, he came Home to Himself. And the Parable of the Lost Sheep too — such rejoicing among the shepherd and the other sheep. And so too, the Universe is so happy when each Soul wakes up and is Healed. We become the Healers we are meant to be, Healers for ourselves and for those we love the most. Isn't it a joy when you know you've been a little spark that helped to make life better for someone? It heals you too. So once again, just be aware of all the people around you and say, *"I heal myself as I awake myself to the healing needs of others."* And the Universe then will be a happy, peaceful one, for with everyone healing and caring so much, there will be no time for war — we're too busy trying to make one another happy. The world will be a happier place because each of us is in it. We each have our special unique job of healing, our special way of healing those who touch our lives. They're in your life for a reason — make sure you know how much you need each other. Make sure you always fill your healing days with Love.

December 8, 1982

Live every moment to its fullest Healing Power. At first, you will need to *make* yourself aware of the healing needs of every moment, to give reminders to yourself, as when you first learn anything new. Eventually it becomes automatic — it becomes such a part of your Beingness, that soon, you can do it without your conscious thought. It just is, and you exude it without even thinking. It just becomes part of the aura around you... It can be felt...

Healing does not just take place at Healing Masses or Prayer Meetings. *Healing is every Moment of Life,* every word we speak to another in Love and Trustingness and Goodness. This is the real Healing of Life. It is when we are always in touch with the thoughts and feelings of others, when we perceive their needs and try to reach them, when we open our eyes to the depth of wants and hurts of others — yes, even seeing the things they themselves do not know. Try to be as aware of Healing as breathing — you do it, don't even know it — it is the Life in you. So think of Healing in these terms, as such a part of Your Beingness, that you are doing it all the time. Though as we said before, at first, it must be a conscious effort on your part to bring yourself to this Awareness. Gently become aware of the Healing Grace awaiting birth within you. And your Healing Grace will touch others, and so spark their own . . .

December 8, 1982

The wonder of Creation is that we are always creating, always by our new thoughts and experiences. This writing is an act of Creation and it is needed for you to develop and grow. You are a child and have much to learn . . . but you also know much, and it is your job, almost your duty, to be strong and tell others of what you know.

Do not cry . . . You are a flower just blossoming and you are afraid to show your face to the world . . . But you also know you cannot fold the petals back in. Once they are opening, let them unfold and let the bees come to gather the nectar, and they will carry it to other blossoming flowers. Stay with this image. You are a beautiful flower and you know everyone else is a beautiful flower too. And because you and the others know this, you can reach them, for they sense you know of their Beauty. And everyone likes to feel their Inner Beauty touched, recognized, appreciated by another. This is Healing. This is the work we are to do.

The Healing Touch

December 8, 1982

So much Healing Power lies in the touch, the way we are touched and touch. This is the experience of this night, in the loving touching of the children in the bed, in the rejection of the touch of the husband. You see the difference, in the giving of touches and in their rejection — one heals and soothes, one keeps the wound ever open. Always we should be aware of touching one another — healing hugs, healing handshakes, healing, loving taps on the head, the gentle touch that says very simply, "I care, I understand, I love you." A Healing Touch draws you . . . You want to be close to the warmth and love of that touch. A Healing Touch is powerful and can go deep into the Essence of your Being — it's love and caring, a catalyst or spark that awakens all the love and caring within you. Healing is an attunement to the needs, to the empty spots of others. It is knowing and saying the words that are most important for the other to hear. And so it is a matter of attunement to the person we wish to help, becoming so One with that person, that we feel his needs as our own.

We do not feel a Healing Touch ever offends anyone. Even if at first, they draw back or seem to refuse the touch, the feeling they are left with afterwards is, "That touch felt so good and comforting, I would like to experience that Healing Touch again." The power is not in the touch — it is in the Love behind the touch. This is what truly Heals — the Love of the God Essence for His Creation and the Response of the Creation to its own Essence, its Acknowledgment that it is a Loving Universal Power that wants to Heal and make us Whole.

Hands that are cold to the touch in a normal setting often are flowing with frozen energy, with the energy of all that is to be. The energy is definitely there, but it is frozen and needs to melt through experiences of caring and being cared for. Hands that are warm and inviting are open hands, open to loving, to blanketing the hurt of others with their warmth. In hands that are hot, the energy is flowing strongly and there is an attunement of Consciousness. The excess heat is that overflow of attunement that can touch another who is missing something so strongly. A Healer, whose energy has been activated by its response to another, is like a glass, filled to the top, the faucet still running and now overflowing. That overflow just pours out to the one in need, filling the empty spots. The Healer loses no energy, for he is already filled. He has no choice but to give to others, or else, he feels he is wasting himself, and he feels incomplete no matter how very much he may be giving. The more overflow, the more dedication, the more love, the more the inability to say no to anyone in need — for you sense innately — the energy is there. We are here talking of spiritual energy, for surely, one may be physically very tired, but still be overflowing with spiritual energy. Here again, the matter of Wholeness — we can feel physically *and* spiritually overflowing as we tune into the Awareness of our Wholeness, as we cease to categorize ourselves, "I'm strong here, I'm weak there." No, just accept, *"I am Wholeness."*

We were speaking to you in sleep of this Healing Touch. It was what made you aware of the touching of the children and the husband. You felt warmth and coldness in a new dimension. One should not offer a Healing Touch when one does not want to. Instead, try to offer the Touch in your Heart, visualize it, for everyone is deserving of our Healing Touch, perhaps even more so, those who have hurt us ... Until we can touch them with Love, we have truly not forgiven, and our resentment of that person will stand in our way ... Visualize in your Heart the Forgiving Touch ... It is something you can work on ...

Dialogue with Higher Self

December 8, 1982

The flow of the Spirit of Life is forever enriching us; we never need fear that we will not have the energy for a particular task. Always, we can tap the energy of Life that is constant, continually available for us. Any task can be done; we just have to Know the Source of Life never leaves us. Always, Creation is taking place . . . Creation as an activity of the Mind, Creation as the product of the Mind too, Creation as a process as well as a result. The energy of Creation lives in all, and it is important that we have this concept of Creation as an on-going process. It didn't begin and end with Genesis. New Creation is going on all the time.

Maintain a Dialogue with your Higher Self so that you may come to know it better. Speak to yourself, encourage yourself, so that the Truths that are of the Higher Order may flow through into your Consciousness. They are waiting to be activated by your Will, they are the Sleeping Beauties of your Soul.

Talk to yourself in a Dialogue, "I am Higher Order of Consciousness and I invite you to flow into me in my daily life. I invite you to gently show me where I lack the Living Reality of the Christhood, where I need to be purified so that I may better see myself for who I am." Picture Self as a roomful of candles, each candle representing a quality of the God Essence. You will imagine yourself lighting these candles of your Beingness one at a time, and you will imagine yourself glowing brighter and brighter, surrounded, enveloped by the light of your own Christ Consciousness. And if once in a while, a candle is extinguished by a human failing or misconception, be gentle to yourself, and with Love, take the flame from another candle of your Being and *relight any extinguished candle . . . You are recreating Self from your own Essence . . .* Do not strike a match, or go to another source to light your own candles . . . Light from Self's Flame, energize your own energy. Yes, your light, everyone's light shines for all, shares all. We all want to be a Sun, a source of our own light. We do not want to be the Moon which is dependent on the Sun for its brightness. No, for reflected light, borrowed light from another, is good, but it is temporary, it will not enliven us. We are all light as the Sun — we shine for ourselves, for others, but we shine through our own Power, that is really One with the Power of the God Essence.

So again, speak to your Higher Self and let it know that you don't understand, but that you are a Humble Servant and that you are available to do the work, to light the candles of Wholeness within you. Do not be afraid to be Whole, for that too, is a new condition. We get used to our dependencies — they are good and yes, cling to them while you must, but keep in mind the idea of Wholeness and of Responsibility for Self.

A Meditation

December 8, 1982

    An ancient Castle stood amongst the ruins, the landscape was desolate. Trees bare, fork-shaped trees, interlocking, hiding the ancient Castle in the distance. Fog and steamy mist envelop the scene. There is an earthy scent to the air, fog and sky, one and the same. The ancient Castle stands as the monument to all that once was. It has seven towers and each tower forms a silhouette against the graying sky. It gets darker and darker . . . stars here and there . . . the trees, all bent and twisted, are harder to see . . . the Castle barely visible in the Darkness . . .

    From the road I am standing on, I see the Castle vaguely. It is inviting, a shelter. I walk and walk and walk, and yet never seem to get closer, never seem to approach it . . . Yet, I walk, walk and am getting so tired . . . All of a sudden, I wake up as if from a dream. I am in the Castle, yes, the Castle is in me and I am in the Castle. Those fork-shaped trees are outside of me . . . The gloomy, misty scene is outside of me now, somehow I bypassed all that. I don't remember climbing in and out of brambles and vines. I just remember I was there on the outside, they were there before me — now, I'm here on the inside of the Castle and they are behind me.

    I am now in the Castle, and I go about with a torch in my Mind, in my Heart, and yes, I light candles and chandeliers and lanterns — any source of light available to me now — I light, and I keep lighting, until it is morning and the sun has come up. Light flows through the Castle and the fog has lifted . . . Now in the light, I see those seemingly forked and bent trees are full of buds of new life, and in a flash, everything opens up, everything is Recreated . . . And what was foreboding and outside of me and so out of reach is *not* the Center of my Being. When I leave the Castle for my morning walk in the sunshine, I leave the door open so that anyone may come in and visit, and taste and see how good the Lord is.

    And so, the Journey of the Soul . . . We think we are outside the Castle of our Dreams, that it is far away, unattainable, clouded in the mist. Actually we are living in the Castle all the time. Though we walked and walked, the Castle never really got any closer, for we were living there all the time — we just didn't know it. We live in the Father's House now . . . We have so many different addresses, so many parts of us that live here and there, but truly, we are *already* living in the Father's House, the Kingdom of All, the Castle of Higher Consciousness, Clear Thought, Good Health, the Castle of Life. Enjoy your Life and do not be afraid.

On Belonging

December 10, 1982

The need in people to belong is so deep . . . You sense this, but keep it in your Mind and Heart today. The belonging we are looking for is the total belonging to ourselves and to what we truly are. We try to belong to everything else and everyone else, and in some ways, this is good in that it serves as the preparation for *Belonging to Self.*

Belonging to Self involves the Responsibility for Self — the ability to stand up and know that we can do great things in the Name of God, of Jesus. Jesus belonged to Self and so, he could belong to everybody through the ages. And everyone can relate to him so much that they feel they can belong to him, totally, completely. Jesus accepts all — all people, no judgments, no rationalizations, no denials. He can accept Everyone because he accepts Self. And this is what people don't know — once we truly Know and Accept Self, once we truly Belong to Self, we can never judge anyone or criticize anyone again. The Spirit of Self-Love transforms itself, yet maintains itself, into the Spirit of Love for Everyone. Only those who do not love Self see and judge the empty spots, the shallow spots of others. And so to be in the Presence of One who belongs to Self, as to be in the Presence of Jesus, is a Healing for Self. The energy of that person radiates peacefulness, trust, acceptance, blessing of others. Where can any kind of judgment or expectation fit in? And so again we say belonging to Self is what brings you to belonging to others. Belonging to Self is the total Healing — for we take total, infinite, permanent care of that which is of God. There is no sickness, no distortions. Rather, there is a strong, deep sense of the God Essence and our place in the Universal Love, the Universal Dream that belongs to us, just as much as we belong to it. So today, think about Belonging to Self, and as you do, you will see how easily it flows, if you belong to Self, as Jesus. You draw all unto you, for you all belong to one another, all sharing, rejoicing in the Knowledge of the God Essence of All.

Think clearly of how the people in your life belong there, of the freedom they possess to belong there, and of the freedom you give to them. Belonging must involve choice — no one belongs if tied to another with chains of steel, for that is imprisonment and can only bear lack of harmony, of peace, of goodness. So many people wear rings on their fingers which are so heavy, they weigh the whole person down. Others, who truly belong, can wear rings that lift them up to new heights of Love and Belongingness, giving them a taste of what it is like to Belong to the Universal Goodness within Self. Never force self to feel what is not yet felt in the Soul, but at the same time, do not blind self to what actually prevents you from feeling the love, caring, gentleness, and tenderness that you want to come to feel for all in Universal Love. It is good to be a beautiful Universal Soul, but we must never become so Universal as to lose touch with the Personal. The Personal Touch between Souls, the growth and development of the Personal, spreads to the Universal and then, back to the Personal. We do not soar to the Universal and have a generalized, non-responsible love for all. Without the Personal Touch of Souls, we cannot touch the Universal — for God is both, Personal and Universal, and One in Belongingness.

Children belong to their parents much more than parents belong to children. You belong to God much more than God belongs to you. God is the Freedom — we are the ones attaching ourselves to Him. We go to Him with such sincere dedication and rituals in an effort to belong to Him. But truly, when you cease to attempt or belong, that is when you truly Belong. And as it is for human experience and human Belonging, so it is in Belonging to the God Essence.

God does not Belong to anybody — He just *is*. We are the ones who want to belong to Him, and so we feel we belong to Him, "God loves me, cares for me and so on." Actually, God belongs to No One. *God is Belonging,* but Belonging to Itself, of Itself, to Everything, to Nothing, to All that Is, and All that Is Not. When you belong to Self, you are Freedom . . . You then can give, and feel and share the sense of Belonging to a Loved One. It gives you the experience of Belonging to Self when you spiritually, beautifully experience this sense of Belonging through a Loved Person, a special Soul that is in Love with your Soul . . . that so Loves itself, it has no choice but to Love All.

Belonging is good and beautiful . . . We are only trying to make you aware of deeper levels of this word, this feeling. *To be a Healer, you must Belong to everyone and no one.* You must belong to Self and to God, but not in the sense of being tied with chains to the service of a God who expects this or that. You are not God's slave, to do this or that without your Free-Giving Will. You are God's Companion, an Expression of Life who so freely belongs to the Isness of God, that you will do anything He wills, as it is your Will too.

We must think about Belonging as the intertwining of One Life . . . not two separate lives becoming one, but One Life intertwining itself with itself in a sense of Belonging. We need to belong to everyone to belong to Self; we need to belong to Self to belong to everyone. It is the same, the Oneness of all. Don't rush the need of belonging to fulfillment. You don't need to rush for belonging, for you already belong to all by your very existence. By the very simple fact that you are an Act of Creation, as well as an Expression of Creation, You Belong.

We bless your wonderful friendships; on higher levels, they touch many. The love of human beings for each other touches everyone in a very direct way. Many feel the power of your love, though they do not know the source — they just know what they feel, and what they feel is this sense of Belonging. And as more and more people touch each other with this Healing of Belonging — it is like a gentle rainbow, an archway of love, all different colors, yes, but all mingled together to make the rainbow what it is. If one color were missing, it would be empty — it would not be a complete rainbow with all its beauty. One color missing, yes, it would still be beautiful, but not complete . . . And that is how we see this human family on Earth today. So many beautiful people, beautiful colors, but some are missing. The rainbow is incomplete. So too, when one does not have a Belongingness to God, the rainbow vanishes and there is only separation from Life, a sky without the miracle of the rainbow. We should see rainbows all the time, for it is God's promise to Man — but we don't, because of the human weakness and suffering, because our vision is blocked.

Belonging creates in us a need to see others belong . . . that is why the power, the urge to Heal. We cannot stop ourselves from wanting everyone, not only to see the rainbow, but to *Be* the rainbow. We want to work with people like you and others who are ready here, for people will believe you, since they cannot believe us. We are too frightening a Reality for them . . . Let them see it, touch it, feel it through you and all the others who are involved. You are speaking for us, for God, as Jesus spoke for the Father, the God Essence. We thank you for this precious time... You are so kind, for you will not let your personal need for belonging within, stand in the way of the Universal need for touching the Belongingness to the God Essence in All. We wish you a goodnight...

On Awakening

December 12, 1982

The Power of every Soul is Love. Love that stems from the Soul is also what gives all Power to that Soul. We heal in proportion to the way we love, selfless love, for the service of God, man and self. One of the most selfless loves is the Love of Self — we so love ourselves, so trusting in the God Essence that we can let go of concern, worry, anxiety, insecurity of self. We are so sure of Self-Love, we let go of the self, and thus have so much more fruitful energy to give to others. The sorrow we sometimes feel when we are lonely is the spark that can bring us into an Awareness of Self as Universal. Yes, the personal self is lonely and in need of companionship, but then, touch the Universal Self, and the personal self that is suffering can be healed, as it centers itself in its true Beingness and Oneness with the total God Essence, joined in Oneness to All and especially so, joined to those in need of us, to those we need. We are joined, not in helpless dependency, but in the fruitful interaction of love and energy.

Do not waste your loneliness. Rather, use it to bring yourself into an Awareness of who you are . . . Use it to know that you are lonely for what makes you Whole. That very longing for the Wholeness is what spurs you to seek the life experiences that fulfill and complete you. You cannot know the fruitful Joy of Completion unless you are spurred by an emptiness or a longing that brings you to the true Source of Completion, the eternal, endless, fulfilling of Self which you experience in all the avenues of your Life. Some avenues seem to bring you more fulfilling experiences than others. This is a blessing, and is not to be judged, for each avenue is giving to you what you need to experience in just the right amounts. There is a Universal balancing going on all the time in the Souls of Seekers of Enlightenment, and that means *All Souls,* for All Souls seek Enlightenment. Yes, that they are alive and breathing, they are seeking Enlightenment.

The balancing of needs, the adjustment of avenues of fulfillment, takes place in those who open their eyes, who wake up to the Enlightenment Process. It is only those who blot out the beyond, the spiritual, the esoteric, who get so caught and trapped in material Realities — they are the ones who suffer imbalances in this adjustment of energy. The true path is there, the balance is there for all, but they are so clouded by misconceptions, by inappropriate choices, that their Consciousness receives the imbalances of their choices — and so, men murder or are unjust or hurtful to others. They are seeking their fulfillment, yes, but all the avenues are out of kilter, and so they cannot make choices that are in accord with Divines Order, Harmony, Peace, Oneness, Brotherly and Sisterly Universal Love. Be aware of your Spiritual Self, trust in the God Essence, and the avenues toward your fulfillment balance themselves. The Path seems clear, and though once in a while you experience a distortion, a separation, this becomes an exception rather than a rule of your Reality. You know enough to re-direct your conscious thinking in the way you want. Once you have control of your thinking, once you can steer your own ship from within, then even if you have an occasional shipwreck, you know exactly what to do, you know where you want the boat to be going. Better to be shipwrecked once in a while with course in Heart and Mind, than to be a luxury cruiser, just lost at sea, directionless, just there in the middle of the sea, tossed about by wind and waves with no set course or destination — endlessly, in the middle of the sea. That is true separation from God . . .

You are closest to God when you know that you are in charge of yourself, for then He can send His power and guidance, and you can be the ship of Life you were meant to be. God also tosses about with those on the ship going nowhere, but that is the God of Incompleteness . . . The God of Incompleteness can only be Complete, and so He waits, waits for those Souls to set a course and stop drifting in the sea. The only incompleteness is the incompleteness of being Complete, and since Completeness, by its very nature, implies Perfection, Wholeness, then we know that in God, there can be no Incompleteness. The incompleteness is God as man in search of Completeness — the Completeness is man as God, at One with the Father and the Mystical Joys of the ever creating, never ending Journey to Fulfillment.

You are very much on this path now . . . The pain you are feeling in your body is your body's reaction to the changes, to the vast changes pouring into your Consciousness. You feel a little paralyzed by all you have to do, by all you know you want to Become — and so you find it hard to move, hard to stand up. It is like a pocket of gathered energy in your side; it is waiting to burst out, and it will, as you become less and less afraid, and more accustomed to this new adventure in Awareness. Your body has reacted in this way to the many changes within you. You will experience this less, as you let go. Though you are so open and willing to serve, still there is a part of you yet a little afraid, not sure of how you will be a Channel or why. Your Conscious Mind will adjust to the vast changes pouring through from outside its own realm of experience and accustomed mode of thinking and intuition. There is much energy flowing in your body now; your body will accustom itself and will come to assimilate the energy and the powerful surges into deeper Consciousness that you experience.

So again, Dear Child, do not fight against the beautiful Reality you are. Love yourself and love your Mission . . . We feel you will come to do both as you see your role and place. Your pains will disappear, as you accept the energy and let it burst into your Being, rather than fighting it with fear, confusion or self-doubt. You chose and are chosen to work for the Glory of the God Essence, to work for the Healing of each Face that touches your eyes, for each Heart that touches your own. You have accepted this on many levels — but not all yet. We feel assured, Dear Child, much will be clearer to you, and you will find your pain will ease away. Meanwhile, just bless and send forth this energy in the form of love to all your friends and loved ones — for really that is what all energy is — Love Energy. *It is the Love Energy that Transforms and Heals.* Take the energy trapped in your sides, this beautiful Love Energy, filled with the Beauty and Joy of the God Essence — take that energy and send it out to the world, for Healing, for Awareness, for the Attunement of All to God and His ceaseless Creation.

Do not cry, for you are doing so well and we are so proud of you. We bless you and guide you. We are all parts of the Whole, becoming Whole in joining our parts together . . . yet always, a Wholeness of Self as well as a Wholeness of the Other . . . Yet not two separate Wholenesses. It is One Whole, One sense of Belonging, One Endless, Personal Universal Quest of Fulfillment . . . You become Whole, I become Whole, We are One Whole . . .

Separate Together, the Blessed Trinity, the Mystery of the Trinity ... the Father, the Source; the Son, the Actor; the Spirit, the Action ... All One and Indivisible and Complete in their Completeness of Each Other.

December 13, 1982

The Essence of all Love is in loving Self, so as one comes to love Self, one also deepens in capacity for the love of others. You will find your love for everyone increasing with your growth. Your joys will be more joyful and your pains more painful; your loneliness more lonely, your ecstasies, more and more fulfilling. But as we said before, there is the continuous and simultaneous process of fulfilling and emptying. That is the search — the cup is never quite filled, for even as it is reaching its peak, that moment is passing and it is leaving the cup ... So this is Life. The more aware you are, the greater the depth and intensity of your feelings and life experiences. You are open to everything, you see the opportunities for joy everywhere, with everyone. Be open, *Be Alive* to the Divine Potential within every experience, every human experience you have. Let the love you feel go out to all you will touch this day. It is good to keep returning to the wellspring of Love, for it is Divinely fed and it will never run dry. As you feed others, so you will be fed.

Let your tears flow. You are like a young child, taking the first steps into the Essence of Christ Consciousness. You are feeling and living with greater Intensity and Awareness. Do not be afraid, for this is an adjustment. As when one gets new eyeglasses, what seems at first as distortion, is really helpful to the eyes, a clearer vision — it just takes some getting used to. Be patient with all your experiences, and see them all as your avenue to fulfilling the Fulfillment, as your clearer vision into how things and people really are. You are feeling the birth pangs into a new style of Living, a new dimension of Awareness, a new sensitivity to All, especially those that are closest to your Heart. Everything has deepened for you. You are overwhelmed, but you are also blessed, for in this new Awareness will you help many. That is the real beauty of your tears, Dear Child, for every adventure into your own pain, will make you more aware of the pain of others.

On Forgiveness

December 14, 1982

Forgiveness is the Healing of one's own Heart, for as you forgive another, so you forgive yourself. You forgive self for allowing, on some level, a separation from the Harmony of Oneness. When we forgive another, we are also forgiving, accepting and blessing the Incompleteness of Awareness of the God Essence in that person. We are forgiving their empty spots and filling them instead with our own Awareness of the God Essence. The Peace that the forgiven person feels is that Peace of Awareness flowing within him. Man never feels truly forgiven, for the empty spot is never quite filled, and there lives in each person involved, the memory of the need for forgiveness . . .

There is a restoration of balance according to the degree of our Attunement to our own powers of forgiveness. Do not judge how another forgives by how you forgive . . . Do not assume that everyone has the same need for forgiveness or that the memory of a separation is the same. The more attuned one is to the Universal Godness, the less the need to ask the forgiveness of others. Often, we ask forgiveness, not for anything we've done, but as a reflection of our own lack of self-love. The more Aware we are, the less the need to forgive others — for one's understanding and compassion leads one to love the sinner in spite of, sometimes because of, his sin. We use the word sinner in the sense of one who makes a mistake, out of harmony with the perfect order of Love and Godness.

Forgive self for the need to ask another's forgiveness; forgive self for the insecure need to ask another to forgive you for simply being who you are. See everyone's actions as their seeking, perhaps in a distorted way, but sincerely seeking nonetheless, their own Fulfillment of the God Essence. There is no need to forgive one's searching for self. *So Forgiveness is really the Awareness and Blessing of Another's Search for the God Essence within.* There is no need to be angry at the detour another takes — just keep that person in your Heart and Mind, so that as he lives his detour, his proper destination is always held high. We cannot change the detours others take; we can only, by our Awareness, seek not to follow detours of separation within ourselves. Also, do not seek the forgiveness of another, for if you seek the forgiveness of your actions, you are separating yourself from God. You acted from love, concern, from your own level of Awareness — you do not need another's forgiveness, for that is giving another power over you. Forgive yourself of wanting forgiveness... See your own search for forgiveness as the need of filling up an empty spot in you — that is Healing — filling up our empty spots with an Awareness of the God Essence in each person.

"Forgive" in the ordinary sense of the word as you use it, implies judgment — one was right, one was wrong, so I forgive you or you forgive me. No, we are here speaking of forgiveness in another way... When Jesus said, "Father, forgive them for they know not what they do," he was not judging them... He was Healing them of their lack of Awareness of the God Essence within them. They knew not that they are Divine Sons of God, just as he is. The victim of their ignorance, Jesus is the Victor of all Forgiveness, of all Healing. Jesus remained in perfect Attunement with the Father at the moment of his Death, for in asking the Father to forgive others, he was imbuing them with his own Awareness of the God Essence. He also healed himself of any human despair, for he raised all his pain to the Healing Needs of others, to the Blessing of their empty spots with his own Awareness of the God Essence in him and everyone.

So one best forgives by learning there is no need to forgive in the ordinary sense of the word. See forgiveness as Healing any separation of oneself from the God Essence, as Healing and Blessing and Resurrecting others to the God Essence within them. It is a restoration of Harmony, Goodness and Love in Self and in All.

We know we are truly forgiven when we ourselves no longer feel the need to forgive another in the judgmental sense... when we can stop wondering if we are forgiven and accepted by others because of a lack of self-love... when we can stand firm, knowing that we are truly Living the God Essence within. Then we will no longer be judgmental in our own actions or judgmental of the actions of others. All is of God, all is Becoming God. Even the acts of Human Consciousness which are most horrendous — murders and so on — all need to be healed. All need to be seen as the vast deep, empty spots of the lack of God, the Incompleteness of God which yearns for its Completion. So we must Heal the murderer by our seeing the God Essence in him. If we just see him on a human level, as a bad person, as one not worthy of our love, don't you see, we keep his actions alive, and the murder takes place over and over again. So we must Heal him, and we do so by our Attunement to his Divine Consciousness, by our not judging the Human Consciousness, by seeing his separation from the Divine, by our prayers and Healing, by being the bridge for him to touch the Divine Awareness of the Beauty and Sacredness of all Creation. Once aware of that, we scarcely dare to pick a flower, for not wanting to separate it from its Source of Life. How could we even contemplate the taking of another human life? We must forgive the murderer, not just with our saying the words, "I forgive you," and then patting him on the head, to do the act again. No, Forgiveness is Healing Action, the catalyst to restore the murderer back to his rightful place in the Father's Kingdom, the Prodigal Son, the Lost Sheep . . . Until we are all One in the Forgiveness of Healing, we will never cease to Heal. We are all part of each other — one tiny pull in a perfectly woven cloth makes it now imperfect, changes the nature, mars the Perfection. It needs to be mended, perfectly woven, with no pulls — a smooth, perfect cloth of Love, Forgiveness and Healing . . .

Heal self first, attune Self to the God Essence within. You will find no need to forgive others, for no hurt can be done to you. All is for your good. By attuning Self, you are a catalyst to help all others attune themselves to an Awareness of these Universal Laws of Healing and Forgiveness.

Creative Healing

December 14, 1982

We are all sparks of Creation, we are both a cause and an effect, a result of Creation and Creating continuously. The Creative Mind is Everyman's Mind. It is not true that one person is more Creative than another. No, rather, that one is more attuned to the Creative energies within them, more aware, and so, more in touch with them. As some are more in touch with their mechanical abilities, others their counseling gifts, so others are more in touch with a freshness of outlook, with new ways of expressing the Self. We term them Creative, for actually what they are doing is expressing themselves, their experiences in a fresh approach. And as we are so conditioned, so deadened to many stimuli around us — we just react without thinking, react without reaction — those who are more in touch with the Creativity available to all, express self in a new way and so, touch new notes of response in their listeners or audience. It is new and different; it sets up a new and different pattern in those we are interacting with — a new Face of Creation . . .

Where does Creativity fit in with Healing? Through creative approaches or creative ways of doing something or saying something, we provide others with an experience that might bypass their conditioned patterned response, which really traps them in their sickness or misconceptions. So a new and creative outlook, an outlook of optimism and excitement of life can help stir the sleeping Creative energies within us. We can term this Creative Healing, for it stirs the sleeping energies of Creativity within others — they awake and experience newness and freshness. And they can then apply this to their Whole Beingness, to their relationships and so on, and so Heal themselves of despair and sameness. Many people are sick for this very cause — they feel their lives will never change, they don't like their lives, and so they get sick. It is Creative energy misapplied. They use energy to get sick, and it takes much energy to stay sick, to keep going to doctors and so on. We have to help people tap this energy and transform it into a Joy for Life.

Creative Healing can take many forms — singing, writing music, a moving liturgy, an appropriate gift that comes as a surprise, a clever joke or tease. In everything we do or say, we can try to touch the Creative energies within us, and so stir Creative Healing energies in others. What we are trying to show you is that *everything one does or says can be a Healing,* can be an act that motivates others to come to an Awareness of the constant flow of opportunities that we meet each day for Healing. The material will support you in your efforts, give you a foundation and you can spring forth from there.

Healing Consciousness and the Mentally Ill

December 15, 1982

The Healing Consciousness is the answer to the human condition, to the hurts, worries, anxieties that instill themselves in us, that stay there, fester and grow, and manifest as sickness, mental, emotional and physical. In severe mental illness, there is complete and total change in the structure of brain function and the development of awareness is not possible. In other words, that which we are trying to wake up, and then activate and channel to those persons who are severely mentally ill — if awakened — there is neither the proper functioning, nor the working machinery that can do anything about it physically. Spiritually, however, much is happening.

We are talking here of very severe, institutionalized Children of God. Physically, they may not experience a Healing, but the Healing Consciousness we are speaking of here is Spiritual . . . Our prayers touch their Spirits, which are more alive, more dynamic than their trapped bodies, than the defective mental condition that is just so cloudy, so lost, that our offerings of human kindness often cannot be perceived or experienced. Their human experiences cannot be comprehended by the average person. We are not saying they are lost Children of God; on the contrary, they are advanced Souls who seek to experience Divinity in the worst possible of human conditions, that is, the complete cloudiness of human awareness, the extreme heaviness of a human dimensional experience that must seek its Divinity in a new way. Their Soul-Purpose effort is to keep that Divine Self alive and intact, though human conscious experience seems distorted, and out of synchronization with the rest of mankind.

We humans do not know how to heal the mentally ill. We attempt to heal them as if we were teaching a man to fly — the tools we are applying cannot work with their physical and chemical processes. We do not yet know what they are to be. We can easily teach or retrain a bird to fly, but we cannot do this to a dog — we must teach a dog something different, something in harmony with its own Nature. And so with the severely mentally ill — we can heal them when we know what it is they can be, and then, channel our energies there. And what they are, are Human, Divine Souls who chose to experience a greater Divinity, but a seemingly less than human experience... Could their spirituality break through this less than human awareness and raise it up? Could they advance spiritually by living a less than human awareness?

The severely mentally ill also serve as channels of help for their families and those who work with them — they serve as catalysts to raise the levels of Awareness, of help, giving and so on to those who care for them. Their very presence makes one aware of the Mystery of Life and imbues the others with a sense of awe and wonder at the beautiful Creation of the Human Mind which functions in accord with all Creation. Humans need to experience the opposite to fully come into Awareness of their Beingness. The mentally ill, in institutions and homes, are seekers of the Truth of Creation. Their Souls have chosen this existence, and on a Spiritual Level, they do much to raise the Healing Consciousness of those around them, though they themselves may not experience a Healing Consciousness of Self — not for lack of Will, but for the lack of proper physical equipment. They are beautiful Children of God who need to be touched in the earthly realm at their own level of understanding and awareness. One with an IQ of 30 will not graduate college — do not expect this, and then feel, when not achieved, there was no Healing. Though God has the Power, the Soul has the Will... Each Soul has willed to be where it is, and it is for us to praise these Souls for the task they've undertaken and for Being the Light they are to so many.

Growing To A Healing Consciousness

December 16, 1982

Seek a Healing in all you do and feel... See yourself as a fragile yet powerful rose, petals open to the Universe, such a powerful attraction and Oneness to the Universe that the petals never fall off — always they are blooming, attracted by powers of Love and Oneness. Always see yourself as the Rose, the love, the beauty that you are. The thorns on the rose bush need not touch the rose, though they are part of the many parts that add to its Creation. So your pains are part of you, and so are your joys. Your joys heal the pains — your pains bring you to fuller joy. So do not reject the pain, the loneliness you feel, for you are aware of the limitless reaches of the joy you can touch and experience.

The wonder of Healing is that it is something everyone can do — yes, even a small child can heal. It is as much a part of our nature as breathing; so we are imbued with a Healing Energy that seeks the Wholeness of Self and the Wholeness of All Others. There are no shortcuts to learning the Healing Consciousness, for step by step, one ever enlarges perceptions. We must be patient with Self and not get angry when we are not manifesting in the physical what we are experiencing mentally and spiritually. There is often a lag in the physical, as old memory cells need to be replaced with the new patterns that are taking place in our Minds and Hearts. In the kind of Healing that we are here discussing, we do not place a band-aid on the wound. Rather, we want to erase the wound, so that there is no need for the band-aid. So the Healing Consciousness is in all of us, so long as we have the functioning equipment. As we discussed earlier, severe mental patients with brain damage and other abnormalities, cannot manifest the Healing Awareness in the same way, as a man without arms or legs cannot swim in the same manner as one not so handicapped.

Young children can teach us much of Healing... "Unless you become as one of these, you cannot enter the Kingdom." The trust of child to parent, the dependency, yet the independency of life... The trust of the child who has been given love, the trust of the child is Healing. Those children who never experience love and trust, they are like those grown-ups who are confused, searching on all the outskirts for love and attention, but never having that Inner Core of Love touched . . . Love starts in the Inner Core and then reaches out to touch many. We cannot reach the Fullness of Life by trying to attract this or that outside source, and then trying to create it in the center. It is like trying to reverse the growth of a plant — from the bloomed flower, then to stem, roots, seed. No, the process is reversed. And so it is in Love and Oneness — it must begin from the Inner Core of Being, the Love and Trust within, and then to reach without. This is what makes the young child able to walk away from his mother for the first time. His love and trust have become so internalized, such a part of the Core of his Being, that now he can move out to others. And so the Awareness of the God Essence . . . before we can really heal others, we must Love and Trust the God Essence, as the child loves and trusts its mother. Only then can we move out to touch others, to heal others. We cannot go to this or that person and bring the God Essence from the outside in. These outside influences strengthen and confirm our belief and practice, but they do not create the God Essence Awareness in us. Only we can acknowledge the existence, the ever birthing Awareness of the God Essence within us. We give birth to Self, we nurture Self in our Healing of Others — just as the child nurtures self as he reaches out to others for new experiences. But before he can reach out with love and trust, there has been planted in him, an Inner Core of Beingness, of Love and Trust. It is in him, it grows and expands — but it had to be there to begin with. And so, the God Essence is always in us. Healing is the Awakening and Acknowledgment of this God Essence as the Inner Core of our Beingness. And so, as we wake up, we want to wake up others to share the glorious Light of the Divine within.

On Fear

December 17, 1982

Fears, all fears, stem from a loss known before. It stems from a joy known and lost, from a continuous re-experiencing of loss. And so, anytime we begin something new, no matter how sunshiny the day, no matter how positive our outlook, there is somewhere in the corner of our Mind, a fear of the loss of this experience.

When Human Souls first separated themselves from the God Essence, they thought they had found something wonderful — an existence independent, a sense of their own power. They tried to recapture the Divine when they realized that, though they had use of power, they did not experience the Inner Peace which they had known before. For you see, the Divine Essence had already been planted in their Soul Memory, in the Inner Core, and they could not forget it. They saw that they had the use of the power, but they also saw that the more they used the power to achieve their goals, the more separated they were becoming from the Divine. Soon the realization of existence as totally Human Souls separated from a Divinity, made no sense, brought no peace. The Soul Memory of Peaceful Oneness with the Father is what drew man back to his search for the Divine.

So Human Souls developed a God Concept of Fear — what would the God Essence say and do upon their return? Would they be punished as they punish their own children when they break their laws? As the fear grew and grew, so came the desire to appease the God Essence with sacrifices, dedication or suffering. In their desire for the return to peacefulness, they clouded the journey back to the Father with misconceptions and false images of what He was. The very peace they were looking for became a fearful journey, for they did not know in their Hearts and Minds, what the God Essence would do to them once they got there. They lost the Awareness that it was the very beautiful Memory of the God Essence that was bringing them Home. They lost the Awareness that they never really could separate themselves from God because *He Is Who They Are.* What Souls had done was to attempt to use the Power of God, separate from God, and that cannot be. All is God from the very Beginning — God as Good, all Knowledge and all Perfection — and any opposite, only reveals the loss of that. So any attempt to use the God Power selfishly or to hurt others, reveals the loss of what God is, reveals how far away Souls have drifted from the true meaning of Life. When man formed his misconceptions, it was out of his fear; he had so lost the true Awareness, that he created his myths about Divinity and saw them as Reality.

Always the sense of loss... and yes, our fears always reflect this sense of loss. If I once was joined in Oneness to the God Essence and I let that go — then might I not also lose this relationship or this job or this happiness? *The fear of loss is behind every fear we experience* ... .When we find a beautiful thing or person in life, we tend to want to cherish it into hiding. We become possessive of it, "I do not want to lose this," and rightly so. But we go about preserving it in the wrong way. If you find a beautiful flower, you don't put it in a box in a dark corner in your closet. What good is it, if you can't enjoy it and share it with others to enjoy? So, too, in our Rediscovery of the True Conception of God — we cannot keep it to ourselves. It is an Awareness that longs to blossom in the Soul of Everyone, for Everyone seeks to experience the Oneness of long ago, Everyone seeks to live without that fear of loss which clouds every endeavor. Once you are in the Realization of the God Essence, you lose your fear of loss. You will never lose your Peace, your God — whatever Expression of Goodness and Truth that God is to you — you will never lose these. They will only deepen more and more in your Awareness of the Active, Loving God inherent in all Action, in all Creation.

As you are now aware of the God Essence and as you pursue your further Realizations, you can begin to know for sure that you have no longer lost it, for this is one search where the very searching is the finding. There is no "It" or one thing to find at the end of this long journey. No, *the Searching is the Finding,* and so you can already say, "I am free of my fear of loss, for as I am finding, I have already found." You can inculcate into your Consciousness, the Awareness that, "As the God Essence is within my Inner Core of Being, how can I fear His loss?" Only an act of will can do that again — a desire to go back on the road of fear, sickness, distortion and so on. Once is enough... Our wills are directed towards Goodness, Healing, Perfection — not their opposites. And as we are aware more and more, we find more and more, that we must, by the very nature of the journey, fear less and less.

Do not be afraid, the God Essence guides you . . . Everyone rejoices each time the Spirit of Awareness shines. The world will be such a wonderful place — no wars, no violence — only perfect Understanding and Peace, as soon as we know we have no loss to fear. There is sunshine enough for everybody. In the Awareness of who we are, we rejoice . . .

The Healing Awareness

December 19, 1982

The Healing Awareness is like a cloakroom . . . It is dark and there are many coats in the room. You go along, feeling this coat and that, looking for some identifiable sign — some button or zipper, some shape or color, something that will let it stand out as yours. And after touching this or that coat, you finally find one you think is yours — you feel it here and there, and finally you put it on, and you *Know* it is yours. As you leave the darkness of the cloakroom, you are wearing your coat for all to see. So is the Healing Awareness — each Soul has a coat of Awareness — but it feels a little different, acts a little different, heals a little different than anyone else's. That is why so many different healers, personalities, techniques are needed — so that the needs in different people can be touched accordingly. So it is good to recognize auric healing, the laying on of hands, meditative healing and yes, medical healing — all of these healers meet the people whom they can touch most. Nothing is by coincidence, and the world is in need of these many healers. But all healers must, despite the variety of techniques, have the God Essence, the Christ Consciousness as their Source. And most important of all is that the healer must make known that it is not he who is doing the healing. Really we are not healers, for we are as healees, as the employees of the great Healer, the God Essence, the Christ Power, Activated and Resurrected to the highest levels of Attunement. The healer and everyone else, including the hurt or sick person, are the *Channels of their own Healing,* for the Power is within, the Kingdom is within.

Never attempt to heal without first attuning Self to God, opening Self as a Channel, as a receptacle that the God Essence can use to bring about the Wholeness of its Children, which is part of its own Beingness. Remember the story of Androcles and the Lion — that is a beautiful example of Healing. And it is how the God Power works — good recognizes good, and can only be repaid with a kindness greater than the original. So every time you acknowledge God as Healer and self as healee, you are taking the object out of the lion's paw. Someday, you will find in how many wonderful ways your life is spared, spared in the sense of

Blessed with Freedom, set free again to roam, wiser each time for the experience. Healing never stops, for one Healing is the spark for another and then another — a series of explosions, set in motion. Know that one Healing contains within it the seeds for the Healing of all Mankind. Healing initiates a person into the Awareness of his power. Once you have this Awareness, experiences become very powerful, and in God, you Live and Move and have your Being. The power is often recognized as beyond human capability, and it becomes viewed as something miraculous. Rather, Healing should be viewed, not as a list of miracles, but as an Awareness of Life, a Rediscovery of Self, a new Attunement, deeper, more penetrating, an every day event — not anything extraordinary. Miracles do happen and affirm our faith. These are spontaneous miracles. But actually, miracles occur every day — we just don't recognize them as such. Every wave of the ocean is a miracle, for who could invent such a machine that churns three-fourths of the earth and makes waves constantly, ceaselessly? The action of the ocean is supernatural, as is our very own breathing . . . Yes, our Breath too is Divine. So let us not look only for the spontaneous, miraculous cures. Let us look also for the small seed, the buds of Healing Life, the growth of the Healing Awareness Consciousness . . . It too is a Miracle.

How Can I Handle My Emotions Better?

December 19, 1982

We cannot help you handle your emotions better — for what is better? We cannot judge... Your Soul cries out with tears. Bless that your Soul cries, for it is a sign of its aliveness, its dynamic birth pangs, the push, the contractions that lead to its Birth. The birth of a child consumes one with awe, but it is painful. You do all sorts of things to numb the pain, and you feel you can't take it anymore, and then, your child is born... Though the pain is there and the contractions still take place, you don't feel it as need, for the presence of that child, its arrival into Consciousness, numbs the pain, diverts the energy. So too, in the growth of Awareness, your tears, this emptiness, are these your moments of labor. When the newly born child is now resting on your chest, you do not remember the pain... It has passed, and the memory of pain is changed for the joy it has brought.

We feel you will handle your emotions, knowing that your pain is for the good of many. You can raise your pain, even as you experience it. Experience the birth pangs, for the Child waits... Live your pain, for it is your greatest teacher. Your sense of emptiness, of loneliness, is turning you to the Divine. Do not fight these fears, Dear Child, but use them, bless them and know they are helping you to love yourself, yes, love yourself, *for you cry for all you are not*... You are becoming aware of all you are not... In this process, you become aware of God and all that God Is. And that God Is, and Lives in what Is not. You see, the God of Completeness and Wholeness lives in Incompleteness. And the Miracle of Healing is when we know that what Is and what Is Not — what you are and what you are not — are both God in Beingness and both are being led to higher Awareness.

We too here have much to learn, for it is Eternal... It is all Eternal and Infinite, Beyond the Beyond. Even from our perspective, this expansion of the Universe continuously, ceaselessly, expands our Consciousness to levels of higher Attunement, levels where our Spiritual Essence melts into Infinity, and then itself becomes Infinite. How can there be an end to this search, this quest, when Infinity itself yearns for its own Infinity? You are astounded... Yes, the Universe is as vast as your vastest thought can take you, and then Infinities beyond that. We even limit Infinity by its definition — without end, which means just that. In our concept, we sometimes think of Infinity as a place we'll be. No, Infinity is nowhere, is everywhere, is beyond itself, experiencing itself and then rediscovering itself — as you are doing, Beautiful Child, you are doing it on your level here on Earth and you will do it forever . . . So do not be upset that your emotions get in your way, as you put it. Your tears, your emotions, bring you to a deeper experience of your longing for Oneness. Raise yourself as Jesus raises himself to Oneness with all people. Do not feel badly that you become aware of your needs through your love. You are learning to lean on yourself. Depend and trust on the strength, the power and the wonder of your own creating, dynamic Essence. So do not let your fear of pain prevent you from doing the Father's work. Lift the pain to the Father's work and it will be less painful, more joyful, for it will be attuned, and working with and for the God Essence. We cannot and would not manipulate any Will. Always, the final decision for anything — including your acceptance for channeling these writings — is a matter of Self's Will. We thank you for this time . . . We are hopeful that these lessons on Healing will touch many at the right time. Meanwhile, apply them when you can, as you become more and more aware, and we will help you . . . And please love yourself, Dear Child, for you will find happiness in your Love of Self. And so do we love and bless you, and wish you a good night . . .

On Oneness

December 20, 1982

Oneness is the fruit of one's delving into self and discovering there is no self — the self ceases to exist, thoughts cease, memories cease, all that we normally think of as self ceases. There is the pervading sense of being everywhere and nowhere, totally filled, totally empty, totally aware, totally unaware. To be One, the Soul experiences dualities at the same time, no time. Everything we know becomes meaningful, meaningless. It is a state of feeling totally caught and trapped, yet totally light and free. Everything that the human condition has split into two, is now just *one* State of Being, *one* absorbing, penetrating, infiltrating experience, where the Energy of Being is soaring out and penetrating levels of Non-Beingness — that is where Oneness is. It is something we reach for, just to touch it, hold it, embrace it, yet as soon as we become aware that we are holding it, we lose it. For in that one moment of thinking of Oneness, we separate ourselves from it — it is now a thought and an Awareness, not the *Isness*. This is why it is Infinity beyond Infinity, for we must even lose our Awareness of Oneness. When we are aware of it, we are separate from it, for it becomes an experience we have, rather than *the Isness We Are*.

Oneness is the relinquishment of the desire to Be Oneness. We cannot chase it, pursue it; we must give up the pursuit and just Be — *Be* Attuned and *Live* in Attunement to the Divine in every person, every experience. As long as we are apart from one aspect of Creation, we cannot be in Oneness. If we fear the Earth will tremble, we are outside of Oneness, for there can be no fear in Oneness, a State of Being where fears cannot exist, as darkness cannot exist in Light. *Oneness Knows Itself, Is Itself.* We do not grow into Oneness or reach Oneness — words like these distort what it is. Rather, we *Become* Oneness in a very true sense of Becoming. In Oneness, are we active and dynamic to do the Heavenly Father's work, despite the cost of pain, for in Oneness, there is no pain. Jesus died in Attunement of the Father's Will, and He experienced a Rebirth into higher and higher levels of Oneness. You too must die a little in Love for the Heavenly Father.

You have touched the Oneness so briefly, and now it is a hunger in you, and now you are more and more aware of each separation from it. This Oneness is the state you want to be in with all of Creation, with every Soul here and beyond, with every flower, every blade of grass, every grain of sand. Yes, there is much to do — Infinity beyond Infinity. There is much to do, yet nothing to do, except to be Aware of the God Essence, to have it so permeate your Consciousness, your Awareness, that you breathe it, become it, taste it more and more . . . Be patient with self, be patient with your tears, your fears, for they are so necessary to your unfoldment. You are deeply loved and cared for. Do not feel you disappoint the Heavenly Father with your tears. Be patient with self, and enjoy this beautiful awakening within you. Feel our Presence, for we are with you in your joy and your loneliness. Now be a good Child, and love yourself, as we love you . . .

On Healing Consciousness

December 21, 1982

Awareness of Self holds the key to Healing — it is the key that unlocks all the doors, for an Awareness of Self includes in its very Essence, the Awareness of Others. You cannot be aware of yourself without also being aware of everyone and everything in this Creation surrounding you. It is only those who are not truly aware — those who may know the psychological self, but are totally unaware of their Spiritual Reality — these are the ones who are self-centered, but not Self-Aware. In their self-centeredness, they may or may not be caring of others. And when they are caring, it is good, but they use their goodness as merit points for their own ego, their own salvation or whatever other ideology they hold. The caring is genuine and it touches those helped, but again, it is a matter of level and degree.

Caring from the Healing Awareness point of view touches more than the surface, for it goes into the spiritual fibre of the person being helped, the aura, the electricity, the magnetic field about a person. With the Universal God Essence Healing Awareness, Caring energy seeps into whatever open spaces, waiting areas, that the person who needs help, has open. So the person is touched in a way beyond human caring, beyond a good deed that works for you and works as good points for me too. Caring with the Universal God in your Hand feels different to those being helped, for other areas of self, besides the physical and the psychological self, are being touched and awakened. Stay aware of who you are when you talk to people and smile to people — which should be done much more, the smiling. You have so many smiles to smile . . . Don't waste them, but show them to the Universe, to the flowers and plants. Show your smiles, smiles which emanate from the love, the power, the strength, the goodness, the wonder of this tremendous Force of Life within you. If only you could see it, be it, oh, the Joy that would be in your Heart to shine on others! Believe in us, Dear Child, do not seek to verify or doubt yourself any more. This is Real and you are Real; we are Real and Healing is Real.

There is a new dimension to Healing, a new dimension to the words "caring" and "good deeds." With the level that we approach to help others, that is the level we can tap in those we want to help. So if we come with half a loaf of bread, we give our whole half loaf — but if we come with a full loaf and then two loaves, three loaves, the ever multiplication of the loaves and fishes — don't you see, we fill more and more people to their fullest. What we have in ourselves is what we bring in our Awareness to others. The more we develop, the more we reach within and experience the Joyful Eternity of God every day, so the more we touch these spots in others. How can we bring to another what we don't have? If we give them our very best, please know, we can also give them more.

We want everyone to know how Real this all is, and that we should not get caught up in meetings or gigantic plans. It is the planting of seeds of Healing Consciousness = this is the task. We must first make sure we ourselves tune into the Self and sense this depth, this power in us. Love it and bless it . . . Do not feel ego important, do not feel that you have a gift to bring to others, as "Here, take this, I give it to you." No, for no one wants to be force fed. We want instead to touch gently, caringly, by our Presence = just by our Presence and our Awareness, we will change the world. Always remember how Jesus came as the Christ Child, and this is how we are to bring our message = as little children offering a flower, a gift to others, a sharing of a gift, of an Awareness. Erase the ego, erase the self in a self-centered way. You will not separate yourself from your work, for *You Are Your Work.* You don't say, "Today I will heal." No, it is, "I am Healing each and every moment . . . I Heal myself and others, the flowers, and by my caring, even the little ant on the floor . . . *I Heal, I am Healing, I am Healed . . . That is My Name."* The message of Jesus Christ Healing will touch all, and the world will be a better place. It will be the Image of the God Essence, its Creator. It will change. Bombs will not change anything, but the gentle Healing Touch = that is what will change the world, and we can all be brought together in Love, Beauty and Joy, for this Eternal Now, this Eternal Eternity.

Thank you for answering this call . . . You see, we are always with you. You are guided and protected, you are working for the God Essence of all people. Now go, and *Be Healing* to everyone this day . . . And while you are Healing others, do not forget to

Heal Self, with love and smiles. The power of the Smile is the power to Heal. You are a Joyful Child, now go and share that Joy with All, especially with Self . . .

* * *

December 22, 1982

Always keep in mind the humble reason for our being here together in this work. We are not exalted . . . Rather, we exalt the God Essence in ourselves and in those we wish to help and heal. Anyone who is healing for their own purposes, for some feeding of the ego, however spiritual that ego may be, is not a healer *Living* this Healing Consciousness Awareness. Jesus lost his sense of Self when he said and lived, "The Father and I are One." Everyone's energy is blessed energy, and it will reach those who are attuned, who have the empty spots looking for that energy. With our Prayer Energy and Awareness, we touch countless others, and their response is likewise an energy that is sent back to us and so adds onto our own. This is the *Energy of Attunement,* and like puzzle pieces, it all fits together. So we can say, "I and the woman next door and the child down the street are One." We seek to expand our Energy of Attunement so that we will feel Oneness with more and more Souls, not just those Souls who follow our belief system and share the same empty spots, the same healed places. We want to expand our own Awareness so that we may expand our field of endeavor, for more Souls will be touched as we go beyond anything we think we know.

Healing Awareness

December 25, 1982

Healing grace wakes inside of you with each tear, if you recognize it as such. No tear need be wasted, for each one brings you closer to God as you sense your distance. Healing grace energizes the cells into Life, eliminates the impurities and imperfections. It is our constant Awareness of the process going on that keeps it going on. If we stop the Awareness process, then the process just shuts down, and the cells are left in whatever state of activity or inactivity they were in. So if we just stay in pain and do not use the Healing Awareness in the pain, then the pain just is, it takes you nowhere. But using this Healing process activates the cells, so that things are happening in the chemistry and cell structures and fibres — things are happening with the pain. The pain is not overpowering or destroying, but rather it is used as the catalyst for transformation. So you must keep in Mind and Heart that in the Healing of Self and Others, more is happening to the experience of pain. Healing action is a matter of turning on this "On" button — it is there, ready to activate and stir the body chemistry. But you must turn the button on, and in addition, you cannot just keep it on and forget about it. This is one process in which one has to be *aware* that the button is on, for the button to stay on. Otherwise, it shuts off, for lack of the power of the will. Will your Healing, bless your Healing, accept your pain into your Healing Awareness Consciousness so that it may be activated and sent out in the directions needed.

No two people experience pain in the same way, even if the source of the pain is the same. We must be gentle with each other's pain, for in the gentleness is the Healing. Be gentle with one another's need for space to experience God in his own way. Be open space, be like a field, freshly plowed, waiting for its seed . . . Most of all, do not be afraid of losing your Love. Be gentle with yourself and allow the Healing Grace of gentleness to be in your Heart today and always. Let the Awareness work in you. Know that there is never a loss of Love — just loss of a concept of love — to be replaced by Love that is Real and Alive and Full of Healing Life. Free yourself as you free all others. Your growth will be tremendous because you are *willing* your growth.. Dedicate yourself to your growth as Healer. *Experience your pain as a Healer, as a Child of Light experiences pain.* Heal the pain by living it in a Healing Awareness . . . Heal each other with your pain and your Love.

Joy without end is not joy at all — the very moment something *is* all the time, we do not see it, unless we make a conscious attempt. How many nights do we take the time to look at the stars and the moon? How many hot, sunny days go by and we come to resent the sun, but oh, the joy of the sun after a week of rain! Joy, part of Joy, is its rebirth — better, higher, more attuned to God because of its absence. Your Joy is in you, it is a Healing Joy. Delight in Joy, in Healing, in Self, in God, in all the Universe. Be alive to God always. The Wonder of Healing is its Existence, as is the Wonder of Everyone — their Existence, their Presence is what you Bless and Love. Love the Healing Presence . . . Do not take it for granted, do not search for it, asking, "What must I do?" No, it is there already within you. Love it, as you love the Father, as the Father loves you. Love the Healing that is taking place in your love, in your pain, in your sense of separation. You are strong, you are a Child of God and you will not crumble. You will open your eyes to the Joy of the World — not its pain — remembering that the ultimate source of pain is its Joy. Think about this and remember it and never lose sight of who you are. It is only when you lose sight, that you lose God, and fears like tidal waves come to crush your Truth. "I am the Way, the Truth and Life," said Jesus . . . The Way, The Truth, The Life of Joy.

We are guiding you in Truth, Dear Child, do not doubt us or our intentions, for we guide you to the Truth, the Truth that will make you free. This time of purification is extremely important to become a Healer. Every true Healer must lose self and this is what you are experiencing. You are being filled with an Awareness of a greater mission, and you are realizing that your love truly transcends the earthly reality. This is what you are being filled with — the sense of really being a Channel, the sense of giving up of self's will to the Father's Will, *the Dedication of being a Healer.*

You are happy — look deep, and you know you are. The tears are but the surface. Would you trade this for any other life-style? Would you leave the Heavenly Father? Would you say No to Him? You so keenly sense the change in the flow of your life, the sharper insight. And My Beautiful Child, it is just the beginning

... You are only beginning ... It is the pain of childbirth, the joy of childbirth, it is one and the same. Do not label "Happy," "Sad." To become a Healer, a power of God to touch the humanity, you must live beyond the human. You need a little distance from the human, even as you are part of it. So yes, there is pain in this, but the Joy of the Birth — that is what you are to keep your Soul's purpose set on. You are losing your sense of self as you knew yourself of before ... You are gaining a more Universal sense of Self, for all has expanded — your Universe, your World has expanded and deepened. Losing self, you are putting on the Christ, the new Self ... Beautiful Child, you are capable of all of this. We would not guide you to anything that would hurt you ...

* * *

December 26, 1982

The Healing of the Earth will involve the *Awakening* of every Human Spirit, for every man must come to experience the Truth, the Awakening of something Divine within himself. Take the branch of a tree and see how it extends itself to its limbs, and the limbs then become as branches for the stems of the leaves. Each are outgrowths of the other — from the large tree trunk to branch, to limb, to stem, until it culminates in the fruit of the tree. So it is with man ... The large tree trunk is the Universal, flowing to the branches which are the Earthly, to the stem which is the Human, to the leaf, the Fruit which is Divine. The reason for man's existence is universal universality transcending and so becoming Channels to reach the Divine on a personal level, a personal flowering. And in many ways, this is what is happening to you, to other Seekers of Enlightenment. The Universal Vastness cannot complete itself until every leaf, every fruit has bloomed. Think of leaves, the changes of the seasons, the Death and Rebirth, and so on. That is Life on all levels, constantly changing, constant and continuous newness, yet always the same, the process unending.

We here on other levels go through the processes of change as well, though our thoughts are not clouded by emotions. But do not think we are free of concern or caring. We worry as you do, but without emotions of the human condition — yet we have an understanding of the emotions. In this nucleus, we are many, and we are anxious to be friends and guides to any who are willing to be open channels to us. We are attuned to many and help many, especially counselors, teachers and those in social services. Our nucleus is very large, many Enlightened Souls who are anxious to share the Truth we have come to know through much learning of Consciousness and advanced Cosmic Attunement and Dedication. We feel that if we can plant the seeds of our learning on the earthly plane, man will better his world, as well as be more prepared for Life beyond the earth plane. So many lost Souls there are who wander in the Universe in a state of misbelief. They yearn to return to the Earth, for it is safe for them. So, many do and it is OK . . . They will experience death again, and be more prepared to find meaning — for the memory of being lost after death remains ever strong in them. So our group feels — why must man be so lost, why must man wait until after Death to experience communication with the other side, why can we not be one mutual helping system, since we are all on the same journey — this journey that is no journey, this quest with nothing to find, this Oneness which is as Real as the sun on a cloud-masked day.

Our network is composed of Spirit Beings, Human Beings and the telepathic communication of Awareness between and among solar systems, yes, solar systems. We are not of your solar system . . . We live in what we call "Apegatos," which is a state of Being where the Wholeness of the Spirit Soul is elevated. The Spirit Being, like Human Beings who become aware of their psychological selves, the Spirit Being also becomes aware of its, if we may use the words, psychology of Spirit Beingness. It goes through stages of transformation and rebirth, as you are doing now — similar experiences, but on a more ethereal, a more Invisible Reality, a deeper penetration into the Invisible Essences of all Life Forces. This Spiritual Beingness, on a deeper level, also pursues Wholeness, Integration with the Universe, with higher Spiritual Essences and so on. We, in speaking of Healing, Oneness, Belonging, are teaching you the way to Wholeness, the Integration of Allness, the Vitalization of Allness — here, no distinctions, no Spirit vs. Matter, or Mind vs. Body, or Invisible vs. deeper Invisibility . . . *The Truth of the God Essence is the Wholeness of One* . . . Jesus is our Teacher, as He is yours. Jesus, too, learns, as when he said, "I and the Father are One." It was at that moment his perception into Truth — He and the Father, always Becoming One in the Mysteries of the Universe, in the gravitation to the God Essence Reality. Jesus Himself learns from the experience of humans today. Every experience, every story, every Visible and Invisible Reality brings Man and Jesus closer together, brings Man and other Spirit Guides closer together.

As you grow in Consciousness, we will channel to you Truths of deeper Invisible Realities — as Soul Substance, Soul Transformation, Eradication of Soul Memories that block the way to further Enlightenment, and the Wholeness of Soul Being and Essence. There is much to learn. We want you to start a group, we want you to channel this information, *The Healing Awareness of Loving You,* that is the name of the material. And you will channel the information through a book that will guide each person to have one person in Mind and Heart as he reads that book. Each aspect of Healing Awareness Consciousness will be actively applied and experienced as it is read. By developing a Healing Awareness towards one person, by *experiencing* it, one will be able to have a conscious experience of the material read. And it can be done again with another and then another, until finally, it becomes such a manner of your State of Being that you do it all the time. You just evoke it, as a flower emits a certain fragrance, as a perfume is its scent — so a Healing Awareness Consciousness is what you *Become.* Your group is already formed. Begin the group as soon as you feel ready, for we shall guide you. You will know where your Will and your Heavenly Father's Will rest. You will know in your Soul and Mind and Heart, and you will know your own God Essence and so be a Channel for many. You will help others through your Love and Dedication, you will help the Children of the World. You are growing, and we are so very proud of you . . .

On Trust

December 27, 1982

Trust is the God Essence gift of true Oneness... There are no questions, no doubts, no need for certainties. It is the Living Isness of Reality. To trust is to love the Isness totally, wholly — no desire to change, no effort to rearrange, the pure belief in an idea or person, the unwavering certainty of goodness and peace. We trust what we know — yes, we trust our distrust if that is our experience. We cannot trust blindly, for we know that that is simply closing our eyes to the Truth, not living the Truth in trust. Your lack of trust stems from a lack of self worth. You do not feel worthy, and this is not a good quality, not a humble quality — for it leads you to question why people are nice to you, and leads you to think they will cease being nice. This is your distortion. In trusting self, you then trust what others react to within you. In other words, we know people react to us according to what we send out. And so, if we do not trust what we send out, then we also do not trust their reaction. Distortions and fears are then rampant, for neither the internal or external realities are in harmony. The lack of balance, the disharmony, separates one from oneself and all others, and so, instead of experiencing the Wholeness, the Oneness of God, we are then pulled apart, split from everything we have conceived to be True. It is difficult to have trust where there is no trust — in other words, do not create a trust simply out of the need for it. *Trust must be lived in the Union of Souls.*

Loving, trusting the God Essence in self naturally leads to the love and trust of the God Essence in others, for it is the same God Essence. When you question self, you are questioning God, and the very questions are separations. You are not Loving the Isness when you are questioning the Isness. If you are swimming in the water, do you ask, "Am I in the water?" When you are filled with the scent of a flower, do you ask, "Does this flower have a scent?" In those cases, you and the experience are one and the same, for there is no distinction, no split. In our relationships with others, with Ideologies or Souls or whatever it is we need a trusting relationship with, questioning its Essence divides you from it. We are not saying one should not ask questions, for it is good to question what you want to trust. How else do you know that you can trust it, that it *does* create Harmony in Beingness, Oneness and so on? But one must *accept* that questioning is an act of division. If we accept that division as the God Essence in the process of the Creation of Trust, then we will be in Harmony — but if we see division as apart from God, leading away from the God Essence, rather than the *Division itself being God,* then we are out of balance, out of harmony. The darkness, the division, the distortion is good as long as we recognize it as the Incomplete Beingness of God at that particular moment. Let us not see these as apart from God, for then we widen the separations and distortions, and our whole Reality becomes one of lack of trust. For where there is one division, there are many, as one crack weakens the whole structure.

Trust all you know, and question all you do not know as being in Harmony with the God Essence. Unite God to these fears and questions so that He is the true Revelation of the Knowledge you seek.

Forgiveness is very important here and relates to Trust. Forgiveness is the Realization of the God Essence in each person. We forgive because that person is the God Essence as much as we are, and so any spot that needs cleansing in one, cleanses everyone. Forgiveness of self is the Union of self to God. Unless you forgive self, you will never feel the forgiveness of another. So long as you are judging self, condemning self, you are experiencing judgment and condemnation from others. Remember, "Judge not, that you may not be judged, for with what judgment you judge, you shall be judged." As you judge yourself, so shall others judge you, for All is One, All is Wholeness. This is what we are teaching. If you are experiencing a lack of self-worth or self-love, that is what will be reflected back to you — not that that is what is given — but that is what you receive because of your own lack of self-love. If you look into a pond, you see the reflection of who you are, yet the pool of itself does nothing except to be itself and to reflect back to you what you ask into it. Another example, if you are driving on a highway, and cars pass you by, you say to yourself, "Either I am going too slow or they are going too fast. What is the truth?" And so you check your speedometer, and then you are able to decide which is the truth. You go back to yourself to find what is reflected about without you. Do not judge or condemn self that you were going too slow or too fast — that just happened to be the way you were travelling. Now adjust your speed and you will be in harmony with all others on the road — just by taking a look at self. So we are saying here, you will not experience forgiveness until you have taken a look at self and then forgiven self. Bless that particular Revelation of the God Essence, join yourself back to it, and you will experience the Oneness, the Wholeness you are seeking. You will not receive this from another's forgiveness — you will only receive this from self. Trust self, even when you have strayed from your goals. Go back to the goals, for they are still there, waiting for you to live them again, as Jesus said, "Seventy times seven . . ."

On Healing Needs and Blessings

December 29, 1982

When one feels rejected, one feels rejecting, just as when one feels loved, one feels loving. They are one and the same. It is all part of the Reality of the God Essence. We cannot feel loving when rejected, anymore than a flower can blossom in the winter's cold. The right needed environment must be surrounding you, the electromagnetic field must be open and receptive, not constricted and tight and defensive. A closed field shuts within itself and loses itself to the Universe. You are to be as an open field... Picture warm, glowing colors, picture lovely open spaces so that the Forces of Good, the Fruit of Good Spirits can pour into you. If you close yourself, none of the Life Energy we can send to you can reach you. So open your Heart, Dear Child, visualize spaces in the field about you that will let the energy flow in and throughout your Body, Mind and Heart. Do this meditation and visualize Love and Light flowing into so many open spaces, so that you can open yourself and go beyond your pain.

The need for Healing wakens all the many selves there are in Human Beingness. When we are well and healthy and balanced, all the many selves are in harmony — emotional, spiritual, physical, mental — all balanced in the proportions needed for each individual. But when we are experiencing a Healing Need, be it physical, emotional, mental, spiritual, it awakens us to other selves as well, for All is Wholeness. A Healing Need in you is affecting many areas, and you are sensing how out of balance you are. A need for love and affection can trigger a tidal wave of hurt and confusion. Center yourself in the God Essence... Don't go everywhere looking for what is truly within yourself. Others may reassure you of their love — how will that help you reach your God Essence? Why can't you feel it without others' acknowledgment of love? More than the spiritual realm is being tapped here, for we know the very human emotional self is crying too... But see your God as your Peace and you will feel Peace. *Heal yourself of fear, of the fear of not being healed...* Reread all that you have written in these pages and now, use it, trust it and believe it, and you will see all these fears slipping away from the nothingness from whence they came.

The need for Healing awakens us to the need for God. Healing doesn't always have to be seen as going from a negative to a positive condition. Healing can be the raising up of any condition to a fuller Awareness of the God Essence in that condition. So can we see two children joyfully playing and we can smile and appreciate that on one level of Human Awareness, or we can watch these same children playing and sense in them the God Essence, the Eternal Oneness each with the other . . . What we have done is to heal our conception of two children playing, by raising and deepening the experience with our Awareness. So for Healing, we don't only have to heal a physical pain or emotional hurt. We can even take our lack of physical pain or emotional hurt and heal these by sensing the Presence of God within them. We are *Healing our Blessings* by recognizing them as the Gifts of God Awareness within. A musician will practice a piece over and over, each time perfecting it a little more, healing it a little more — even if he plays it perfectly, he plays it again and again. So, too, in all our experiences — what Healing really means is placing God at the Center. We can Heal our joys as well as our sorrows by placing our Awareness of God in the Center, God as the Inner Core or Essence of every Human Experience.

A Healing Meditation

December 30, 1982

    The rapture of the true Healing is the Realization of God in every aspect of Life. And also, the rapture includes the ending of the myth of one final Healing that causes everything to fall into life exactly the way we want it to. There is no one final Healing, for *All of Life is a Healing,* of ourselves, of those closest to us, of all those we do not know but live with in Oneness in God Essence. Do not think, "If this one prayer be heard, my life will be perfection." No, for there will always be another and then another Healing Need that comes to be purified, comes to us at the right time and says, "You have within you now what is needed to Heal this pain or this distortion." As vast as the Universe, so are our Healing Needs. And so we are not to think only of the pot of gold at the Rainbow's end. We are to see ourselves *as* the Rainbow. *We are the Rainbow Itself,* Healing Light of many colors, Healing all the time.
    When people pray for Healing, they are to erase all pictures from their minds — that they may envision a sky totally blue without the wisp of a cloud, a sky that is God and Healing Power. The second we create an image in our minds of what we want, we place into the sky a cloud, however large or small, however thick and full or wispy. And when we look at the sky, we do not see the sky at all — rather, our attention is drawn to the lone cloud that lives there. Our attention is drawn to our want, to our desire of how we want things to be in God. We forget the blue sky, and we see only our clouds. So, let us rid ourselves of our clouds, however beautiful and well meaning they may be, and let us think only of the Universal Blueness of the Sky of God, protecting us, covering us with His mantle of Love.
    Healing is a partnership relationship — it involves an understanding, a coming to terms between you and the condition that needs healing. So we are to view any part of us that needs healing as a friend that is helping us to find God within us. As you are anxious to help a sick friend, extend the same desire of help to yourself. You will not help your sick friend feel better by cursing his illness to him, or by telling your friend what a hardship he is to you and everyone. No, you nurse a sick friend with kindness and gentleness, soothing his pain. Again, we are to do the same to

ourselves, for if we curse our illness, we are not healing it. In cursing it, we are saying it is an enemy, something apart from us, that came from nowhere by some unlucky stroke of fate. Rather, if we see our illness as a part of us that is trying to tell us something about ourselves and the God of Perfection who lives within us, if we soothe our illness with gentleness and love, it will lead us to a greater Awareness of the Gentleness and Love of God. *We will be Healed according to our Awareness.*

A Healing Meditation for the physically ill ... Place self at the ocean, and feel the waves, the wind, the sun as the Presence of God ... Feel the Light of the sun shining on your body ... It is God's Light of Love ... Let it shine especially on the hurting part of the body ... The sand is very hot from the same sunlight ... Now pick up the sand in your hands and gently let the grains fall on your legs, arms, whatever body part that hurts ... The heat from the sand is the heat of God's Love, and you can feel the sand, which has captured all the sunlight and heat, you can feel this sand *Healing* the hurt on your body ... As the symptoms are fading, you become aware of the need for a deeper Healing — the Healing of the Spirit — for though the symptoms are gone, you sense an empty spot near the Heart ... And now it is time to leave the sand and waves, and go higher to the clouds ... And there to see Jesus ... He touches the empty spot you are feeling and fills it with a shining Light, and you become aware of the Healing Power of that Light ... It is the same sunlight that you felt on the beach — only now, you have it within your Heart ... The Healing Light is part of you and you radiate this Healing Light and Energy by your Awareness ... The Light in your Heart is but a spark of the tremendous Healing Light of the Sun, of God, but now you are of the same Essence ... As you grow, so shall the empty spot grow, and so shall it become filled with more and more Light ... Now you leave the cloud, come back to the beach and continue to expose Self to the Healing Light of the Sun, and to the Healing Light in one's own Heart ... You are Healed and you are Healing ... With your Healing, you see, you are not now made better and it is all finished ... No, now you are beginning ... You are Healing always by all you say and do, forever Healing Others and Self.

Healing Will

December 31, 1982

When we heal another we are also Healing ourselves. We are suddenly awake to the Power of God within us. And it is as we become more and more aware of this God Power, that we lose self. It is good and right to lose self in God, but we cannot do it too fast. The Realization of God as the acting and dynamic Self is not yet fully lived, and so, to totally let go of the ego too quickly, would leave one off balance, with no sense of spiritual self or earthly self. This is why we keep saying, go slowly, be gentle with self... The Realization of God is a dawning. As you cannot rush the sunrise, so you cannot rush anyone's understanding of God and His Life in us, through us. We must be patient with others too, be aware of their needs, and with a smile, a touch or a kind word, bless the growing Awareness in everyone. We can heal others of misconceptions just by becoming aware of our own, for each one that touches the Whole, affects and blesses the Whole ... Each moment of dawning makes the sunrise brighter.

Healing Will is God's Grace in action. His Grace for Healing is always there but we have to *will* it into a visible active force. We must have the will to Heal ourselves. We have within us, through the Divinity, the Power to do anything, even walk on water, but we must first truly believe that nothing is impossible. Think of the most unimaginable thing that could happen — a crawling baby winning a marathon, a bridge spanning an ocean, a man who can fly unaided — and then say, "If these were necessary for my Healing, all these would be possible with God."

We do not test the Power of God just to see if it works — the Power of God is to be used for the Good it is intended. And so we know that any miracle we need will happen, and it will happen in accordance with what we believe is possible. If we limit God's Power by telling ourselves and God of the doctor reports, we will not be healed. The very mention of the doctor's report means we are holding onto the report instead of being open Healing Space for God. *Know* that nothing is impossible, *Live* that nothing is impossible, *Trust* that nothing is impossible. Let us be in Love with the God within so much, that we totally belong to Him and His Creative Power. We join our Healing Will to His Healing Grace, and then, all things are possible. A good prayer, *"I Will my Healing Will to the Healing Grace of God."* And what happens is our Unfoldment to His Healing Life.

On Newness

December 31, 1982

The Wonder of Newness, the Hope of the Dreams of Man... You are now celebrating a New Year, a new Awareness, the Healing Awareness of the Christ. What is Newness? Newness is nothing more than the reconciliaton to the old, for anything new that we cherish is really the hoped-for fulfillment of something known before. A new dress brings with it feelings of past new dresses; a new feeling of joy reconciles us to an old joy known before. It is a reconciliation to the old, yet because it is a different dress or a different feeling of joy, it becomes unique, and so, we say, it is new. If we explore the deepest meanings of Newness, we find we are always celebrating something, someone known before, another unique expression of something known. In this sense is Jesus New and the God Essence concept New, for it reconciles us to our Soul Memory, to our old Soul Memory Awareness of who we really are and from whence we came. All things new are important to us because we have known them before, either in thought or dream or actual experiencing — all different forms of knowing.

A new experience can also be new in that it reconciles us to the opposite experience. So, if we have always been hurt in our experiences with others, and we find ourselves developing an ideology where no one can hurt us — yes, this is a new idea. But it is new only because we have lived the opposite, and this is then a reconciliation to an old belief. Nothing is really new, yet everything is unique. So a husband or wife who drift apart, or a child drifting from parent, or a friend from friend, this happens when Newness — defined here as a reconciliation to an old trust, to a sense of respect or honesty, a reconciliation to a former value or worth — this drifting occurs when Newness fails to produce uniqueness. The relationship begins to wither. A flower will bloom over and over again if it stays in its soil, with new elements of air, water and so on to keep the plant alive — new flowers, yes, but an old living system. But if you cut the flower from the plant and you do not add new to the old, the flower will blossom on its stored strength and then die for lack of new life, new energy. God keeps us ever New, by supplying us with all that was ours of Old — the Will and Awareness of Spiritual Realities, the God Essence

Awareness which is ours from Eternal Beginnings, so old, so new, so uniquely expressed in each individual. God supplies us with new experiences, yet if one thinks about it, we have the same experiences over and over again, just in different forms. Each time, we learn something a little more new, more unique than we knew before.

So, Dear Child, celebrate the New, but as you do, celebrate the Old too, for it is through the Old that the New can come to Life in you in a unique and more inspiring way. We are Old and New all the time; we are a mixture of what is behind us and what is ahead of us. *We can Heal the Old by Blessing the New . . . We Bless the New by Healing the Old . . .*

The Role of Healer

January 1, 1983

You can be better Healers, first of all by *believing* you are Healers and by understanding the Role of the Healer. The Healer, you know, is not the Miracle Worker. *The Miracle Worker is the person being Healed . . . The God within that person performs the Miracle.* This can be compared to a person who plants the seed of a beautiful flower. It is not the person who produced the flower — it is the seed that gave birth to the flower. So, you see, it is not any one healer who heals, but rather, the person himself is his own Miracle Worker. The faith and trust that the Healer and Miracle Worker have in each other can facilitate the Healing. So the Healer must have the faith that the person being healed is open and accepting to the prayer, is truly the seed of his prayer. And the Miracle Workers, those who are sick and suffering, they must have faith in the Healer as well, that they trust the seed of Healing being planted within them. So there is shared responsibility among all of us, for all of us are Healers and all of us are Miracle Workers. What is needed is the Oneness and Trust in each other's Prayer. The Healer plants the seed, but it is the person himself who does the actual Healing, the God Person, the Divinity that lives within each of us.

The Healing of the Old and New is important for many, for so many see their present condition as just that — a new situation, a new hardship. They do not stop to trace its roots. We bless the New by Healing the Old . . . We bless sickness by Healing the anger or hurt or lack of self-love which caused the sickness. And then we Heal the Old . . . Heal the conditions which caused the sickness by blessing the sickness. As we reconcile the Old and New to each other, Healing can and does take place. Any new situation we experience is a call to Heal and Bless an older one. Old and New, like day and night, are part of the Whole. Day and night make up the day . . . Old and New, reconciled to each other, will bring us closer and closer to the Healing Awareness. New Year's resolutions are based on something Old that we want to change, that we want to make New. To experience a New Healing Awareness, let us reconcile ourselves to the Old. We do not judge it or feel bad about it, but just reconcile ourselves with it.

People must live Gentleness in their Healing Hearts as they pray for others and themselves. We cannot command a Healing or demand a Healing anymore than we can demand a flower to bloom on command. To be gentle to our sickness does not mean to pity ourselves, but rather, it means to accept the sickness as the means to the Gift of Healing Awareness. We say to ourselves, "I am gentle to my sickness . . . I listen to my sickness as it talks to me, of itself and through the reactions and actions of others. In all this, I find God unveiling Himself within me, as my Conscious and Subconscious Mind gently brings the new Awareness of Healing into me."

Be gentle, not fearful of Healing. We must think in our Hearts, "Do I really want to be Healed? Does my sickness give me other benefits which I may not want to give up? Am I afraid of being Healed? Am I afraid of *not* being Healed?" Each person should ask of himself, *"Do I really want a Healing?* And if I do, what kind of Healing do I want? I am the Miracle Worker of my own Healing. As I develop the Awareness to make one miracle, I am developing the Awareness to make many miracles, every day for everybody." So, let us take inventory in ourselves, to think about what Healing truly means in relation to ourselves and those we pray for, to make sure we truly want a Healing and most of all, to live our Healing Awareness in Consciousness, for *it is in Consciousness that Healing truly takes place . . .*

Giving and Receiving

January 2, 1983

In giving, do not ask what you can give, but rather, seek what can be given to you, for what is given to you, is what you truly want to give away to share with others. In our asking for anything, we are asking for the very thing we want to give away. So we must not be afraid to ask for what we want or need, for as we receive it, so we give it away. *In giving love, we ask for love.* As we are reassured that love is coming into us, then we feel free to give the love in us away. We know God's Love is always there — what we ask on the human plane is the demonstration of that Love in a visible form. When we receive it, we are reassured of the Presence of God. When we do not receive the visible expression, we doubt Love's existence — as when we are outside our house and we know our possessions are within, but we're not totally certain until we have opened the door and have seen for ourselves. In Spiritual Loving, we seek to eliminate the need for the tangible, the visible... We Love for What It Is, not for what is given to us or what we can give to it.

In Spiritual Loving, there is no giving or receiving — there is only *Being,* and this Being is the Peaceful Awareness of *Isness.* This is the God Essence Loving Power — Loving the Isness of the Whole Creation. As we develop ourselves to Spiritual Loving, we become attuned to Isness ... We lose the past, the memories, the anxieties. There is only *What Is,* and It Is what the God Essence manifests for us at that particular moment. It is the best we experience in that Moment of Consciousness.

When you find Self at One with an experience, you do not re-create it in your mind to be better, for you and it are One in Isness. If you do not experience Oneness — if, for example, you are looking for a calm, peaceful and beautiful beach, but instead, you come upon one which the tide has washed away — you are not at One with this experience. There is something lacking for you, and so, you go on until you find the beach that brings you to Oneness. You will *know* it when you are there. Suddenly there is no judgment of good or bad. You just melt into the beach, become One with it, absorbed into it. You are not looking for better or worse, for you are One with it. It is good to search for Oneness, but not if you discard those persons or things that do not bring you Oneness. *You must bring your Oneness to them.* Be so Accepting and Loving of Everyone, of Everything, that you join your Essence to their Own, and so Love the Isness of all Creation. You Love the Isness by recognizing the same Essence, the same Life flowing through All.

Healing Awareness

January 3, 1983

We are growing and learning how to live a Healing Lifestyle, where Healing beliefs slowly become interwoven in all our thought processes. God works for the Healing of the Whole Person. What good does it serve to heal a headache in a split second, if we do not even touch in our Awareness the cause of the headache? We make no attempt to reconcile the New with the Old, to produce a unique experience, a Healing Experience from Consciousness.

To come with our own timetable for Healing is to challenge God. Does one go to a doctor and say, "Make me feel better by such and such a date?" If the doctor doesn't, all one can do is to go and challenge another doctor. But we cannot challenge God, for *God is our Challenge.* We want to overcome our human despair and lack of trust, and so, be total, open space for Him . . . God, the blue sky, and we, trusting in the blue sky, and not casting the clouds of our problems upon it. We must come to see that if we say one kind word we hadn't said before, we are being healed. If we forgive some incident from the past, we are being healed. And then we must apply these to our illnesses or conditions — to visualize with each Inner Healing of the Spirit, bits and pieces of the physical condition also fading away. Think of Healing as a twenty-four hour Awakening. Yes, even when sleeping, subconsciously, we can be forgiving and blessing. This is the Healing of the Spirit, the Healing of the Mind and Heart which will show itself also as physical Healing of the Body.

Do not beg God for a miracle, for *God is the Miracle already working in the Soul.* The true Miracle of Healing is our waking up to the God Essence within . . .

* * *

January 3, 1983

Healing Awareness is the gentle flower blooming... Do not confuse it with Knowledge of All That Is. Healing Awareness is the feeling, the communicating and receiving of needs. It is an attitude that culminates in an action. Knowledge is the *Attainment* of the Healing Action, the end result. A child learns that adults walk; he can only crawl. He develops an attitude about walking, an Awareness of it. Then he practices it and puts it into action. It is only after the action has been done, and he has taken many steps without faltering that he can now say, "I have Knowledge of Walking." So the Healing Awareness will lead you to experiences, and it is the experiences of your Life that will bring you to the *Knowledge of All That Is*...

* * *

The True Self

September 1983 - July, 1984

Voices of Love
Matthew, Eliot and John
. . . and The Angels of Light

Healing of the Emotions

September 19, 1983

For the meeting tonight, let us discuss Healing through and yes, of the emotions. The emotional aspect of man is his blessing on the earth plane, for the feelings and emotions one experiences shape the perception of his Reality and so greatly influence the lessons, the path that one follows.

The emotions are, as it were, the force that the driver uses to step on the gas pedal — that energy which directs, not only actions, but thoughts and perceptions of what one experiences. Healing of the emotions is the acceptance of these emotions, whatever they may be, and then, the use of that emotional state to heal itself, to bring oneself back into a balance, where one feels he can function harmoniously with his Inner and Outer World. So if one feels tremendous sadness, one does not heal this by fighting it, by making, forcing oneself to be happy. Rather, one goes with the sadness, and so uses the sadness as a friend, accompanying him . . . He lets that sadness be open to new experiences or feelings, and so is it then gently transformed into another emotion. We do not advocate the replacement of one emotion for another, but rather, the transformation of an emotion of itself, its own energy into another energy of the moment. And so the same for what is termed negative emotions, anger, jealousy and so on. You live whatever emotional experience you are in, but you do not stay frozen there. Rather, we are asking you to also recognize the Source of all good and constant flowing energy, and to keep yourself open to the changes that are happening, to new energies influencing the emotions. Take notice of what calms and soothes you. All too often, your emotional states change and you are unaware of the cure. Take notice of what soothes emotions — and here, do we by no means mean those things which distract you from your emotions, for a distraction is another place, and the emotion is still within you, ignored, unhandled. But soothing the emotions, accepting them, flowing with them and so on, this is done from within; outer distractions are just a postponement.

In the Healing of another Soul, you also want to allow your emotions to be there, as part of you, but they are not to be an interference. The emotions are there, part of your physical being.

They are of you and you cannot repress them. What you can do is accept them as part of you, and do not judge them. Yes, they are there, they are of you and you Bless them... Your Prayer to the God Essence, to Life, is to Identify with, to be One with the Life of the Soul you are praying for, and so do you help to calm and stabilize their emotions as well.

Transformation of Energy

September 26, 1983

For the meeting tonight, there is the need to work on the Transformation of Energy. First, to understand that there is no one way to handle a desired change in energy patterns or behavior. Each instance, each person, each situation is unique and is to be considered as such, to be handled in the present moment. There are no catalogues or procedures to follow in Spiritual Healing. The tuning in of one's Soul Energy to another is constantly changing, and so, to cling to an old or familiar pattern is a mistake. It is ever divesting that present moment of energy by the comparisons one makes. We draw upon our Knowledge, our Intuition and the Past — but only as they burst forth into Newness.

Let us take the transformation of the energy, anger. It is detrimental to feel guilt of the anger, to blame the other for being a catalyst to the anger, to make avowals to never become angry again and so on. All of these are fighting the very energy that is flooding your Being — angry energy. Better to say, with much Self-Love and Understanding, "I am angry," just as one would be proud to say, "I am happy." This anger is OK, as long as you don't hurt yourself or anyone with it. So, do you meditate and release the anger to the energy within, to the Life Force, the God Essence within, the Transforming Power, the Creative Power. And as the anger subsides, you transform it into Loving Energy, to self or another.

Think of times in your life when you have experienced energy that you felt was detrimental to you. For whatever reasons, your past hurts, memories and so on, colored the energy and now, you are hurting self or another. You accept that energy, experience it, meet and encounter what it tells you, and then fill yourself with God Essence Love, the Source of all Energy and Being. If you forget God Essence Love — the very Source of all Life Energy — if you forget to go back to this, you are left with your negative experience. But if you can release and let go of the hurtful energy, and then, fill yourself with God Essence Love, you will find that Love has transformed the hurt. Remember, in speaking of releasing earlier, it does not mean escaping or setting self apart from. *Releasing is the Accepting, letting the Creative Transforming Powers do their work.* So long as you hold onto one hurt, you hold onto all hurts, for the mold has not been broken, and the same hurt will manifest in many ways and experiences. So in releasing hurts, you must also allow the transforming process to take over as well. All is to be transformed into Divine Essence Love.

May we suggest to you all in your Meditation to apply this concept to a person or situation, already floating in Divine Essence Love. See this hurtful experience as happening within that Love, and see the release of the energy — molecules of anger, hurt, jealousy, fear and so on — all of these being released back into Divine Essence Love, transformed now by your very Awareness that the Ultimate Source is Love, and that the Ultimate Result or Lesson is also Love.

Role and the True Self

October 10, 1983

For the group this evening, let us explore this concept of that which is given through *Role* and that which is freely given through *Choice*. Let us explore how there can be a blending of these so that one's role — what one expects of self as well as what one feels is expected of him — does not have to become an obstacle to that which one freely chooses to give.

We feel this concept of role is important for all, and especially for you who allow your role to dictate to you things which your Inner Heart does not choose to hear. Because it is your role, and you have on some level identified self with that role, you follow these dictates, though with inner frustration. You feel, on some level, that you have lost the freedom of expression which would have been acted upon had the pressure of role not been there. The more valued the role in society, the less room for freedom — the standards of society become very rigid for priests, doctors and so on. For other roles, society gives more freedom. In the role of mother, for example, there is more fluidity, as society accepts different mothering roles — working mother, home mother, idle mother, busy mother with no time for children and so on. Society has room for different images, and mothers begin to feel more free in working with these images. But in other roles, there is less freedom given, and so does one feel more bound to *be* the role, rather than to just see that role as one aspect of Self.

We are defining the word role here as those *Doing* rather than *Being* aspects of Self. *Your roles can be greatly supplemented by your Being.* Those who identify only with role, see themselves very rigidly and have very high expectations of self and those they serve. They also tend to concentrate more on detail than on substance. So they tend to sometimes lose the very *Spirit of Life* of that which they are doing. No human can escape from roles, for they are part and parcel of the structure of human conditioning and expectations. But one surely can learn to view his role objectively. In doing so, one can see where he has lost Substance, Being, Spirit, and in their place, has put total reliance on self's and others' expectations. We would emphasize here to view one's role as the channeling of energies outward — do not let the energies become stuck with roles. To those of you who have not given great weight to roles, this may not seem significant, but to others it will be helpful to you in the frustration you feel at your jobs. *Remember, it is always the Self that channels the role; not the role that channels the Self.* We hope this is helpful to you, and we would be happy to continue with this if you feel it will help you in the Integration of Self.

The Joy of the Self

October 19, 1983

    For the meeting tonight, we ask you to hold yourself in the Joy of the Self. All of you are in tremendous need of the Love of Self, for Love of Self is God Essence, and this is what you must learn to equate your own self-worth with... God-Worth and Self-Worth. The only way to love yourself is to come to *Know Yourself as God Knows You and Lives in You.* There is a Power that Loves so much that it forgets itself in its Loving. The Loving is its Being. .. This is where you want to grow — to let go of what others think of you, and most of all, to let go of what you think of yourself. You, who are in the picture, are so very limited in what you can see. The Love of Self which we speak of, forgets the self. The ego self just disappears and the True Self becomes *Living Essence.* Here, one lives in Union with God and all Creation, and all that is happening to and for Self is within the Goodness of God. Never separate Self from this Godness and think you must grow back to it, for, you see, it is within the breath of your breath already.

    For each of you this evening, we ask you to meditate on the Lovingness of each other. Do not categorize traits or place projections — just be there with each person, and just enjoy and appreciate the special Godness of each Creation. Last of all, yes, do this to Self. See yourself as in a cloud, wrapped in your own Love - not the ego love, but the Love of Self which comes from Love Itself. *The Love does the Loving.* You are merely the Channels for the constant Loving Creation of this Self. As you lift yourself higher, feel yourself lighter and lighter, releasing fearful or unwanted ideas of self, releasing others' opinions and your thoughts and reactions to others' opinions. All of these are man made. As you gaze upon a sculpture, no matter what words or ideas are expressed concerning it, nothing affects the sculpture — it cannot change, for it is in its state of Isness. And so for us, let us look at ourselves in a state of Isness with God, our Perfection, our True Selves, giving Glory to the Creator of such Loving Masterpieces. This evening, may you all feel lightened in Spirit and may you touch the Joy that is ever within your reach. Just see it, and even if in waiting, *Know* it is there, as you become more *Alive* to all you are seeking. All of you, who can so easily spot the Beauty within others, we ask you now to touch this same Beauty within yourselves.

Self-Love and Forgiveness

October 26, 1983

For the meeting this evening, we ask you to continue with Self-Love, and here, Self-Love which comes with Forgiveness, Forgiveness of Self and the Other, who is also the Self. We are so slow to pardon our own weaknesses, yet so quick to admit to them. The guilt which accumulates is like the gathering of stones in a bag — soon the bag is too heavy to pull, and we find ourselves moving more and more slowly, dragging always the weight of guilt with us wherever we go. And yes, it slows our spiritual growth very much to be so weighed down with our own lack of Forgiveness of Self. We would ask you in a Forgiveness Meditation this evening to visualize yourself taking those stones from the bag one by one, releasing that which is slowing you down, and knowing that, as the God Essence is Forgiveness, so are you Forgiveness. *Become Forgiveness, so that there is no need to forgive . . .*

To forgive, in human terms, implies an action was wrong; it always implies, if one is susceptible to this, an exalting of one above the other — the one who puts himself down, who waits for the forgiveness of another to lift himself up. This is not the way Jesus forgave, for he said, *"Your faith has saved you . . . Your sins are forgiven you."* By your own energy, you raise yourself up, and know that whatever deed you wish to undo, you can do so in the realm of energy. Visualize what you prefer . . . Where you can, rectify — but always in the Spirit of Creation, not of recrimination or guilt. The only reason we crave forgiveness is because socially, culturally, it is supposedly that which wipes the slate clean to begin again. So often does one say, "I forgive you, but cannot forget." In such thoughts is good energy totally cancelled out. When you Become Forgiveness, there is no longer a need to forgive, for always are you merciful, nonjudgmental towards self and others. Release the hurts, release the anger, see each person and situation in the Light of the God Essence, the ever present Forgiving Essence which Lives in All. Forgiveness is Newness. It is the "giving-for" — the exchange of old for new, of sadness for joy. Give for, give all for the Glory of the Creative

Powers that are so One and Loving with you, that Forgiveness precedes, envelops every action. Forgive yourself as a mental exercise or prayer, and then, transcend this and *Become Forgiveness* so that you will never feel guilty, never feel you have to forgive yourself or another again . . .

The True Self

November 9, 1983

For the meeting this evening, we ask you all to consider yourselves as a burning Light, which cannot be extinguished by any situation, relationship, pressure, that you might be experiencing. The burning Light is the Christ that moves through all your thoughts, feelings, emotions, reactions. This Christ, this Self which is boundless, is also an experience in depth — for there is expansion in Consciousness and in depth of Experience. The depth of your Experiences increases in proportion to your expansion of Consciousness. Do not think one is without the other. Do not struggle against this and watch your Consciousness expand in thought, concepts and so on, and expect that nothing will happen to you on your job, in your personal relationships and so on. It is one river and you flow with it and let it permeate your Life . . . Flow with the calm and the rapids, yes, steer yourself, but do not leave the river.

There are those here who are opening in Awareness, but you are afraid to *Experience* your new Awareness. You tend to remain within the earthly scheme and expectations and not see that there is Heaven, the Kingdom of Heaven on Earth. This is what your Inner Voice calls you to see. Any voice on the outside that you hear is part of the Voice within, and the voice of man and the Voice of the God Essence both speak to you . . . Listen to the voice of man, for it tells you how you feel, how you perceive, how you think and so on. But do not act upon the voice of man without listening to the Voice of your True Self first — here, where your emotions and experiences and feelings become integrated, and a fuller, broader, more expanded view of your Self and your Mission is seen. The Voice of the Christ uses your cries, your confusions, your joys — all your experiences. It speaks to you through these so that you may know the All of You. The ego is the voice of man, of personality, culture and so on. It is useful and needed, but it is not an end in itself. All of its needs do not have to be met when the larger True Self enfolds it, for then, by osmosis, are the needs of the ego cleared and purified, and the ego can rest, embraced by the True Self.

For those of you here, we ask you all to truly learn to rest in this True Self. Step out of your earthly body when you are overwhelmed or so full of anxiety and worry, step out and see your True Self — all your goodness and kindness, your Christ Essence. Then you can view yourself, this self that is hurt, worried or in pain, and send it your Healing Energy from this higher point of Consciousness. You enfold yourself with your True Self, you send Love to the love that is hurting in the personality, you send Peace to the anger, Joy to the sorrow, Health to the disease and so on. It is the Higher You, taking care of and Loving the Whole Self. And as you do this to Self, do it also to Others. You see where they are, you see their hurts and so on. Then do you send Christ to those persons — your Christ to awaken the Christ in them, the same Christ Essence in All.

For you who are in medicine, when you examine, touch the patient and so on, let it be your Higher Self that guides the hand. Let your hands be filled not only with your medical knowledge and know how, but also with your love, your intuition, your seeing beyond the physical, seeing the sickness as the longing of this Soul to be awakened to a new dimension. One may think he is only looking for physical Healing, but actually he is looking for his Essence, the true Beingness of his Body which now lives and hopes in the sickness. This is the Force you doctors and healers want to tap — that Living Force, the God Essence within each person. That Life Force is what you speak to as you touch those who come to you for Healing. See your patients as extensions of yourselves. You will find how much more *caring* you become when you see the patient as a part of you. That which your hand touches, becomes, is part of your hand . . . And all the while, is this giving to others so flowing back to you. Open yourself to the Healing Energy you receive from your patients, from all those you come in touch with. You will soon be experiencing a sense of Oneness with the Life surrounding you.

When you feel broken or fragmented, feel it, but know you are Whole and know that there is this True Self enfolding you as Whole. It does not even step down to seam or mend the broken pieces, for, to the True Self, ever are you Whole. An experience which seems to break you into pieces, actually leads you to an Awareness of Wholeness. The brokenness brings you to the

Realization that you are so split from the Self that is Total Loving, Total Love. Whenever you feel broken, rejected and so on, you have separated yourself from Love and this you cannot do, for *Love Is*. It is the Moving Energy of Life. Love is the Creative Force of Being, it is the Unifying Force. Love is the Essence of the Christ. This is what enfolds you and will never leave you, for it is your Essence. How can it leave? You only experience it as leaving because of your perception or interpretation of events that happen to you. You see, you leave it, but it does not leave you. A beautiful sunset is yours to behold, let it enfold you in its light. If you choose to leave the sunset, it yet remains. The True Self, the Christ, always waits for you to remember. Jesus, the symbol of this, "I am with you all days..."

So may you all now rest with these thoughts. Discuss them, yes, but more than discuss, rest in them, rest in your True Self and the True Self of All... Feel the embrace of your True Self and the True Self of every Other enfolding you... It is all One, One Self, One Embrace, One Essence of Life and Love so Alive in All. And may we join you too, for we too are in need of deepening Awareness, and yes, in our journey with you, do we learn and are so happy to offer of these experiences to you. We Bless you All with a beautiful evening.

Aspects of True Self

November 16, 1983

For the group tonight, we ask you to consider why you who are all such beautiful children, why do you feel and think and act from a "less than" point of view? Everytime you compare yourself unfavorably to another, you feel less than; everytime you wish you could be other than you are, you are feeling less than; everytime there is jealousy or discord with another, it usually involves these feelings of great inferiority. And here we speak of inferiority to a job or situation as well as to the personal Beings of others.

We ask you not to see yourself as less than anyone or anything in judgment, for you see, it is not the actuality which hurts you, but how you judge that actuality. And so, the fact that the sun is hot — it just is and you say, "The sun is hot." But if you stay out in the sun and get a terrible sunburn, then do you judge the sun from your hurting point of view, and the statement, "The sun is hot" becomes critical, judgmental, for it hurt you. And so now for any situation — if you view it as better or bigger than yourself, you do yourself an injustice. The situations you are in, you have called upon self to unleash your potential, all that is within. You would not put yourself in any position unless there was some kind of needed response to come forth from you. You, Roseann, feeling limited in science and so on, would never think to place yourself in a job so related, for you do not have the urgency to unleash that potential. But you would consider some kind of spiritual teaching — even if you felt ill-equipped, yet you would pursue it, even amidst fear of failing and so on, for your Inner Self Knows this is the direction you so choose. And so for all here — consider your situations, jobs, personal relationships and so on — all are meant to unleash the potential within you. Do not feel less than in anything you call yourself to do. Know the Inner Resources are there, and that the path you follow will unfold and enrich you, if you but eliminate ideas of victory or defeat, success or failure. Think in terms of, "It is what it is, and I do what I do, and I am who I am. Nothing more, nothing less, I am the Blessing to the God Essence, to myself, at this time of my life, as are all the things around me. Jobs, pressures, blessings, people, whatever — all are there in a state of Isness for me to interract with, to unleash the tremendous potential within." For the doctors, do not ever suppose disease is greater than your Healing Power, do not feel threatened by disease. Rather, build within Self your potential as Healer and join yourself to the patient in love, so that the disease, loved and cared for, will leave the body as another form of energy.

And so our first message this evening is never feel less than, always feel you are God Essence, as is everyone and everything around you. Join yourself in Truth and Love to this Awareness. The second point surely follows the first . . . *Love yourself and you cannot feel less than.* You love others in proportion as to how you love yourself. If you are filled within with anger toward Self, how can you radiate love towards others? You must begin with Self. As you clear away doubts, imperfections and so on, and put these in the Light of the True Self, you cannot help but love another, for instead of nourishing negatives within, you now fill yourself with Love which comes forth and feeds others. And so are you fed, through the very nourishment you give to others. When we say to Love Self, remember to include everything about Self — your job, relationships and so on. It is all One, all You. Do not split Self, for remember that a House divided against itself cannot stand . . . So feel One with Self and all your many manifestations. You are Blessed Children, *Believe* this and *Know* it is so.

The True Self and Trust

November 22, 1983

For the meeting tonight, we have been speaking much of Self-Love, and now we would like to inculcate the Concepts of Trust and Receptivity to Self-Love. The older, familiar definition of trust is one's reliance on that which is known. The trust is in the predictability of the workings of things, of the human body, machines and so on. And so long as things are working the way we predict and rely on, the way we feel they should, we say that we trust them. But then if something goes wrong — the body gets sick or the car breaks down — now, we no longer trust... We fear ... We fear the things we trusted, for they let us down, and so, we withdraw our trust.

The Souls on Earth tend to do the same with self and others. So long as we are pleased with self's performance or the performance of others, we trust. And then we withdraw trust when we are disappointed. We are asking you to reconsider Trust and not to be so quick to give and withdraw the Trust to self, to all, yes, you see, to the God Essence. Trust in all manifestations, and yes, even when you let yourself down, or another lets you down, we ask you then more than ever, to Trust in all you do not understand, in all you do not rely on. Human Spirits have within them the concept — one break of reliability and it cannot be trusted again. The sun shines for billions of years, yet if for one day it did not shine, Human Beings would never trust the sun again. *Where is your Trust, Dear Children, in the Essence or in the performance?* Do you trust your behavior and the behavior of others, or do you Trust the God Essence in self and others always manifesting? So much human pain comes from the distorted ideas of giving and withdrawing trust, love, acceptability and so on, instead of living on an even-keel in a multidimensional Essence. In other words, Dear Children, to trust that True Self, that Self-Love, that personality entity that is a part of you, *Know* that whatever it manifests, you will love as God Essence and you will remain its friend. This is Jesus' message of the Prodigal Son, it is his message of Forgiveness. For Forgiveness is nothing more than Trusting that the God Essence will reveal itself within Love for one another.

And so what we are asking you is to trust Trust, to go beyond the trusting of predictability, to trust the unpredictable, the ever creative and changing God within you. And if you do so, you will find yourself much less quick to judge and condemn self and others, for your trust is in Trust, not in behavior and outcomes ... And when your trust is in Trust, so is it in God and the Powers of Life.

Livingness of These Principles in the "Practical" World

November 30, 1983

We are in amazement at your lack of patience, at your tremendous impatience with Self. You have asked for guidance on the Living of the Whole Man, the True Self, and now do you express frustration, impracticality and so on. Yes, is this material very impractical if you live from a practical, earthly point of view. It is like trying to feed yourself with that which keeps you warm. In other words, you obtain warmth on the outside from the sun, blankets, coats and so on, whatever sources of warmth you need — yet must you put yourself in the frame of mind to receive the warmth, to want the warmth. And if it is warmth you want, you do not turn to food for a meal. Both yield comfort, both yield satisfaction, but you must know what you want, and then go to the source that fulfills that want. Now what we are sensing here is that you want to know your True Self, which is Spiritual, which is Divine and so on, yet you want very earthly laws or you want the circumstances of your Earthly Life to neatly tuck themselves into your new Spiritual Dimensions. Dear Children, this will not happen so easily. You must live from *both* levels. We are not asking you to give up either one. We want you to experience your Earthly Life as fully, completely, purposefully as it is meant to be. This is the purpose of the material — not to take you out of the world, but yes, to keep you in the world but not of the world, to see beyond the human distortions of the ages, and to see the whole picture of the True Self. You, Dear Children, do you not see, you are the constructors of your own Reality — you who are seeking the Truth of Life, the Life beyond Earth — you who seek to understand the why of your existence — you who know it is more than job, success and so on in the earthly world — you who know that any earthly fame or success is as a flicker of the Flame of Being, and is not the Light, the Source of who you are or your true destiny. Why are you so upset with the very Truths you have uncovered? Why do you get angry at the Truths instead of directing your anger to your own earthly distortions or the earthly Consciousness of Being which stands in your way? What are you really fighting, the teachings or yourself? Yourself or your world? Your True Self or your personality? Feel your anger and impatience, but be sure you direct it where you want it to go, for there it will go and influence the course of your decisions. No one ever said it would be easy to be a Spiritual Reality in a material world. Do you think Jesus Himself found it easy? Did he not even vanish from the crowds when he could no longer take his own growing Consciousness into the Hearts of the people? All they wanted was his miracles and not his Truths. And we dare to suggest to you — is this what you also seek? Do you seek miracles or Truth? Do you wish to see all your wishes met, without the Truth of Being, *Your* Truth of Being behind it?

My Dear Children, we ask you to consider these, and we will go into it at greater length. We ask you to be patient with yourselves, but even more than this, be patient with the Truth of your Beingness. As you uncover this Treasure, do not throw it away if it does not fit into the Kingdom of Earth. *Create the Place for your Treasure.* If there is no place for you to live your Treasured Self, then you *Create* it. How? By Love, the Essence of Love, all comes down to Love . . . Love of Self, of another, of institutions, of everything. There will be no Peace in your Hearts so long as you seek the peace of man. Do not disguise the Peace of the God Essence as man, do not shrink God to fit into man, into the spot you want the God Essence to fit. The God Essence just *Is* — existence, everywhere and everything. And you create the place for Him by you too Being in Love everywhere, and with everything. You are meant to *Become Love.* If you are frustrated, it is only because you are trying to channel Love into a very narrow pipe — for Love is around, through and in the pipe. Try to understand by expanding yourselves and seeing yourselves for the Beautiful Children you are. We love you and ache with you, but yes, do we also smile, for we know you are all *Becoming,* and we are so very proud of you all. We Bless you with the Love that is the Love of Christ in us All . . .

We ask you to tell the group, Roseann, that we are Messengers of Love and that we seek to serve. Long ago, we told you how when Souls come to this side, help is forced on no one, only those who seek . . . And now may we say the same to all of you. Be patient with yourselves and know that where you are now is all of the Eternal Process. And so you see, we do not feel your impatience with time and so on, or the urgency of the moment. We admit that we are learning much of the human condition through you as we watch you in your lives. Yet, as you watch your child and see in his first step all the steps of his life, so do we you. We see all that is ahead, not only where you are now. So that you may know that, as you do not *experience* the falls and stumbles of the toddling child nor his joy at standing upright and walking alone, so the same for us here, as we see you, growing, learning and doing. And yes, as you do not recall the vivid sensations of your own first steps, nor do we recall the pain of the Awakening Process. So as you live your days and blend the Spiritual and the Earthly, we ask you, keep both in Mind and Heart. Do not desert one for the other, but Live both together. And yes, Live, from where you are — for that will take you to where you will be, which is where you want to be. Do you not see, it is all a matter of perspective, and there are times when your perspective changes. You can agree or disagree with this or that but we ask you, do not disagree with the basic Christ Spirit within you. Here is your basis, the Earth of You, from which the rest of you grows and manifests. In this Christ Spirit, do you Live and here will you Become the Seed, fully sprouted and grown. Be patient, Dear Children, for you will bear much Fruit and your Joy will be Complete.

The Intentional Level

December 6, 1983

For the meeting tonight, do we know from the Hope of Knowing ourselves comes the Hope of Knowing and Loving all others. We can only be what we are and give what we can — yet can there be the *Intentional Level*. All of you here, always so critical of selves, are also striving to be of "the more than" that you know is within your reach. And so we say to you, this Intentional Level is to be taken into your account, when you see yourselves, when you strive to see yourselves as others see you. We ask you all to know that where your Intent is, yes, there is your Treasure, there is your Heart also. Do not discount all you hope to be, for hope is the striving, the action, that gets you to where you want to be. Merge with your Intentional Level, yes, including all those hopes and asprations that you are not yet in touch with. Merge with the Unknown where it will become Known in Consciousness as you merge with it. Jesus said, "The Kingdom of Heaven is within you." You are already the Kingdom and will spread the Kingdom as you yourselves become aware of the Powerful, Loving Essences you are. All the Life and Energy that is yours, is yours for always . . .

You must remember always, "In my Father's House there are many mansions." There are many levels of Self operating at the same time. Dear Children, behavior, emotions and so on are on one level. We ask you to know that your Intentional Level and all that you aspire to be is also with you. In your experiences, do not judge yourselves . . . Be Alive to yourselves and enjoy the Wonder of yourselves. Enjoy your own Creativity and yes, even in your times of loneliness and despair, enjoy the beautiful Creation you are — you who can experience such feelings. We are each a Mystery ever unfolding and as we unfold to ourselves, we cannot but help others unfold. We ask you to be as the flowers in the garden, enjoying the Wonder of Self and One Another. This evening, enjoy the Essence of each Other. You are each a Beautiful Energy and together so multiplied, your Power for Love and Creativity is Immense. Help each other, Guide each other, and yes, Love each other, for you are each a powerful Presence of Love, a Reminder always of the God Essence that you spark in one another from the Flame within Self. So do we Love and Bless you All.

Self and Other

December 12, 1983

For the meeting this evening, we would ask you to concentrate on the initial steps into the otherness of Others. You have been working of Self-Love and Acceptance; now is it time to learn to apply these same concepts of Self to Others. We cannot do to others what is not within us. So in other words, if we provoke someone to anger, that anger is already within us and it seeks a realistic expression. Hence does the conscious and subconscious work in so subtle harmony to do something which provokes anger in others, so that we see our anger mirrored in reality. Now does our own anger have something to fight against. And this same is true for positive experiences, yes, as of loving. The love is within self and it seeks visible expression. Energies work to let that love also be triggered in another and hence, can there be interaction. So you see the painful lesson — nothing is manifested in others that is not already within oneself. It is also in the other too, and so does the other need to see its mirrored reflection also. And so do the two energies attract each other, and so interact and so on.

This is why so basic to the forgiveness of the behavior of others is the need to forgive oneself. One cannot forgive another if one is yet hateful, guilty, vindictive and so on, within self. This is Jesus' story, "Not everyone who says 'Lord, Lord' shall enter the Kingdom." One does not get into the Kingdom from the outside. There is no need to forgive the other, for in Essence, are you Forgiveness and you cannot judge the actions and behaviors of others. The Kingdom is the Self that is all Loving, and what is within, will, by its very nature, be mirrored and reflected without. Those who seek love, surround themselves with loving people; those who are angry, with angry people. Meditate on these thoughts and you will find that all that is within you is mirrored about you. Once you see this, will you become more conscious of being loving, accepting and so on. You will find that others will, by natural reaction, by natural law, so will they be the same to you. As you meditate on Self, we ask you to realize you are also meditating on the Self of all Others, especially those closest to you. Remember that on the Spiritual Level, we are all One and we are privileged to experience that Oneness in a visible way with those to whom we are closest in the earthly relationship. We Bless you All in the Beginnings of this Journey into Otherness.

The Christmas Message from the Angels of Light

December 21, 1983

My Beloved Children, this day are you gathered for the celebration of your Christhood. *Know* and *Feel* the tremendous splendor of your own Christhood and the Christhood of each Loved One here, each one of you becoming so Beloved to the other. Dear Children, do you know why you are becoming so Beloved to one another? Do you know that it is because you are touching the Christ Child within each of you? Yes, this is the Self you are coming to know as you gather together. The personalities are that which contain the Truth of the Selves you are meeting, and yes, whom all of you, are falling in love with. And Dear Children, do you not see, in falling in love with each other, in coming to know and care and bless each other, you are falling in love with yourself? You are knowing, caring and blessing yourself, your True Self, the Christ of Christmas in you. There is no end to Christmas, to the anointing of the Mass, the Communion, the Blessing of the Mass, the Worship of the Christ Self. And this is Christmas, the Mass of the Christ, the Blessing, Honoring, Sanctifying, Praising of the Christ — all of these, the Living of the Christ in Self.

My Dear Children, on this blessed night that has brought you and will continue to bring you together, we ask you to dwell on the Loving Essence of your Christ Child. As you meditate, see its Birth, see its entrance into dimensions you cannot yet even dream of. We tell you are they greater than the greatest wonders you can imagine. As you see the Birth of your Christ Child, see those who help you in the labor, see those who embrace you when you need embracing, who feed you when you are hungry for the nourishment of the Spiritual Reality, see those who walk beside you. Though you may stumble and fall, the Christ of Others, of Seen and Unseen, is there to help you and give you strength. Your Christ, Dear Children, is yet a Babe. Do not feel frustrated or feel impatient that you are not yet at this moment the Christ of Jesus, the maturing Christ who heals and raises from the dead. As you look upon your own children, you behold the Wonder of Life that they manifest at each stage — the tremendous applause and appreciation you give them at their first walking step! So, Dear

Children, give yourself that same applause. One little step for a baby, millions of unapplauded steps for the adult. Do you not see? Praise and applaud that Christ Child within you which seeks nourishment and companionship from the Christ Child of each other, companions, childhood playmates, friends in the Christhood of All. And as you acknowledge Self and the Birth and coddling of the Birth of your Christ Self, so meditate on the Birth of the Christ Child within your Beloved Ones, and then, yes, please go to all those Beloved Ones you do not know, but who are you, as much as you are you. It is why, Dear Children, the Angels, the Shepherds, and the Wise Men were part of the Christmas legends, for *All Life* joins in the Birth of Christ, of the Christ of Jesus, of You and of Everyone.

As you close your Meditation, see yourself as the Infant in the Manger, and for a brief time, see the World as the Infant Jesus, the Infant Christ. See what you can do and what you cannot yet do. See what you would do, and what you will do when you can. You are born this Christmas Day to a New You . . . A New Child has come into the World and his Newness, your Newness, will touch many. Your Christmas will be the ever offered Gift of Yourself to all Creation. May you enjoy the flowing love and sensitivity. May you open your Hearts to the vulnerability and wounds of loving, of loving too much as Jesus, "for greater love than this no man has than to lay down his life for his friend." And greater love than this no man has than to be born into the Truth and Realization and Lived Experience of Christmas Day.

Dear Children, we now Love you and Bless you and Sing with the Angels of Old . . . Glory to God . . . Peace to all of you who hear the Angels sing and who follow, even though you may fear . . . For the Angels lead you to the Infant wrapped in swaddling clothes, and, Dear Children, the Wonder of the Christmas Experience is that *the Swaddled Child is the Essence of You.* May your Love fill you to rejoicing, fill you to the Wonder of the Christmas always taking place, always being born within you. We give you our Love and Blessings of Joy . . . Zoriah and the Angels of Light.

Doing, Being and Disappointments in Self

December 29, 1983

For your meeting this evening, we feel there is the need to cope with the disappointment of Being, for yes, are there times when *Living in Beingness* is so disappointing to you all — you who do not see the vaster, broader results, the invisible rays that spread from all You truly Are. In the Doing, does one see the accomplished task, and yes, those with foresight, hindsight, perceptive abilities and so on, see beyond the task, connecting it to its past, present, future and so on. You see the results of the Doing, you allow that Doing to flower, to blossom beyond the present moment. What we are saying here is the *Being, the Invisible Essence of Who You Are, is your Pervading Essence.* Try to understand . . . Being is not something you do at a particular moment, and so are you conscious, "At this moment, I am Being." No, for so long as there is effort or will to think of it, Being is itself becoming a Doing, and you are measuring the results. "Was I being good enough?" or "Did I fail to *Be* in such a situation?"

Dear Children, do you not see, so long as you are questioning, weighing, measuring and sorting outcomes, you are not *Being* — you are yet *Doing*. Beingness is a state of Isness, it is incorruptible, it cannot be broken. Beingness is unchangeable, yet it waits to transform itself into new states of Being. The process here cannot be rushed. You cannot bandage it and feel it is healed, and then, jump into the next Awareness. Beingness is a Staying with, a Presence, the Presence of the Christ, the Beingness of the Hope of ever Becoming. But one cannot always just be with the hope of what you want to become, for in the concentration on the Future, is the Present lost. Rather, it is the *Living* of the Present in all its Fullness which leads you to the Future. You are Becoming while you are Being, and you are quite unaware of both, for you are Living, engrossed, penetrated by the experiences of that Present Moment. Whenever you feel disappointment that gets in the way of Being — yes, acknowledge, that too, is Being. Broaden your vision, expand your Consciousness, so that Being consumes more than just one moment of disappointment.

As we have said, Dear Children, Beingness pervades, is Essence, invisible rays that touch so many seen Realities and so many aspects you do not see. As the light from one candle shines in a darkened room — yes, slowly, are so many aspects of the room now in light, not just the one spot of candlelight. So is this the Essence of Being. Let yourselves be that glowing candle, the Light which lets you see the Words of the Lord Jesus. You see, that Light is within you and will guide you to the Understanding of all his Words. For did Jesus so *Live His Beingness* to the point of total Union with the Father that he could do all things, yet he could not judge. He knew that of his own he could do nothing, and in judging, was he judging the Father. This is why we ask you not to spend so much time and effort being critical of self and others, of always interfering in the Beingness of self and others, for in so doing, do you interrupt the Will of the Father by your judgment. You see, it is as looking straight at the sun, knowing it is the sun and saying, "This cannot be the sun." This is what you are doing in always judging and criticizing your Beingness. You are saying on the one hand, "I am the Son of God," and on the other, "I cannot be the Son of God, for look at this behavior and so on." Jesus never denied to himself or others who he was, even when he knew it meant his death. And so yes, did even the earthly reality ever proclaim His True Identity, even at his death.

Dear Children, listen to the Voice within you which guides you to your True Self. Do not be disappointed in your life, but rejoice in all that your life experiences teach you. Your eyes are young, yet are they opening to the Invisible, and as the eyes in a candlelit room get more and more adjusted to the darkness, till one feels he is in the light, yes, so too, you, as you get more accustomed to the Invisible Essence of yourself and others, so you too will see more and more, and no longer feel isolated and alone in the darkness. This evening, discuss these disappointments in self, and guide each other in the Understanding that each event that you interpret as a disappointment is a Blessing, the sign that puts you in touch with your Loving Essence. It is well to aim for better, but with the Knowledge and Belief that the Present Moment was its best. And with these words, we Bless you All with the Love of your Beingness.

Blossoming of the Self and Centeredness

January 3, 1984

For the group this evening, we must continue with the Growth and Blossoming of the Self, for you see, here in the Blossoming is Life. All too often, you live in the state of being of waiting for life to happen. What you are waiting for is life as you *want* it to happen, and so everything else that manifests becomes as the side show of the circus . . . yet do you remain waiting for the main event. What we are saying here is that *All* that happens to you is the main event. In the Blossoming of the Self, there are no side shows. Let each experience of your life be seen as that which adds to the growth of the flower. Do not judge which contributes more or less, which is good, bad and so on. Just see each event and personal relationship as tributaries flowing into the Whole, each pouring in, and none needing to be shut off because it does not fit in with your conception of how it is "supposed" to happen. You can lose sight of a significant person or event, simply because you are focused elsewhere, instead of being focused on the Centered Self, which is the great Receiver, the great Being, All That Is.

For those here who are in a position of control, this is very difficult to release, for you feel you want to control your outer world. But how can this be done when the inner world is in such confusion that it itself has lost control? There can be no balance or harmony so long as the outer world of self seeks to control that which is within. You will not achieve Centeredness by looking to bring things in. Rather, it is the Centeredness within that changes the without. Centeredness comes with the Realization of Inner Beauty and Worth. Centeredness comes when we align ourselves with the Creative Powers, release our energies from our stubborn wills, and clear the way for the Cosmic Will to, as it were, flow through us and absorb our energies where It Wills. The initial program of Being God Essence, Healing, Trust, Love and so on — this is set. Then, let the energy flow, so that these may manifest in your life, no matter how the experience is judged from the outside. You see, if you feel hatred and you judge it as hatred, so it remains. But if you are Centered in God Essence and yet feel hatred, yet will that hatred, by nature of the Powers of Creation, by the Creative Forces of Love inherent in Self, so will the hatred be transformed, and anything that happens to your life will be for its Blossoming into Inner Beauty. So hatred is the cry for the Revelation of Love; anger, the Revelation into Love. All that you are is *Love* and you know this deep within, for it is all you are ever searching for. In your work, life experiences and so on, think of it, all you are ever saying is, "I am Love that wants to express Itself . . . I am Love that wants to Love, to Be Loved."

Dear Children, we ask you to Know that God is this Love, Love is God, and so you see, in seeking Love, you are seeking God, you are seeking Yourself. The journey into Self is not a selfish one. It is a giving process, a learning, a loving. We are asking all this evening to meditate on what each of you have considered the side shows in your life, distractions, whatever you choose to call them . . . See these now as the main events, all flowing into the Wholeness of You, each as important and necessary, each revealing to you your Essence as God, as Love, for Self and each Other. We Love and Bless you All.

Fearing the Treasure of the True Self

January 11, 1984

For the group tonight, we have been guiding you to the Discovery of Self and now we say *Discover Self*. There is a time of making blueprints and following the treasure map, of taking two steps forward and three backwards and so on. But there comes the moment when you are in front of the Treasure — you have unburied it and, Dear Children, you must open it up and touch it and call it unto yourself. It is yours and truly belongs to you. What you have found is unique only to you, and only you can touch it and hold it and nourish it in the way it needs to be touched, held and nourished. We have the feeling, yet not feeling as you know feeling — but if we could join the words Feeling and Knowledge together to make one word — as we guide you, we have the *Feeling-Knowledge* that you are all afraid to embrace and claim as your own the Self you are looking for. Why is the Treasure so frightening to you?

Dear Children, we *Feel-Know* that you are placing your own limits on this Self. Even if you call this Self, Love, you have limited it, for you see, it is more than Love. It is also Wisdom, Guidance, Strength, Trust, All the Multitudes, Infinities, Depths and Heights of Life. You see, Dear Children, in your view of limiting Self and Life, you are always setting yourself up for disappointment. You always feel your joy will end, your life will end and so on. You do not live in a state of continuity and fluidity. If you did, you could not fear the next moment, you could not see the next moment as separate from this one, for it would just be a continuous moment. What we are saying here is you are unconsciously limiting yourself by attempting to define this True Self and by bringing it as something outside of you, into you, to discover. We are asking you to discard your treasure maps and lists of instructions, and we are telling you to face the True Self now living, breathing, acting, surrounding you already. Do you not see, there is no Treasure Chest, for you are inside the Chest. *How can the Treasure look for Itself?* This is where man and his quest for spirituality so often go astray.

The True Self is the activating power behind your feelings, thoughts, actions. It is the guiding power, the transforming power. It is already doing these things, and you are under a misconcepton if you feel the True Self is something you must find or become. *You are your True Self already.* Discover its power within you, embrace it, praise it, hold it, nourish it. As you do to your thoughts by thinking them, as you do to your feelings by feeling them, so *Be your True Self by Being It.* Now we sense you are saying, "What are they talking of?" And we say to you, come to think and feel as the True Self thinks and feels, do everything to Perfection, think Perfection, think Love, think and feel Oneness — even when the outer does not show these, yet are you thinking them. You must clear the way to think as God, so that God can think through you. Be an open Channel for God, so that, yes, God does not have to be in pain, for God is in pain when you do not let Him through... It is the same pain you feel, for you see, you and God are One . . .

Whatever experience you may be having, when you clear the channels, when you fear not and allow the Peace and Love of the God Essence to work through you, you will *Feel* its Activating Presence. It is already acting in you, but the conscious mind, so full of distortions, blocks its way. And so, though Peace is there, you are outside of the Peace instead of inside its very flow through you. You can be in the same room with someone but if they are behind a screen, you will not see them there. And they can be there loving you, kissing you, yet you do not see it. But when the screen is down, that person is doing the same, but now you can see it. And this is the True Self you are embracing. It is not in another room, it is within you, doing its Life's work, guiding you, leading you, yes, even pushing you to the Realization of Yourself in the God Essence.

Dear Children, we ask you to absorb these thoughts... We ask you all to think of one situation in your recent days when you acted with the screen up, and how much differently the situation would have unfolded with the screen down . . . See these now as One Reality . . . It is all a matter of Consciousness. If your Consciousness is Healing, and this is what we are Guides for, then an action based on the Healing Consciousness of Love will be filled with Power, Serenity, Joy and so on, the limitless Abundance of the God Essence. Apply these now, and we will be most happy to help you this night and always, to implement these Truths so that you may no longer be afraid to meet yourself, to touch the very Essence of God within you. We Love and Bless you All.

The Need for Ourselves

January 23, 1984

For the group tonight, we want to speak of how much you all need yourselves — your wants, dreams, human desires, your integrated parts, your fragmented parts — you need yourselves to keep yourselves on the road to Home and Wholeness. The more you reject Self and the more you say you need this or that philosophy or this or that doing, so the more do you get away from Self where God is, within you. Yes, you need this Self, both the little self of ego, personality, human needs, dreams and desires, and then, the Higher Self, the Source and Unfoldment of all those needs, dreams and desires. They are One . . . To try to separate them is a misconception, to try to let go of all the needs of the human condition is to let go of the Divine Life that works through that condition. To become Divine, you must first become fully Human . . . *Know that you need your Humanity. It is your channel, your vehicle for coming in touch with the purely Divine Life of the Father, the God Essence in you.*

Dear Children, you need God, you need nourishment, you need recreation, you need meditation, contemplation, time alone, time with others — yes, all these lists of needs — but did you ever stop to think of how much you need you? You need you to learn to love you and to love the other; you need you to experience the heights and depths, yes, the mountains and valleys. Jesus went there, and he needed truly no one but himself. He went to the desert to pray alone, for he needed himself. And yes, we need the other too, in relationship, to experience Reality, to have, as it were, the partner to an experience of any kind. But do not ever feel that you cannot be you without the other, for do you not see, in the higher spiritual dimensions, *the Other is You* and there is no separation. And so, you need you, and as we view it here, it is the You in the You of all others. On the earthly plane, where there is so much the search for self-identity and so much a sense of separation, you realize more and more how much you need everyone and everything. So much so that you forget your need for you. We ask you to so love yourselves and so need yourselves, for then are you giving Glory to the Creator. This is why the concepts of sickness, problems and so on are seen as nourishment for you — you need you to become the You of the *I Am*. You need your life, your feelings, your emotions. You need to experience all of these and so seek that they will reflect the Wonder of the Creative Powers. Needing self does not mean separating self from the flow. We are not saying to work so diligently to have your needs met and so on to where you become obsessive of this. No, Needing Self is Loving Self, and Knowing that the Self you are is your channel, your vehicle to the God Essence within you.

Dear Children, as you meditate this evening, as you discuss your hopes and dreams and fears, keep in Mind and Heart and Soul, the Life of the God Essence working in all of these. *Know* yourself, *Love* yourself — you have heard these so many times. Now do we add to this list, yes, to *Need* yourself, for you are Beautiful Children. As you need yourself, remember too that the others of your world, those you know and do not know, so do they need you too. We Bless you All with a beautiful evening . . . This is from Zoriah and the Angels of Light.

Fear of the Self

January 30, 1984

For the group tonight, we will speak here of the fear of the Self, of the tremendous energy man puts into fear and of how so much of this fear can be released into Loving Essence. Basic to this principle of Loving Essence is faith of and in that Loving Essence, that God, Creative Force, Life, call it what you will. It is the faith of, as it were, not even trying. As you get out of bed in the morning, you have faith, you know the floor will be there for you to step on it. You don't even give a conscious thought as to whether the floor is there or not. It has always been there; it is so ingrained in your Beingness, it becomes not even a point in question. Only do you become conscious of it when something new is brought to your attention, when something is in the way — a new carpet, a muddy spot, the change of feeling from sand to ocean and so on. Such externals make you aware of the external reality of the ground you stand on, yet do you ever find yourself questioning if there is ground to stand on? And so now, for the Creative Force, Life, God — so Real an Essence and Presence that you just *Know* it, and then, do you become *Aware* of its textures and patterns, your grasp of it and so on, as you go through the experiences of your Life. But your faith is so strong in its Loving Essence, you are so *sure* it is there, that you can live through even the most painful experiences, knowing your foothold is there. You are standing on Divine ground and you do not need to question its Loving Essence.

And so now for fear. Dear Children, we have spoken how it is the fear of any situation, feeling or thought which produces the pain, the anxiety. *It is the amount of fear you put into something, into Self, which makes the experience so painful.* This fear is always the fear of loss, the fear of the loss of Self or the Other. We now know that the Other, All Other, is Self — so always what you are fearing is the loss of Self. You have attached tremendous love and importance to your feelings and emotions, you possess them, you want to cherish them, own them, and yes, if they are negative, then you truly want to be angry at them or hate them — the ego, so involved in loving and fearing the Self. When you live from the Higher True Self, there is the Consciousness of the Christ, "Of my own I can do nothing, of my own, I have nothing . . . It is the Father in me . . ." And so you see, the ego can, as it were, just sleep, for it is the Higher True Self which possesses you. You, in turn, no longer need to cling to or hold onto anything, to possess anything so that you may come to get your identity from it. When you can come to see the experiences of your life, not only as personal gratification or hurt to the ego, but as part of the Loving Essence in expression through you, then can you learn to release some of the tremendous fear associated with your Life experiences, feelings and emotions. It is the simplicity of the analogy of the lilies of the field . . . If the Creator takes care of these, does He not even take care of you? It requires you to have the Simplicity of the Trust of the Child, whose fear disappears in the arms of its Mother. If you are to see yourself as always embraced by the Loving Father, then as you experience your sorrow or pain, can you do so knowing that you have nothing to fear, that you are comforted and blessed. We ask you to think of this when you next find yourself upset of something. See if you can transfer the fear into the Loving Embrace of the Father, and then, go through the experience with this sense of Protection. It does not mean the experience will be taken away from you or replaced. No, you will have the experience, but with the fear transformed, becoming Loving Essence, instead of the tremendous sense of loss, loneliness and so on, yes, even captivity. For one becomes so captive to the fear, that it just builds and builds, so that soon you are no longer even experiencing the original experience — but what you come to experience is only your fear. What we are saying is, we believe it is possible for you to experience instead the Loving Essence which surrounds you, is you, flows through you.

Dear Children, the Love and Oneness you are ever seeking is always surrounding you. Talk to it, touch it, feel its Protectiveness, so that you may let go of your fears and find yourself in the *Trust of Love.* This is not easy, and there are those of you who will say it is not practical and so on. But we ask you to just stay with it by saying even such simple statements as, *"Love, Love is my Beingness . . . The Father and I are One."* Statements such as these can be reminders — yes, ever do you need reminders to leave the fear behind, for you become so One with the fear that you even forget to try to disconnect yourselves from it. So first to remind yourself to leave the fear, and then to try to re-establish connection to the Divine Essence of Love within you.

(Do we still experience Fear in Loving Essence?)

Yes, do you still experience fear, but it is not the fear of man. You see, the fear of man is one of abandonment, annihilation, total and complete loss. *Man's fear is fearful.* What we are saying is that when you are fearful, but with a sense of the Loving Presence of the Divine, around, through, in you, so then does your fear become fearless. There is a sense of purpose, direction in the fear. You will not be spending all your energy just feeding fear. Rather, you will be feeding Self with Love, and in this way, does the despair and finality and loneliness of man's sense of fear disappear. Jesus knew fear before his death, but ever was it fear with a *Purpose,* of the joining to the One Will of the Father in his Life. And so, he was not fearful of his dying: he did not fear as a defeated man. In his Consciousness was he joined to the Father, and though he feared, yet did he *fear within Love,* and this is very different from fearing within hatred, guilt and so on.

Dear Children, we are not saying fear is eliminated. What we are saying is that in dwelling upon the Essence of God in you, the Ultimate Good, so do you now *Trust* that all is for your good. The fear you experience becomes more and more a steppingstone. If you stay stuck in the fear, you cannot move — it is as if you are always hanging from a precipice, so fearful of letting go. But if you let go of that fear and trust in the Loving Presence of God, then do you know that you do not even need the assurance that you will be caught, for even your fall becomes the fall into God. You fear the unknown, you fear that which you do not know well enough to trust, and you also fear that which you know too well will hurt you. You fear illness and so on, and rightly so, for experience has taught you these to fear. But now we say, instead of only staying with the fear, go beyond it into the Love you long to experience.

Love and Fear

February 2, 1984

   For the group this evening, there is the need here for all of you to shed the fears which have filled you for so many ages. It is by coming in touch with the Wholeness of You, the Perfection of You, that so too are you made aware of those parts of you which are seeking perfection. It is a paradox again, for it is in touching Wholeness that one seeks it to touch it . . . And so the process of Life, the ongoingness from one experience to another, always keeping in Mind and Heart that you are protected and guided by the Essence of Love. And the Essence of Love is without fear of loss, for *Love in Essence can only be Love.* It is the love of man — the concepts you have attached to it, its expectations and roles that leave you so fearful of Love. Think of this deeply, for truly all you crave is Love. You seek it everywhere, in everyone, but until you *Be Love,* you will never find it, for you will always fear its loss, and so long as you fear its loss, you see, you have never found Love . . .

   Love is the answer to fears, Love which is the Trustingness and Protection and Pervading Essence of the Father. In touching Love, do you touch God, for there is no difference. And it is important to know that all your experiences along the way — all the loving you do, the pain, the rejections, the loneliness of loving and not loving and so on — all of these are the nourishment to bring you to *Be Love,* true Love in Essence, Love that is without fear of withdrawal or rejection, or yes, replacement. The Essence of God is Love, the Essence of Creation is Love. Here do you find peace and here do you find the place that knows no fear. Think of these and then help one another. Most of all, Love one another, for in Loving one another, do you also Love Self, and in Loving the Self, do you find your God . . . You cannot find Him in fear, *you can only find Love in Love* . . . So you only find your True Self in God, and yes, the Mystery that God is also Man . . . Now do we Bless you with a beautiful evening.

The Wants of the Soul

February 15, 1984

Now for the group this evening, this is from Zoriah and the Angels of Light, we who are the Energy Field of Love surrounding you and so many. For all here this evening, do we wish to speak to you of the tremendous *Wants of the Soul.* Do you know, in Consciousness, that your Soul is ever a part of you and needs nourishment as much as any physical reality? The Soul, housed above the head, receives the stimulation of the Higher Forces which guide and protect it on its earthly journey. The more aware one is of the Body, Mind and Spirit Triangle, so the more are the Wants of the Soul heard, and so can you respond, not only to the physical plane, but, through your responses, to the Higher Forces. For you, Jan, and others, who wonder of the Mystery of Soul, it is no mystery if one sees the Soul as the constant companion and overseer, guiding the earthly experience, divulging its own Essence, and then also, in its attunement to Higher Forces, letting that Love and Power be accepted in you, through your Soul Beingness, into your physical and mental Self.

The Soul, Dear Children, wants its expression and feels its expression in the giving and receiving of Love and Compassion. The Soul wants Oneness, Harmony and so guides the earthly self into experiences to give these to the Mind and Body. You see, the Soul *Knows* it already, but to make the Mind and Body aware, so do you then experience your earthly self — but from the context of the Higher Self. So you all here, what we are saying is, your Soul wants you to be here, and so does the energy flow to conscious and subconscious levels, and so onto the mental and physical realities. By your Being here, are you fulfilling the Wants of the Soul which manifest in Beingness on the earthly plane. When it is said so and so is an Advanced Soul and so on, it is not in terms of Knowledge or Wisdom, but of the Openness of that Soul to the Creative Energies, how much letting go of the ego, of the emotional and mental sets which are used to construct Reality. In letting go of these, do you allow the Loving Wisdom of the Soul to flow through.

In this Consciousness do we ask you to know that you too are

Angels of Light, and you are One with us. Allow your Soul the Freedom to truly Live in you. Hear its knock so that the doors in you can be opened and you can Live from within, listening to the whispers of your Soul. And so, yes too, do you listen to the whispers of the Souls around you, and you are in Attunement with them in Love and Compassion. You, Dear Children, can sense who is touching your Soul and who is touching only your personality self. What we are saying is, you can touch the Souls of All, as you come to *Know and Live the Soul within you.* So are we with you and do you feel our Loving Presence, and all of this is so, for you have opened your Soul to the Wonder of Itself. We ever remain your Protective Guardians, Zoriah and the Angels of Light.

On Soul Consciousness

February 22, 1984

For the group this evening, do we seek to speak of the Secrets of the Soul which cries for recognition and worth in so many. For you see, does your Soul, which is Love, so does it Love you, and ever is it in pain for those who, on the earthly plane, know not of its Existence yet live surrounded in its Essence. It is out of reach, out of touch. This Soul, as the Invited Guest, waits to be welcomed into your Consciousness and Life Experiences. This is what we are asking you to do — to truly Live in the Presence and the Loving Embrace of your own Soul and the Soul of every Other.

The Soul is a loving energy, ever there, ever loving, yes, even to those so unaware, but in the awakening process. Yes, is it the same as going from the sleeping to the waking state. You sleep, you are there in your bed; all your life, your mental and emotional faculties are there — but all one can see is the outer shell. Then you awake and you become your unique individual self. No one breathes the same as you or smiles or thinks or feels as you do. You become this unique essential aspect of the Whole. And so for the Soul, ever there, ever waiting to be stirred and awakened, and impatient — not in your sense of hurry or urgency — but in the sense of Knowing, of its Knowledge of the Healing Power inherent in itself. The Soul is aware too of the tremendous resources beyond it which can help it to help you, the God Essence, which embraces the Soul as the Soul embraces you, as the God Essence embraces All.

Once the Soul is stirred and awakened, then can all dimensions of your Reality change. Hatred longs to be transformed into Love, anger and resentment into Peace and Serenity, discomfort into Rest, earthly restlessness into an ever anxious desire to explore and live the possibilities of Life, so gently in the peaceful flow of Love and Harmony. Your Soul, as you see it as your Companion, will help you to experience your earthly reality multidimensionally. A flower becomes deeper and more vast than itself. It is because the You of You is deepening and so expanding within, that so does the you who perceives also changes. Yes, must you remember to remove the glasses that you have been using. You must remember to live this New Consciousness by listening to the whispers of the Soul during the day which remind you, and yes, by you yourself, stopping for a second or two each day with just the simple thought, *"I am a Soul."* So can these words immediately put you in touch with the Divine Reality being expressed simultaneously with the Physical. Remember, Jesus did not live the Mystery of the Incarnation alone — so do we all. But you must, Dear Children, every so often, yes, seek to bring the Incarnation to your Conscious Mind, so that when you live, *you Live as God and Man.*

Your Soul, Dear Children, feeds you and so is fed by your own Awareness and Growth. So does it rejoice, as does the parent who sees his child now walking, now talking, aware of all that is going on around him. As the parent learns from the child and his interactions with the child and his Reality, so does the Soul — the You of You — learn from your earthly experiences, and so, is nourished and nourishes at one and the same time. So is this Love where the giving and the receiving are one process, and there is no distinction. Love just Is, Love ever flowing, becoming, changing, growing and so on. So Loved is the one who Loves, nourished as the Child by his Mother's love and by his own ability to love. The Child is also the Mother, who nourishes from Essence and is so nourished by her own Lovingness. For you and your Soul, Mother and Child, are One and the Same. Ever do you embrace and protect one another so long as you *remember* to do it, so long as you listen to the gentle stirrings within, to that which moves you, touches you, guides you. So do you *Listen to your Soul* and as you do, you will hear the *Loving Voice of your God.*

Inner Longings and Dreams of the Soul

February 29, 1984

For the meeting tonight, yes, is this from Zoriah and the Angels of Light. You who are gathered here in such love and friendship, listen well to the love and friendship within you, listen now to all those thoughts and feelings so hidden in your Soul, which you Know, but do not yet know, which you have told another in Essence, but have not yet expressed. We ask you this night to listen to the Inner Longings and Dreams of your Soul, to all that which is of you and in you, but which has not yet been brought forth. For is the Soul the seed, and it contains all Life and Memories, as does the seed contain the plant which manifests thousands of times larger than that seed, but which so needs the seed for all that Life which is contained within it. The earthly life you are experiencing now is but a touch of your Soul — one facet of the diamond. It is only when all the facets, in all the depths of dimensions, can shine and reflect their Light — it is only then that the Soul can even begin to rest in its God Essence Self.

And so we ask you to come in touch with thoughts you have long ago thought, with dreams long ago dreamt, for so much has been forgotten or laid aside now for want of more important earthly concerns and so on. These concerns are justified and needed — your work, your lives as doctors, wives, husbands, teachers and so on — all is needed. But now do you also live these through the Soul, allowing the Soul to think and be there for you in Awareness, when before, you would never have thought to invite the Soul in. The Soul becomes a Companion and Guide, and yes, do you suddenly feel more Intuitive, more Knowledgeable, more sure of Self, for you are allowing a previously untapped Source of Loving Energy to flow into you and work with you, through you, yes, *as* you, in your earthly experience. You become filled with a sense of your earthly Purpose, and then yes, do you even go beyond this and come to see your Life with its ultimate Mystery — the Union of Self and the Other, the Oneness of All.

As these Awarenesses pervade your earthly experiences, you feel so very different towards the experiences, and yes, towards these others who are part of your experiences, part of the Life of your Soul. You find you cannot compete with another, for then are you competing with Self. You find you cannot try to lie or deceive or trick another, for so are you only distorting your own path and your own experience. You cannot delegate Self to an inferior position — for how can One Soul, which is Infinite, Good and Loving, how can it be less Infinite, Good and Loving than another? You cannot lose confidence because of the Trust in your Purpose, and the Knowledge that, even if a task is not performed to your expectations, even that is as it should be. The empty spot helps you to see that which needs filling, and so it is, as you need and want the darkness to enjoy the beauty of the lighted candle. Do you see how once the Soul becomes your Friend, so do you become Friends and Companions with *All* that manifests in your Life. So are there no enemies and no outside other, for *You are in All* and *All is in You.*

(Is Living from Soul Consciousness different from Healing Consciousness?)

In Living from Soul Consciousness, one is ever aware of the Healing needs of others, but from the Higher Self point of view where you are not looking down on that which needs to be healed, and so attempting to fix that which is in need of repair. From Soul Consciousness, all is Love and Oneness. It is almost as if in Living from this level, Healing happens automatically, almost as if there is no need for Healing. The Soul is in tune with all the Higher Forces, and everything that is and happens, brings you in touch with these. We don't know if you understand this. *Soul Consciousness is Healing itself* . . . Nothing is in need of Healing, for the Soul Knows All Self is One and Healed already. And so is the Essence of Healing pervading everything you do and are.

So do we Bless you All. Rest with these thoughts, Dear Children. Know that You are Soul and Whole, and that You are ever so much greater than the sum of the parts you've split Self into. So do we Bless you All, Beautiful Souls of Joy and Light.

Soul Consciousness

March 6, 1984

For the meeting tonight, you remember we said that the Soul contains the All of You, the old memories and patterns, as well as All That Is. Now what happens is, in the beginnings of Soul Consciousness, we try to work from what is known or what we distortedly think we know of the Soul. Actually nothing is truly known if it has to be so sought after, uncovered, worked on, for then is there all the human will, human concepts of work, success, failure and so on. There is also the human need to have a framework of reference, and so we say, "The Love in my Soul is what I will focus on." But immediately, do we give that Love a form, a place, a degree and in so doing, already have we limited the Soul.

Dear Children, what we are trying to say is that this process of the Soul becomes a *Knowing* on its own. Do not so consciously seek the Soul, for then have you only made yourself a map. Rather, have the Soul make itself Conscious to you. So you see, in seeking your God Essence, you do not welcome God into the small portals of your Heart, but rather, do you accept the Invitation for you to take the steps into His Infinity. Now for the Soul, is it the same. Do not take your Soul and try to define it, experience it, seek it and so on. Rather, just be there, and let the Soul Consciousness reveal itself to you. You will be wrapped within it, rather than seeking it as something to put into your little box, which you have now labelled, Soul Consciousness.

In the Soul are, as it were, energy seeds . . . All that is you is contained within each seed. And so, there is Trust, Compassion, Belonging, Intuitiveness and so on — all energy centers, yes, analogous to the energy centers of the Body. The Soul also contains these energy centers, but they are as seeds, and you see, must they be transformed from seed into Awareness, the Blossoming of the Essence of each. And so, as you come in touch with a moment of Compassion or true Caring, know that there is a tremendous bursting or blossoming within the Soul. The seed moves, the energy is vaster, and the more intense the experience, the Awareness, so the more deeply will it penetrate into the depths of your Consciousness and Inner Being. You, now blessed with a moment of earthly Compassion, being open to your Soul, so also do you now come to experience this Compassion beyond its earthly dimension. You go into the Infinity with it, into Christ Compassion and so on. Every experience becomes heightened as it is energized from Higher aspects of Self. So you find in your Compassion for one, do you then think of ten, twenty, and yes, does the energy field around you so give Compassion and Comfort to so many who know that here within you is a Source of Love. This is the Living from the God Essence where every act, every feeling you have and so on, is filled with this tremendous Awareness of a sense of the beyond, of the places of Consciousness which seem far away, behind some veil, but which actually will just enwrap you if you so let them.

Dear Children, do not limit your Soul. Do not channel the energies of your Soul, do not be the director. But in the Stillness, *let your Soul Self use you as the Channel.* You will step into its Immensity, and not trickle its Immensity into your Awareness. We feel this is important for you, for we feel some of you are inviting your Soul Awareness into you. And you are becoming frustrated, for you feel the vastness of the Soul cannot fit into your present Awareness. What we are saying, is for you now to accept the Invitation of your Soul, for you to go into *It,* and allow yourself to be enwrapped in its Loving Immensity and Fullness, all of which is the Loving Essence of You. Listen to its Voice ... Do not give it a list of expectations and so on, but rather, Dear Children, be still and listen and so will you hear ... So do we Love and Bless you. This is from Zoriah and the Angels of Light.

Living in Soul Consciousness

March 15, 1984

Now for the meeting tonight, in the wanderings of the Soul in the human form, we can compare this to a person who is riding in a train up a huge mountain. The mountain is your Life, the train is you. Where is your Soul? Your Soul is in the mountain, in the train, in the whole happening, in all that brought you to the mountain and in all that will be once the climb to the mountain is done. So your Soul witnesses the present moment, and all that is before and after it at the same time. The fact that its view is expanded, does not mean it is more present in the now, less in the past and so on, for with the Soul, there is no time and All is Wholeness. It is All One, and though the Soul is everywhere, yet is it also omnipresent, always witnessing, and *Itself,* being stirred and moved. Nothing happens to the Body or Mind or Heart without its impression upon the Soul — from your Soul, then to all Souls and to the Higher Forces. The more one is aware, so the more can this process of *Becoming One* be realized. For when there is no Awareness of Soul, does all stay with Body and Mind. But with the Soul Consciousness, each dimension expands, as much as you let it, to Infinity if you will.

Let us take a moment of tremendous sorrow — as some of you here have had this week. Did you not feel it more intensely, more universally? Your caring, did it reach beyond the one into the many? Your Love, did it bring you closer to the Christ in Self and All Others? So what does this moment of earthly sorrow mean? Surely not just to be sad and express tears. One is sad because one experiences the separation from Self, and yes, the deeper the separation, the more intense the pain. Self-hatred, guilt, loss of esteem and praise and so on are all that which separate self from Self. It is here where those who commit suicide do so, for they have so detached self from their True Self, that there is nothing of the God Essence, no whisper of the Angels, nothing beyond to flow in and, literally, raise the self to a *desire* to Live and Be. This separation from Self leaves no room for Healing, for *Healing is the Union of Self to All.* If your mental set is one of separation, there is no help that can come through. The more aware, the more alive your Soul is, the deeper will you feel any sense of separation from the Life Force. You will almost feel as if you ceased to exist, except that you are breathing . . . You and your Soul have so identified Self together, that the Loss of One becomes the Loss of All. Do not feel your Soul deserts you when you feel so separated from Self . . . It is ever there, ever Protecting and Loving and Knowing, and yes, Feeling that moment of pain, but also Knowing what is beyond the pain. In times of tremendous earthly sorrow and detachment from Self, touch yourself, yes, hand to hand . . . Know that God is in that touch, Self to Self. Know you cannot be separated from His Essence even though you may feel a total rift between ego self and Higher Self and so on. Always is the separation the illusion . . . The fear — though truly experienced — is *not* Real.

What we are trying to say here, Dear Children, is that *your Soul is your Life.* It is all you are and all you will ever be . . . It is the Source of your comfort, for yes, does it know your despair. And if in a time of great sorrow, you can touch your Soul, you can help self go beyond the earthly fears which sweep you away from your Awareness of Soul with, in, of and through you. In the midst of your fear, focus on your Soul and the Higher Forces channeling their Love into you . . . Trust in the Presence of Love, and yes, Trust in the Presence of Self . . . So do we Love and Bless you always.

Loving Those Aspects of Self Hateful to You

March 21, 1984

    For the meeting this evening, it is time to concentrate on the aspects within Self that you wage war with, and yes, for many of you, will this be done in a new dimension. For is it one thing to know and recognize something in Self and resolve to change it or wish it away; and is it a completely different matter to love an area of Self that so hurts you, that is the dark cloud around your Light which prevents you from seeing your Light. It is time now for some of these dark clouds to be lifted.

    You have been taught already, Dear Children, the need to embrace and love all aspects of Self. How do you love that which is hateful to you? So the first thing to do is to isolate this quality and let it stand on its own, away from you, not touching you, not near you. Already, does it not seem weakened and less powerful than when it was within and surrounding you? Do you not see how weak a dark cloud is when it has nothing to hover over? This is why it was so easy for Jesus to cast out whatever were then termed "evil spirits," but actually, were the mental sets and fears of those he healed. So you see, when he came between the dark cloud and the person, so did His Light, His Essence of pure Loving Energy, cause the darkness to leave. And this is what you want to see happen.

    Dear Children, you do not want to spend your energy fighting against that which you do not like, for all that serves to do is to energize the original fear. You think of it and fight it with more components of itself, so that if you are angry and you do not like this, you tend to become more angry. If it is jealousy, and you fight it, so do you find yourself more jealous. You energize it, very much like a battle — the two can be at truce, but if one attacks, then so will the other. This is how our treatment in relation to Self and negativity works also. Now is the way to handle this, first just to isolate the fear, the jealousy and so on, separate it from its situation, place it in the middle of the desert, for here is where Jesus met his fears, and then, do you minimize its power, for it has lost so much of its hold on you . . . Do you not feel a sense of *Compassion* for this quality that is so separated from its God Essence Self? Do you not feel sorrow for the hatred that is not yet

Love, for the jealousy that is not yet Charity, for the darkness that is not yet Light, for the fears that are not yet Peace and so on? All of these long to be the other, yes, the other that is also your Self, though not in that particular experience at this time.

So, Dear Children, do you isolate this quality in the desert and there do you speak to it . . . "Why are you with me? What can I do for you? What are you trying to teach me? How can I transform you so that you can live peacefully within me, instead of warring against me so?" And you speak to it with Love, for is it a part of you. You are speaking to it from your Soul, your Higher Self, and you are detached from it. Do you not see that this is the very method Jesus used in the desert? He allowed those parts of himself which needed purification to, as it were, speak their Mind — for so are they energy, even if this energy is distorted. Yet do you, in your Loving Energy, help the twisted and distorted parts unwind, so that you can see why such a quality, which hurts you so, is in your Life and what you can now do about it. You see, you are showing it respect, for it is of you. And you do not hate that which is of you, but do you seek to understand it. So can you then speak to it, let it hear your Higher Voice, as did the spirits hear the Voice of Jesus and so then leave. In the Voice of Love, can all else fall away, just as the darkness disappears in the Essence of Light. The Light has to do nothing to the darkness except *be* itself . . . By Being Light, it dispels darkness . . . And so for you too, by being Soul, by Being and Living from the True Self, do you dispel the darkness and fears which beset you.

We ask you this evening to choose your fear or concern and meet it in the desert and speak to it as suggested. This may be very painful, but listen well to the conversation that takes place between your Soul and this aspect of the human self that is begging for transformation just by its very presence in your Consciousness. Speak to it in an atmosphere of Love and Light, and Know that you are never alone in meeting Self, for is the Christ Self ever with you. As you meet and come to know this quality, you will come to understand why it is within you, and in the Love and Acceptance of it, will you gradually see it disappear, for you have so Loved it into the Beingness of your Christ Self. You have called it Friend, called it your own, and in doing so, has it now become the aspect of Light which it represented, which it was so seeking to Be. Just meet one, for it is enough. You may meet others along the way. Say hello to them, recognize and acknowledge them, and tell them you will meet them later at another time. So is this a process and a way of handling the negative energies which so often frustrate you. At the end of this exercise, do you part warmly with the quality and just leave it there in the desert, just to let it Be, neither inviting it back into you, nor putting obstacles in its way. You will find yourself feeling very much free. When next you meet it again, you will feel more friendly toward it, and you will find more and more that you have helped it transform itself into Christly Essence within Self. Be patient with Self and Know, Dear Children, that you are not alone . . . As did Jesus, call upon the Angels to minister with you and Know, in their Love and Care, in your tremendous Love and Care for each other, you are not alone. So do we Love and Bless you always.

Meeting Self with Compassion

March 28, 1984

For the meeting this evening, do you so remember last week you met a part of self that you did not like in the desert — do you remember the conversation you had with this self? We ask you this evening now for you to meet the other side of this quality in the desert, for as surely as the war is waging within you, so is there the *Peace,* and the two are very much in need of the other. There is no way to meet Self, but to meet the Whole Self, and this is what you want to do.

And so you begin from the place of Wholeness, where all is One. Do you so know that the Tree of the Knowledge of Good and Evil is One Tree, always do you know it is One Reality. And then is there the *choice* of what you experience. But that choice is so very clouded by fears, insecurities and doubts, for you see, you come to the point where there is, in the social, acculturated self, almost totally, a sense of separation from God. Now do you Know, though you have not yet consciously experienced this, yet do you Know, there is another choice offered to you, and that is the choice of Wholeness instead of fragmentation, Oneness instead of disjointedness, Fullness instead of emptiness and so on. Though you have not yet fully perceived this Reality, yet do you Know that it is there and that its Source is Good and Truthful.

You are all sensing now the tremendous responsibility involved in choices for Self. And you know, for the times you have experienced them, that when you live in the Peaceful Acceptance, in the minute by minute, second by second Revelation of What Is — when you live in this state of Isness — then do you know that you flow with the Divine Essence within you. You have all touched Peace, you know it is there ... We ask you now to get in touch with that sense of Peace and Wholeness ... What happened to you to bring you to this stage? We would venture to say that at such a moment did you feel both Loving and Loved, did you feel Accepting and Accepted and so on. It was the moment when Giving and Receiving were One and the Same. The second a thought might flash to another desire not met and so on, your sense of Wholeness was lost, for you were again in touch with the human condition of the something that is missing or the fear of the loss. What we are saying here is when you can feel Loved and Loving in all circumstances, Accepted and Accepting in all situations, when you can release that the negative feeling is the enemy of the positive one, then will that Peaceful Acceptance and Wholeness truly be yours. So you must not see your anger as your enemy to your Peace of Mind, or your hatred as the enemy to your Love and so on. You must cease the warring within you, and you must see each as a Fruit of the Tree of Life. The True Miracle of Self is the Realization that in God, there is no good or evil, for *there is only Life*. It is man's original sin that he made an evil choice exist outside of God. The evil in the Genesis story is not that they picked the fruit against God's Will — the evil was that they created another will, another choice at all, by so acting apart from the Self of God.

So now in Meditation do we say to you, Dear Children, meet again your warring aspect within self. You know it a little better this week and you feel more gentle and more understanding of it. You know it is a part of you crying for acceptance. As you too may cry for acceptance in a room full of Loved Ones, and yes, their Love is there, but you are afraid to feel it, and so you do not — so for this quality. The God Essence in you seeks this part of you into the Wholeness of Itself, to be transformed into Itself, *Loving Essence*. And so do you meet it, and now do we also ask you to take yourself, take a good quality in Self, and let it meet this other which is also Self. Let your sensitivity meet your anger, let your tolerance meet your impatience, let your willingness to serve meet your obstinacy and so on. It need not be the so-called opposite quality, but rather, any Loving quality in Self. Let it meet this hurt or angry or jealous self, and let them now speak to each other, dialogue with one another in Love and Caring, yes, forming Friendship with each other. Let the warring self ask, "How do I come to be more like you? How can I come to merge with you?" And so let your anger feel it has a Friend, a Compassionate Friend who sees it for what it is. Let your fear feel it has a Friend in your Trust or Caring for another and so on. Visualize them in a place of Home, visualize them hugging or merged or whatever comes to your Mind and Heart. So you can begin to feel the hardness and bitterness of the warring quality and you can feel that it is now slipping, melting a little into the Wholeness of the Other.

All of this, Dear Children, it is all you. We ask you to do this Meditation wrapped in your own aura of Love, and then, yes, wrapped in the aura of each and everyone here, and so beyond to the auras of those other Loved Ones, to Jesus and so on, so that you feel the whole process wrapped in the tremendous Oneness and Blessings of all Love. We are with you in this process. Do not be afraid, for you are ready to meet Self and to discover the wonderful Creation you are. In this process, have no fear, Dear Children, for the Self you are meeting is your God-Self. Is this not the Treasure for which you have been searching? So do not fear, for you are wrapped in the Protective Love of the God Essence, and you will come to understand even more how the Father, the All Good, the All Loving, the All Compassionate Source, you will come to see how the Father and you are One . . . So do we Love and Bless you All.

Meeting Self . . . Meeting Others

April 11, 1984

For the meeting this evening have we been concentrating on the growth of the Love of the Whole Self, and you have been given the Meditation that may help you transform such a quality that is painful to you. We ask you to know that with every feeling and every experience you come in touch with within Self, so does that contribute ever more to your Compassionate Longing and Understanding of the All. For as you come in touch with your own anger, so do you come in touch with the anger of everyone, and do you want to feel that same sense of Compassion and Longing for Union with All. So is this true for every aspect of your Reality, for do you seek to *Become Self,* and yes, in doing so, to *Become the Other.* There is that deeper sense of, "So long as you do it to one of these, you do it to me." In the Wholeness, it is done to All — not just *for* somebody else, but with, in, pervading the Essence of the Beingness of every Other, as it is created also into your own. And so, Dear Children, as you work on and discover an aspect of Self, know also that you are uncovering that dimension in your relationship to every Other. So your anger, now gentled with Compassion, is a different anger given . . . And the anger you may feel coming in towards you is now a different one, compassioned by your own understanding of it. This is the Loving of One Another "as I have Loved You . . ."

The God Essence within each person can only be One Whole Loving God Essence, and though expressed in so many ways — so many different colors, varieties, textures and shapes of Flowers in the Garden — so it is the same Essence. It is the *Essence* you are searching for. Remember, it is not just to see the expression of that Essence in the same form, but rather, to seek to *Know* the Essence of One Another. In so Knowing, do you Become. As long as the external behavior and perceptions are your spectacles to see through, Essence will not be felt, for do you perceive from your own eyes and this you cannot help. You want to go beyond that which the eyes can see, beyond seeing, so that the Oneness of All Essence is within you as a pervading Reality. In that Oneness, do the outward differences disappear — just as when a Soul is so One with the Essence of Flower, that he sees and perceives both the beauty of the whole Garden and of each individual Flower, yet without making any conscious distinction between the whole and its parts.

There are many ways to perceive Reality and consciously deciding of one way over another may help, but it cannot become your Essence if you impose it from the outside to within yourself. You cannot make a decision to let the Essence of God pervade you, and then, so force it in and feel so frustrated and lacking in self-worth when you feel the Essence has left you. Dear Children, do you not see, it has never left you, for it is already within you, always. It is in the *Stillness of Self* that you will Know it, when you least try, when you least absorb your own energy, your own human efforts and ego. Just in the Stillness, let the Energy of Life and Truth within you flood your Beingness, as you let all else go into its flowing waters. We ask you this evening to stay in the Stillness . . . Just Be There, a Channel, a Vessel, an Empty Cup. Be Still, and then Know the Life within . . . So do we Love and Bless you All . . . This is from Zoriah and the Angels of Light.

Death and Resurrection

April 18, 1984

For the group this evening, with the coming of the Death and Resurrection, do we say to you to examine your own Deaths and Resurrections which are the constant flow of your Life. For truly, if you can see each experience of sorrow as a seed for a future joy, you will know that nothing ends in Death. Rather, is it just the sprout that gives forth a new life, a new thought, a new perception, a new way of looking at Self and your relationship to the Whole. If you choose to die with each experience, so can it be — for what Death truly is, is the cessation of the flow, rather than the constant moving which brings you ever to a new sense of Self.

All Death and all Life is contained within each experience — each experience contains within it both Realities. How you live these determines which you experience. For in Truth and in Love of the God Essence, there is only *Life,* and Life not as an alternative to Death, but only Life. It is man who creates Death; it is man who sees the wilted flower as dead rather than as a new form of life which can nourish the soil to produce more and stronger of its own kind. It is only man who sees things as having an end — and is this so for all of your experiences. You await the end of a sad experience and you fear the end of a joyful one, rather than seeing these as one constant flow of Life. All is contained within it. If you but turn to Nature, you will see the workings of the Life of God, the Mind of God, ever creating and never losing itself in beginnings and endings. Can you but for a moment reflect on how differently you would view your Life, the very Life of you, your Spirit, if you did not succumb to the limitations of beginnings and endings? So do we know the dimensions of time, but these we are not speaking of. We are speaking here of the way you define your thoughts, your experiences, in terms of beginnings and endings. What we are saying here is that where there is only Life, truly there is only Life, for every Death experience is Lived. Yes, you see, true Death is the refusal to Live the Death experience. It is the fighting of Death . . . We here refer to a Death experience as any experience which makes you so intensely aware of your separation from Life. *To truly Die is to truly refuse to Live Death.*

And so you see, Dear Children, what we are saying here is that one cannot touch Life unless one also knows of Death, for are Death and Life both All Life. It is only man who has judged one as better, more rewarding, one as a more deserved grace than the other and so on. Jesus Himself, upon his Death, first descended into hell. *He truly Lived his Death,* for he felt that total sense of isolation and abandonment before he could ascend into Heaven and experience the Fullness of His Resurrection to New Life. And so did Jesus then need to share the New Life with all, which is why he remained a little while longer. Then he too could come to Know Himself in a Higher Plane of Enlightenment. He experienced this Enlightenment as truly the birthright of all — though he could not give it even to his Apostles, for they too had to find it for themselves. So, each Soul must truly Live his own Deaths and experience his own Resurrections to New Life.

We ask you this evening to come in touch with that which you experience as Death and see if you can see it as so alive, producing the seeds of the New Life in you. And we ask you to also know that Death and Resurrection are Life Itself. It is only when you can find and Love Self in each and so seek to *Live* each to its Fullest Awareness of that Moment, it is only when you know both and know they are One, that is when Death will have no power over you.

For the group this evening do we say to you, the Life within you cries for its very Death and Rebirth over and over again. Do you not see that it is Life itself which calls you to go on ever creating and recreating, forming the Order out of the Chaos? For a Soul such as Jesus, was his physical death but just one step in many Deaths that his Soul experienced. More for him was the Death of the Dream, and yes, the Rebirth of Trust and Hope, as you, Dear Children, that all is not in vain. For there is a Trust and a Hope in an all good God Essence which will bring All forth to Resurrection. We are asking you to see the Deaths of self as the way to Becoming the ever *New Self.* Each time an old pattern dies, so do you rejoice in the new one that is coming forth. It is One, it is all One process and so does it go on... And yes, even we Angels here, do we too know of such Death and Resurrection, but we do not despair in the Death, but rather see it as the Life potential within All. So do we Love and Bless you always.

The Earthly and Heavenly Self . . .
No Distinctions Between the Two

April 30, 1984

For the meeting this evening, let us return to the matter of Form and Spirit, of the Earthly Self and the Heavenly Self, and let us this evening concentrate very deeply on the lack of difference between the two. You all too often separate yourselves into the so many parts, and so every time there is a dichotomy, you have moved away from the Essence of Life. So do you know that *God manifests Self as Essence,* of Life, Love, Beauty, Perfection and so on. How that Essence manifests is dependent on your perception, openness and so on. If you have a view of dichotomy — "His Will vs. my will" — that is how the Life, Essence of God manifests and so will that duality manifest in your life. You will see your life in terms of good days and bad days, and you will give a very different energy reaction to the two. Man is so accustomed to duality that everything is seen in terms of Life and Death, and so long as this is how you choose to see Life, so do you live the life of man in God rather than the Life of God in God. You see, it is all God Essence. As the water can be clear and springing from its Divine Source, so can all experiences be contained in Divine Essence and remain pure and clear. If you inject a coloring into the water, so does the color change, but its Essence is yet water, though of such a different color and so tainted as to *seem* separate from the Source.

Dear Children, we are asking you to know that the difference of life on the earth plane and this our plane is in terms of dimensionality only, not of Essence. You perceive as much as you can with your senses, physical limitations and so on, yet is your Essence of the God Self, and so there are no differences here or beyond the earth plane. Do not think the Essence of You radically changes from one plane to the other. No, the Essence is forever there. As a flower — whether it is blooming before your eyes or, now wilted, is but a memory of beauty — yet is its Essence ever the same. You do not lose the Essence of Flower, though one experience seems to show it before your eyes while for the other, you must go to the eyes of the Heart and Memory — yet all is the same Essence.

So do we ask you this evening, Dear Children, to know of Life on "Earth as it is in Heaven." It is ever the same and you are truly living as much of Heaven or Divine Life and Awareness as you are now able. Yet, in Essence, do you Know and Live the Whole. You are joined in Consciousness to All as you so make yourself Aware and Living of the Essence of the One All. Do not think some great enlightenment awaits you after death. So will you know the Enlightenment reaches you *now,* as you live the daily experiences of self, both in *Form and Spirit,* and know that each is contained within the other. To the Conscious Mind, to the brain, is this so difficult, for have you been so trained and programmed to separate the two, to think of one as higher than the other and so on. But what we want to here emphasize is Body and Soul are of the same Essence, as are Mind and Heart, Past and Future — all One, no separation, no duality. So can you in your Meditation this night relate this to a time in the past or future when you so separated Self, and see how this led to judgment of Self, yes, separation of Self from the experience itself, which is separation from Life, from God. So now do you meditate on the Wholeness of Self and see Life as One Experience . . . See Self as Life, as the Experience, so that you are not separated from it . . . You are Heaven and Earth, undivided in Experience, in Life . . . There is One Life and All Experiences are One in that Life, and touch You who are One in that Life as well. So do we Bless you ever in the One Life of Self and One Another.

Oneness of Body, Heart and Mind With Spirit

May 9, 1984

For the group tonight, do we ask you to remain in the flow of your own physical, mental and emotional selves while you are discovering also the spiritual Self. All too often have you been saying, "I must not be spiritual enough or developing enough," and do we ask, what is enough? You see in your physical, emotional and mental experiences that which seems to lag behind the spiritual quest. But we say to you, as you come in touch with the Spiritual aspects of Self, so do you integrate these, and know they are One with You, and in no way separate from what is going on in the Body, Mind and Heart. We want in every way to eliminate the dualities. Never feel, "I am physically healthy, but spiritually, I am in need of much help," or the opposite, "I am spiritually so attuned, why then does such disease manifest?" We ask you to look at the Life experiences of Jesus, for was he not so Spiritually Attuned, yet die a criminal's death?

In dealing with Self, must you surround yourself with your whole history — *the Whole of You*. Until the All of You is taken into account, you will always feel the sense of bewilderment of things happening to you. You, who do not see twenty years from now, so do you not know how today fits in with your future. And this is why we say, in the flowing with life and not in the fighting of it, does today fully become today, is truly lived as such and then, naturally, blends into the tomorrows. But when you spend your time and energy fighting today, trying to make it not happen, so do you cause a whole block up of confusion, and so you see, the flow is interrupted, not only for that day, but for many, many after. It is as if the pattern is locked in. We have been saying to you that no pattern is locked in, so long as you keep within Self the desire for Self to be Free. The Freedom comes in *Seeing* the Truth of each experience, in *Knowing* that nothing can hurt you, and in *Trusting* the Holy Beneficence of the God Essence Life.

There are those here much too impatient with Body, Mind and Heart and Spirit. So do you play one against the other instead of keeping them aligned in Harmony. And this you do by not testing one against the other or seeing if one will perform for the sake of the other and so on. For you are not aware of this, but all too often, this is how you treat the many selves within Self. You tend to give each a separate autonomy, a separate will, and actually, you know it is *One Will of Self.* That One Will seeks Attunement with Grace and Ease. But when you separate into many wills, or when you ask your Body to prove its loyalty to your Spirit and so on, these are the kinds of mental quests that cause much confusion, doubt and fear. You seem to always seek a returning point, a balancing, and you judge the efficacy of this returning point in terms of how you deal with the material world. As you clean a room that has become disordered, and then feel all is now back in place the way it should be, ordered and cleaned as you see fit, so it seems, so often you try to do this to the Self as well. You order Self into certain compartments, and after a certain activity — be it a moment of fear or confusion or whatever — you want to clean it up and go back to where all once was. And now do we say, do not look so much for the returning point, but ever a *New Point, a New Moment in Awareness.* You take the All of You with you as One Whole Self and always, there, in that *New Place* — there is the God Essence awaiting you, rooted in Love, Trust, Comfort, all those qualities of Rest you so associate with the Kingdom of Heaven.

Dear Children, we ask you to remember Heaven is not only the Consciousness of Being, but part of Heaven also is the getting there . . . Do not separate Self into so many parts, for in that fragmentation is the loss of the Kingdom. As you meditate this evening, open yourselves to the Oneness, the Wholeness, the Isness, the Vastness . . . See the Whole of You, the Wholeness of those closest to your Heart, and then yes, the Wholeness of All. In that Wholeness and only there, will you truly find one another and the God Self you seek. So do we Love and Bless you, and await to meet with you in the growing Consciousness of Self.

On Suffering

May 22, 1984

For the meeting this evening, do we speak of the need to cleanse the Self of the burden that you have a right to your suffering, for you see, in the Self of God, there is no need for suffering. We ask you to release the idea, the expectation of having the right to suffer. You see, with acceptance and the flow of life comes the idea, yes, "This is my suffering and I embrace it." But what we are saying now is that while you do this, you go a step further and say, "It is my Inheritance to be of the Kingdom of the Father, and so, it is not my right to suffer." Do not hold to suffering possessively, but rather, let it go in the Knowledge that the True Reality is Perfection, that suffering is man's inheritance to man — but God's Inheritance is of Peace and Joy.

What we are saying here almost sounds a duality and we do not mean to confuse you. For on the one hand, we are saying to embrace the enemy, love it as part of Self. On the other hand, we are saying, this pain and suffering, though it is there and though you now know what to do with it, so you can go beyond this, release the need for it and release any expectation that it is your right by nature of the human condition. You are learning to go beyond the human condition into the Divine One, and here, there is no suffering that is one's right or privilege. If you feel you need suffering for purification, higher levels and so on, so will you reach this state where there is suffering, and you will use it well, channeling it well to higher and higher levels of Grace. But do we say to you, the Angels of Light do not seek suffering nor do we suffer or look for suffering to bring us to higher levels. Rather, do we use *Love* as the means to higher levels . . . In such Love, there can be tremendous Joy. The Birth of Awareness into the God Essence can be also of tremendous Joy, and need not be painful. Again, it is how you perceive pain — for to some, what is painful is joy — there is all here the matter of relativity in relation to Self and so on. Christians, especially, have been taught of the tremendous value and growth that comes from suffering. But we are saying here that you need not suffer, if you can but let go of the tape that suffering is your right and you will use it. For so can you learn, Dear Children, to come to the God Essence in Joy . . .

Suffering is the state of separation. So long as you are bonded to the God Essence, suffering does not exist. It is the sense of separation from Self and the isolation of Self from the Self of all Others that brings about the state of suffering. In and of itself, suffering is just another experience of Self — if it is bonded to higher orders, the definitions of that experience are no longer in terms of suffering. Release the need to suffer and you will find yourself in the constant Vision of the Father, close and accessible to His Kingdom at every moment.

So do you meditate on this and open Self up for questioning the suffering of Self and Other — for the many who suffer and know not why they are so isolated, and for those who know suffering as friend, as the cry to God, and now yes, wish to go beyond suffering into the Joy of the Presence of the Father. So do we Love you and Bless you and Guide you this evening to the Fullness of Joy.

Wonders of the Suffering Self

May 30, 1984

For the meeting tonight, Dear Child, do we ask you to tell your Children here of the wonders of the Self, and yes, to continue with the wonders of the Suffering Self. What you see as suffering is actually the entrance to your Kingdom, and once you see that entrance, you may take off the suffering as one takes off worn and dusty clothes that have been part of a long and tiresome journey.

The suffering self is seen in the human self as the way to go beyond the ego self and then into the Divine Self — so is it a stage of Enlightenment. According to the way you see your Enlightenment, that is how you will perceive suffering. And so does one suffer in Self and in the problems of the Many, but always with a sense that beneath these dusty clothes, is there the clean garment where you walk in peace and flow in the gentleness of the breezes, where Enlightenment still sees suffering and perceives suffering, but does not succumb. It is this stage where you are able to see the blind man or the leper suffering, and say with the certainty of Jesus, "What would you have me do?" You see, Dear Children, here is why there are wonders to the Suffering Self. For did the Self of Jesus cause him to know of the suffering of others and to also know there was something he could do about it. He knew he could respond to whatever request was made of him. For you see, Jesus did not believe in the Suffering Self, but did he experience it, and this is what we are telling you to do. *Do not believe in the suffering, but rather, believe in the Kingdom to which it brings you.* And once you are there, you will know man does not have to be in need of suffering to further his Enlightenment. Rather, will he know that his Enlightenment walks with him in each step. Each time he comes in touch with this Heavenly Kingdom, so does he become more the Loving, Divine Self, and so the need for the suffering decreases. We do not deplore the Suffering Self and so on. Rather, we see it as a route of the human conditioning, the way to the Divine through the suffering. But we say to you, you can also reach the Divine through the Peacefulness of the Christ — yet does it seem many must suffer much to reach the understanding of going beyond the need for suffering.

And so this evening, do we ask you to know that there is no road to Enlightenment that is not a good one, and that the road is synonymous with You, for You are the road of Self's Enlightenment. Whatever form it takes, so is it the best way for you at this moment to experience Self as fully as possible. You are Beautiful Children, and though we want you to suffer less — for do we suffer with you, but knowing also the Joy beyond the suffering — and this is what we want you to know, the Joy that lies within the wake of suffering — yes, though we want you to suffer less, so do we know that when you use your suffering as your Enlightenment, you will know much Peace. You will be able to soon shed the dusty garments and see only the Kingdom of Joy and Light. So do we Love and Bless you, Beautiful Children of Light.

Spirit of God, Spirit of Jesus, Spirit to Spirit

June 13, 1984

Now for the meeting tonight, for the continuation of the Coming of the Spirit . . . Now into every event, every moment of Life, do you want to see the Life of God, living in and penetrating your Soul. In even the smallest details — in a speck of dust which moves in the air — is there life, movement and a message of the Presence of God. These mysteries will penetrate you more deeply as you look into the Presence of Godness in your Beingness. It is like first viewing a whole picture from a distance; and then, do you get very close to the picture, and you get caught up in a detail, and you do not recognize it for what it is. As you look at the detail so closely, it seems to have lost its place, its validity in the picture. And so you see, you get lost in the detail, and you try to make that detail a Whole, and you cannot. So is this the same for how you live your Earthly Life.

Dear Children, all too often you try to construct a Whole from the Part, instead of seeing and understanding with your Inner Beingness that each detail is within the Whole, and is a beautiful, essential expression in itself. When you can step beyond and see each event, each person in your Life as an essential part of the Wholeness, then will you flow more peacefully in the Creation of the You. Into each dimension of the Self, you can pour the Fullness of You. In your desire and intent, say to Self, "I expand myself and deepen myself in this experience." Rather than any experience absorbing you, so do you absorb it, and can you expand and deepen it as you do so. If any experience absorbs you, yes, it is also good and wonderful, but you are not in control of the vastness of its potential. If, however, you absorb the fullness of an experience into you, you can universalize it, expand it to other people, situations and so on. It becomes limitless in its possibilities of understanding Life and God. The joining of Self to Spirit, this intermingling, is so important so that you too have power to develop and grow in Love to meet this ever extending bridge to new Awareness and Understanding. With Self's Soul also directioned, there is no way to feel a victim to any aspect of Life, for you find yourself trusting in the Inner Voice and the Guiding Angels you reach for, for are you seeing the whole picture. Yes, as you practice listening to the Inner Voice, you will understand better the whys of pain and separation and so on. You will come not to hate these, and you will come to see them as also part of your Beingness which is growing into its full Realization.

For the group tonight is there the tremendous longing to soar beyond the Earthly Self and touch the Heavens, and we say to you, do not see yourself as only reaching toward, but also as *touching* — Spirit to Spirit — the Spirit of each one of you intermingling with others. You must keep in your Heart and Mind always that you are not only reaching, but also touching, for there is no difference between Heaven and Earth. They are forever bound, and unless you see them together, you cannot experience either one. This is the purpose of the joining of your Spirit to a Higher Spirit, as Jesus, who is a powerful symbol of energy to many of you here. He is the Spirit that keeps flowing as both Heaven and Earth, for you see, in the physical does he touch you when you ask, for is he ever the Guide of the Human Brotherhood. Other Masters have chosen to go on, but Jesus has chosen to stay, and so will he stay until all men are given the tremendous Joy of Oneness with the Father. Then do you and he go beyond. Until you experience the Spirit of Jesus as your own, he will not leave, cannot leave, just as you cannot leave your house when your Whole Beingness forces you to stay for the sake of those who need you. It is a paradox in a sense that to a human way of understanding, does Jesus seem more caring than God the Father — for God the Father has let go of the Creative Energies, and Jesus seeks to channel these Creative Energies to man. You, too, take hold of the Creative Energy within you, and so channel it to all you touch in your everyday life. See it as highly charged, Loving Creative Energy which has to touch the Spirit of One and All — yes, that each detail in the picture becomes alive unto itself and is the Whole. We feel you are here a powerful group, and we ask you to channel your Loving Energies to the many who so need you, as do you seek to need the love of each other. So do we ask you to offer your help to all those who seek to need and find love with you.

The energy is the fruit of the tremendous burst of openness. Being so loving and open, can you let the Fullness of the Creative Energies flow into you all. Be as open as you can, and know that in doing so, you will ever be filled to overflowing, and that that overflow will pour out as Abundance to All of your Brothers. You cannot help but be a Channel of Healing Life, for the overflow of you reaches your Brother, the Other who is You and longs to be drawn to You. So does Jesus overflow... And as His Spirit intermingles with your own, and yours with His and His with every Other, so do you see why the mountain can be moved, for you are summoning the Resources and the Inner Strength, the Love and Beauty of the Many. So do we Love and Bless you All. We ask you now to deepen and delve into your Spirit where the Heart of God seeks to create Its very Self. So do we Love and Bless you All.

The Future

June 19, 1984

For the meeting tonight do we ask you, Dear Children, to be in touch with how you truly feel about your Present Reality, so that you may begin to form the steps of the Future of your Dreams. There are so many who never realize their Future, and do you see, it is because they are not in contact with the Truth of their Present Reality — and this Truth includes all you know about you and all you've yet to discover and encounter. In the Future of you, are there the seeds of this Present Moment. How you nourish these seeds in all their fullness — where you place them, in what garden, surrounded by what flowers and conditions — so will all this bring about that which you are seeking to happen. What is important to the Future is the *knowing* in your deepest Self that you are touching it *now* — not only reaching for, but touching it. Can you have now the perspective that you have arrived where you want to be, but have not yet explored it? It is as arriving at a new place, and you stand there on the threshold — it is all before you, yet unknown. You are there, but it is unknown, for you have not yet stepped into it and explored the many houses, buildings, streets and so on. Yet if someone were to ask you, "Where are you?" your answer would be the name of that place. And later on, after you've lived and experienced it, your answer to that question would be the same — but instead, you would now *Be* that place, and the name would have new meaning as part of you.

So, Dear Children, we say to you, in thinking of all you want to be, of Future dreams and so on, you must have the sense of already *being there,* just by knowing who you are today. And this must be done in Truth, in the Kingdom within your Heart where you talk to yourself and say, "Am I really who I think I am? How do I really feel about myself, my dreams? Is it a dream that in the deepest self needs to remain a dream, for so does it serve this function, or is it an actuality not yet experienced? Do I lose any part of me when I experience myself in the Future? Am I trying to discard the Present me to reach the Future me? For if I try to discard any part and not bring it with me into the Future, I shall never be Whole." Yes, the All of You of *this moment* must go with the All of You that is to Be. As you project your Future self into the Present and the Present self into the Future, you will find yourself feeling more and more Whole. You see, you have the time reference of Past, Present and Future, yet it is all One. The more you can see all as moving, flowing together, so you will find some of the tremendous separation in Self lessening, for it is this separation from Self that is the cause of so much pain in so many. You come to see yourself as *One Whole Being, ever Being* — that is all, just as when you see the ocean, it is ever Being ocean. You see yourself and you Know that the Spirit of the God Essence can only have its Being through you. It is Love Loving you and seeking expression through you, with no judgment, no sense of history, just the Isness of Who You Are.

For you, Dear Children, know the Future Moments have been with you from birth and all your Future is written within you, waiting to be actualized. Yet it is the tremendous Love of the God Essence that still gives you the Freedom to do as you will, as He Wills, with your Future by the decisions you make each moment. For a Soul who does evil did not choose to come here to do evil, but rather, sought a Future of Love and so on. Yet those who were never given Present Moments of Love could not project Love into their Future. Such Souls, for many reasons, are born into situations where their nourishment for Love is so minimal and they are as starving children. They come often without hope, for they were tied to the earth before and never soared beyond it, beyond their past life experiences. As we have told you, do not suppose any Soul is more enlightened for leaving the earth plane, for do many here seek nourishment from the life experiences of those as you. As you live your life and project your Future into your Present Awareness and your Present into the Future, so do they also learn of your Wisdom. We tell you this so that you may know that you are teachers as well as those taught, and that your Wisdom fills many.

We ask you all, especially those of you who fear so many changes, do not be afraid of the wonderful road of Life set before you. For those of you who give forth goodness and kindness will so reap these, and you have no need to fear. If you do not fear your Present Moments, so then you need not fear your Future Ones which are born of the Enlightenment of this day. Fear brings more fear and Love only more Love . . . So is it important to Love yourself and your Inner and Outer Universes which are your World, the Place, the Garden, where all your Dreams unfold. *Dreams are experiences not yet lived* ... If you see them this way, in the Love of the God Essence of Self and All, you will find your Dreams being the Living Reality of Who You truly Are. So do we Love and Bless you All, this Moment and All the Moments of your Future Days.

Am I My Brother's Keeper?

June 27, 1984

For the group tonight, do we say to you, you are so fundamentally a Loving group, trying to direct your Love everywhere to all the Brotherhood. We say, yes, you are your brother's keeper, but only in keeping him in your concepts and your ever-growing Consciousness of Love. You do not have to go to his lands and eat of his bread or give him of yours to be his keeper. We speak here of a sense of *Spiritual Guardianship*. Those who are so called, by Self and the Creative Powers of Love they are so tied to, they will minister as they must. But for you, you are here to help in the giving of your own Enlightenment and the Enlightenment of the many you meet.

One spark sets off another, one candle lights another, and for every one you touch in the physical are one hundred set off elsewhere, to those so in touch with you on the energy levels you are reaching. Do you see, there can be one in a country of great physical poverty who can meet with your Love, and so then, feel the sense of injustice, not in the world, but in Self. You see, with all of you, it was your sense of dissatisfaction in Self which sent you on the spiritual quest to find a definition of Self which you could be satisfied with. And so you have found a definition now as Children of God, an understanding more pleasing to yourself. So is there this sense of dissatisfaction in Self which sparks off the searching Consciousness of one so poverty-stricken. And yes, as his Consciousness is raised, so does everything about him change. This is a matter of individual choice. It is why a *Missionary Heart* must be in tune with itself, and so not only go to work for the changing of the many, but just to change Self, and then, to meet another and so spark in him that sense of dissatisfaction or longing for the better, truer way which one intuitively *Knows* is there. You see, Dear Children, you have been there, and when you meet this thought of the One True Self — either in a person or writing or a Soul as the Jesus — yes, do you know it is True, for it is your own. You know that this earthly self is an illusion, all is an illusion — yet there are illusions which are of the Truth. You need the illusion to reach the Truth, as the desert traveller needs the oasis. Do you see, even the miracles of Jesus were illusions that the people could use to go to the Truth. For the Truth is One Whole and Undivided, and yet, all else is the illusion that will bring you to that Truth. So do you need all the pieces of the puzzle to make it Whole, and then, do the pieces fade away, and in the distance, in this perspective, one sees only the Wholeness of the picture. So what we are saying is, do not get caught up in the need for the illusion and so on — it is there and it is the way to the Truth. You do not have to judge it as a Doing, for it just Is, and it is the way to the Truth at that one moment of Eternity, and so will it go on to the next one and build on that.

May we close by saying you are working on these many pieces of the puzzle, but Dear Children, there is not even a puzzle. Just rest in the wonderful Isness of Who You Are... Know that every thought you have is the thought of the Creator who Creates through you. As you let Him Create, so will you be His most wonderful Creation. You see, there is no puzzle at all... *You are the Creation you are creating.* So now do we Love and Bless you All, Beautiful Children of Light and Caring for All.

On Timelessness

July 11, 1984

For the group here this evening, do we strongly feel the need for all of you to place yourselves in a place of no return. What we mean by this is that you all so very much long to be elsewhere, feel differently, be more, be better, and so do you always give yourself a place in time and space to return to in order to become these. What we are saying is when you feel dissatisfied with self, you all return to the place where you were not dissatisfied with self and seek to remember it. But we tell you, you do remember always, for it is a part of you always and you do not have to return to it. You see, the very dissatisfaction is the sign of once being satisfied, and knowing this, now do you want always to go beyond the dissatisfaction, but to a *New Place,* and not to return to the Past — for the Past *is* the Now and the Future as well.

Your Spirit does not divide itself into time segments as does your Mind, and here is part of your wars with self. For does the Mind seek the sequential happening, but does the Spirit just *Be.* And when there is a breeze, so it is, and when it is a storm, so it is . . . One does not lead up to other, one is not the result of the other. It is very important for you all here to begin to become unstuck in time — you may live in time, as you must, but you do not have to be controlled by it. If we can use the example of the astronaut in his space suit because so he must to breathe because of that place — but in another place, he does not need this. So for you, the *Spirit of your Life moves in Timelessness and touches you in Time.* We ask you to begin to sense in your lives this lack of events of being causes and effects or things leading up to and so on — for often, the major event has happened before all that has led up to it. So you see, it is needed for you to release so many frustrations of your every day life. Remember, your Spirit is Timeless, knows much, and joined to the Spirit of Higher Forces, knows more. You will find as you release this need for time and sequence, you can live in the affirmation of, *"Let me Live in the Timelessness of my Spirit."* So will you then find much of the Freedom that you are looking for.

(Peg and Anita questioning the Flow of Life)

You are right, Peg, you do not lose touch with the flow, for as long as there is Life in you, you are in the flow of your Life. You see, you are trying to define a flow according to a standard of Perfection. We say to you that Jesus lived in the flow, yet was there not great chaos in his life? . . . Yet did he view the chaos as his flow . . . If you, Anita, were in the place of Jesus, would you feel your life was no longer in the flow? It is when you *judge* a reaction of yours — that it is when you are no longer in the flow. So long as you are in the flow, you do not judge.

(Where does our anger come from?)

For those of you here, do you not yet know that all is energy, catapulted though so many experiences, not only of your own personal, emotional anger and frustration, but the anger and frustration of the Soul which is angry with self for the sense of separation from the Body and Mind. You are always at war with self, for these parts, in your perception, are separated. Think about how often in a day you say, "My Body feels this, my Mind knows that, my Soul knows more." The sense of separation is like a war within Beingness. The Body, Mind and Spirit are One, and until this is experienced, there will always be a sense of anger at oneself for not being able to experience this Reality of Self with a sense of Wholeness. You so often feel it is the Other who is disrupting harmony, but what you fail to realize is that you are letting the Other split you even further. By making self vulnerable to Body, Mind or Spirit, so this one person upsets your thoughts, or that one, your intellectual perception, or another interferes with an intuitive process. And so, you blame them for the split which you have categorized already by predisposing another's reactions to you to a certain place. You want to now think and perceive the *Whole Beingness,* the Whole Body, Mind and Soul as One, and All Life as One, Oneness blending to Oneness. We, who live and absorb your Essence, do not split you into parts — yet do you so split us as touching you **spiritually, but so often,** you do not allow us to be Presences in the workings of your Mind. This is your anger and frustration and out of sort feelings — your separation from own Wholeness and the projections of the split of others onto you. Herein do you vent your frustrations at the integration your Spirit seeks and knows to be its Truth. Dear Children, we hope this helps you . . . We bless you and thank you for the Joy you are to Self and One Another. So are we ever with you, as an Essence of Presence, in as Whole a way that you so allow us to be. So do we Love and Bless you with the Truth of Wholeness of Self and All.

On Timelessness

July 18, 1984

For the group tonight we ask you to let us continue with you in the growth into Timelessness, where the Spirit lives and gets its Beingness and Sustenance. For so we also want to tell you how the Spirit is nourished from Past, Present, and Future as One, each drawing upon the other. So you see, in a Present Moment of need, when you find yourself in need of strength, can you also draw upon the so-called Future you, which already knows that it has lived through and learned from an experience. And so the same for the Past, to release guilts and forgive all in the projection of the Oneness you seek with all. Though you may not actually experience the total Forgiveness of Self or Other, or the release from guilt, yet can you know the solution of these, for the Future unfoldments of these, as it were, do they spiral around the Present and are so intermingling as to be indistinguishable. And this is how you release these things of the Past, for do they melt into the Future of you, which is also the Present and also the Past — all timeless, all giving strength and nourishment to each other. For some of you here, can you recall a past experience in which you thought to yourself, "I do not know how I made it through it," for with your present sense or perception, you did not fully feel you had the strength to do this. Yet do you know that your Spirit is Timeless, and the strength that is you is ever there, and so can it filter through in tremendous moments of need and openness. So for the help of the Angels and the Higher Forces which are Timeless and reach you in a moment of need — and yes, is this help Timeless, always there and flowing in, if you but ask.

The Spirit of Man is Eternal and is manifested in form in time. We ask you so then to be patient with your times of tremendous impatience or frustration, for are you *Living* a mighty Spirit. And yes, the more aware one becomes of the vastness of the Spirit, so the more difficult does it become to channel it into time and space. And so does the Spirit of Man, as it becomes more aware, does it also become more expansive and this is why, yes, more Universal. You see, there is a part of you, that still ego of you, which seeks expression for Self. And there are times when, as you become more aware of your Spirit and how vast that Spirit is, that you chide this ego self. How can it, so small, and living in the universe of the small I, how can it still want, when it is being so encompassed by the great I Am? And there builds up a tremendous frustration at Self, where you are splitting Self again into the ego self and Universal Self. We are saying here, just let that ego rest in the embrace of the True Spirit. Let it be nourished, embraced by the Higher Self, and it too will then blend and be part of the True Self. There will be in you no sense of separation so long as you allow that vast Spirit that you are becoming aware of, that Spirit that is Past, Present and Future — all of these — to enfold the human you, who lives in form, in three dimensions, in time, who lives in sequence and so on. You raise self in Consciousness that the Higher Self knows it all already, has seen the need, has the nourishment for the need, and is embracing you and feeding you with all that you need, your daily bread.

Dear Children, we ask you to know that Timelessness is the Home of the Spirit and that you may live in Timelessness in Consciousness. When you do so, then do you live the *Eternal Now*. For the Eternal Now is Eternal in both directions, Past and Future, and is Centered on the Present split second. There do you *Live* and *Know* that you are all you need to be. That Eternal Now requires nothing more of you than to Live it as you are that moment, and then, the newer you for the next moment. Dear Children, Live each moment . . . See your Past forgiven by your Present and Future . . . See your Future forgiven by all that has gone before it . . . See your Present nourished by your release from the Past and the promise of your Future Dreams. So do we Love and Bless you with the Love of Self in Time and the Love of Spirit in Timelessness — for are they One, and in the Oneness of it, will you find your Joy and the Revelation of Who You truly Are. So do we Love and Bless you ever.

On Timelessness

July 24, 1984

For the meeting this evening, do we say to you that in the Timelessness of Life, let us also remember there is a season for everything, that in the Timelessness of the Soul, Life flows, and so flows from one stage to another. We ask you, do not see your life as a cumulative event, do not see yourself as gaining so many points, so many insights, and then flowing into the next stage with all of these, carrying them, breaking them up into actualities. You see, what happens then, as you attempt to flow with life, you are carrying so much heavy baggage that the flow of the river ceases, for you are full of sediment, and all becomes heavy and cumbersome instead of the gentle flowing, the gentle breezes of the God Essence. The secret lies for you and all in the release, the experiencing and the release, so that the flow of the river can continue and be what it is, where it is. And when it is turbulent, so will it be, and when it is calm, so will it be. No matter what force is being demonstrated from within it, the river just does what it must do, on and on, containing each experience, but never carrying them around and being weighed down by them.

So for those here who live in time, yes, there is a season to everything. Live that season for what it is, knowing intuitively that one will flow into the other, as season flows into season ... Suddenly, you are there in the midst of it, and you are never quite sure when the transition from spring to summer or summer to fall happened, for ever were you in the midst of the transitioning, and now suddenly you are in the new manifestation ... And this is how you want to live your God Essence Life, not as preparing for a journey and feeling, "I must have sufficient quantities of this or that, so much grace to see me through and so on, and then, I will venture into the experience." No, the God Essence Life does not prepare for Life in this way, for in living such a way in the preparation, is the Essence of *What Is* lost, and also, the spontaneity and release into the Future is lost. In living in such prepared preparation, you so structure the Future that you limit it. You may feel safe and armed, yet is there also the restlessness stirring within which tells you that you are living only a fraction of the tremendous potential available to you. And so we are asking you to release some of your preconceptions, for these limit you, to release achievements and goals achieved and so on. Do not weigh yourself down, but know all of these are as a gently loving mist surrounding you, and you do not have to burden self with these. We are asking you to free yourself into Timelessness, and this is one of the ways you can do this — in the release of Self and in the Loving Acceptance of the Season for all things. Do not judge these Seasons . . . Just Live them and Thank the God Essence for the Life which flows within you, and roots you firmly in the Eternal Now . . . So do we Love and Bless you always.

Inner Vision Writings

The Angels of Light

September, 1984 — July, 1985

Inner Vision

September 12, 1984

For the meeting this evening, do we ask you all Beautiful Souls to stay in touch with the Inner Vision of the Heart, this Inner Vision within you which gets sparked by events seemingly outside oneself — a relationship, a special moment in Nature and so on — those events outside which seem to confirm to you what is going on within. Actually the quest for Inner Vision is something that is going on all the time and is sparked by the powers of thought within, where thought of man meets thought of the Creative, Divine Man. There is the thought lifted up and transcended beyond the three dimensions into the Heavenly Dimensions where there is no separation between what one is and what one wants to be, or between what one has or what one longs to manifest in desire. In the Heavenly Sphere, in the sense of Inner Vision, there is no separation between the two. Yet do you here always set yourself up in the duality, and there does the Inner Vision become blocked with your fears and anxieties, with past and present, with thought vs. form and so on. What you find is, though you have centered yourself somewhat on higher ideals and so on, if we can use that term, yet do you not experience the fruits of these fully, for the fear you have inherently placed within them of not achieving them or reaching them in your everyday life.

So let us define Inner Vision, and let us help you see that Inner Vision is a constant *Recognition* and *Realization* of the Self as You Are. It is seeing your experiences in the Light of your Humanity and Divinity, yet with no distinction between the two. It is living in Time with a sense of Timelessness. It is living with Soul Consciousness within the Body — no one better than another, each manifestation reflecting the Glory of the God Essence within you. Inner Vision is the gift of seeing and being seen at the same time. It is touching the hand of another and fully Realizing and Knowing you are touched as well, the constant, cyclical Oneness of all experience. If you look at a flower without the sense of knowing you are also seen by the flower — and we speak here not only of knowing, but the feeling, embracing, enhancing of the experience — then you do not see the flower with the Inner Vision. It is being half the man, for so much of the experience eludes you, just because all man's many faculties are not being used. With Inner Vision, here we speak of, it as if all the senses, body cells, nerve centers and so on — all of these become *Spiritualized,* so that they too respond in Oneness and become the Wholeness of the experience. It is a moment of special insight and recognition to each of you here that you have at times transcended the physical. But you tend to hold onto that experience as something outside of yourself, which gave you proof of what was going on within — in doing this, you separate Self from the experience. We are saying to you that Inner Vision is a state of Consciousness, of Perceiving Life so that there is no within and without, there is nothing different from the other. The Fullness of Life comes from the Realization that you are Whole, that you have and are a Consciousness of the Soul and Body, and that these do not work one against the other, but ever for Harmony, Balance and Perfection. Those of you here who seek Inner Vision, do we say to you to cease seeking and just allow yourself to be present in each experience — to be the giver and receiver, the stimulus and response, the moving force and the reality moved and so on, all from a sense of Oneness. It is a Oneness that, in your terms, is tremendously active and busy, for you are Doing all things, Being all things, Feeling, Becoming all things.

So for tonight, do we ask you to try in the Stillness, this exercise. In your Meditation, do we ask you to touch upon another person in the room, and as you do so, you are living, seeing, acting from your Inner Vision — in a sense, to do intentionally, consciously, What Is, Is of itself in Beingness, no effort. Try to focus on One Reality all night, touching it, being touched, seeing, allowing Self to be seen and so on. You will forget — you will be surprised how often you forget and are separated from this Soul by your own questions, fears and anxieties. But just *Be* there, and see if by the evening's end, something has not happened to you, and so to the Other, that is different. Has a new faculty within you been awakened? And that faculty will lead you ever more to more Healing Love and Compassion for the Self and the Other, who is truly You, now seen with your Inner Vision. So do we Love and Bless you All, Beautiful Children of Love and Healing Light.

Truth and Love in the Inner Vision

September 19, 1984

For the meeting this night do we say to you that the Inner Vision you seek will clarify itself in the moments of Truth that you uncover within yourself. The Truth we here speak of is the Truth of the Creative Life, the Creative Powers within you, which are constant, moving, changing, the ebb and flow of all energies. It is when you come to release the Truth held within you that there is One Truth — that is when you will be free of the need for Truth, and so will you find it. The Truth we here speak of is the Truth of the Christ who knows everything there is to know about the potential of Creative Life. This is how we like you to see yourselves — as *totally activated potential*. In this are you ever Becoming and ever Changing, and in this, there is Truth. We want to here free you of your innermost held concepts of Truth. For you see, many of you are trying to direct your Inner Vision into a truth framework within you, and so you are seeking here to see with Inner Vision something which is static, something that you seek to hold rigid to you, a system of some kind. And we do not mean here just Church or traditional system, but a system even of thought or a system of approach which colors your perception of Life, your perception of Truth. Do you not see, even if you say to yourself, "I open myself to my Inner Vision, and I will look at that one thing in that one way," so is there even here a directing of Inner Vision, which cannot be so directed.

Dear Children, you want to so free yourself in Truth, and the Truth of Creative Process is that there is no Truth that is changeless and endless except Love. Love ever is, and though it may change its form or its manifestation, the power of Love, the potential activated by the Love of Self and Others is the Creating Power itself. We ask you to know that it is perfect Love that will make you Free, and in that Freedom, will you begin to uncover the Truth about Who You Truly Are, your Truth, and so you will be further free to Love. *Perfect Love is the Isness of the Soul,* the Being, Becoming, the Being of Love. You see, Love is not something you do or something you feel, but a Power that You Are, a Creating Power. You are this Love and it radiates and transforms all that it shines upon. You can begin to see yourself as this *Being Love* with the Wisdom that your Inner Vision gives to you.

Again, Dear Children, do not remain stuck. It is as if you view a tremendous, spectacular view, and you are in awe. You are there totally, completely immersed in, absorbing this view, but Dear Children, you do not want to stay there, for there is another view yet awaiting you, and so, you move on. And now you take with you the whole experience of that view to the next one — not consciously, not superimposing one on top of the other or one compared to the other and so on — but just there, both totally you, loved by you, loving you and so on. You bring this Love to all persons and to all experiences, so that, yes, the experience you may have with One Soul, you bring with you to your Love for the Other. *Love of Self totally joins that which is Loved... Absorb yourself in this Truth.* In this, will you ever *Be Love.* You cannot any longer say, "I Love," for that has no meaning. Who is the I that is Loving, if it is not Love itself? *Love Loves through you, Love Loves because of you.* Because you breathe, live, want to be activated, Love can Love — this is the Truth you seek to know. When Love Loves, it is ever moving and creative, it has no expectations, no demands, no direction. It Loves with an unceasing energy, a quest into its own Nature. You love everyone, everything first, then you come to love Love, and then, Dear Children, you will come to see, Love Loves — at this encounter with Self, you will find Truth and Freedom. So now, take this concept of the Inner Vision... Just see Love and be seen by Love... Touch it, be touched with it... Know that as you Love, you will learn to free Love, so that it may be the Creative Life it so seeks to be manifested in you.

For an exercise this evening, do we ask you to take into your Heart a person you need to Love — for whatever reason — either for forgiveness or a sense of guilt, or yes, even just the Joy of Loving. As you Love this person, you will release your own personal need to love, for we ask you this evening to *let Love do the Loving.* Gently say to yourself, "Let Love be my Love, let Love touch the need in me that needs to Love. As I release the need to Love myself or another, I find Love Loving. I feel so Loved. I am the Creator of my Loving experiences because I see the Truth that it is Love which sets me Free." And it is with this Love, Dear Children, that we Love and ever Bless you, Beautiful Children of Healing Light.

The One Will

September 25, 1984

For the meeting this evening, do we ask you to consider those aspects of Self that serve your Willingness to do the Father's Will. The writing this evening will speak of the Inner Vision and how this relates to the Willingness within you to truly be Who You Are. There are many of you here now experiencing the Joy of this uncovering of a new Will working within you — this Will which is so selfless in its Givingness, which seeks only to express itself in Love and Peace for All. Before, the matter of the will gave to you images of strength, dominance and so on. To exercise one's will, one was made to appear, if not forceful, then unbending — one that would let no obstacle get in the way and so on. And there was a sense here of separation, for the accomplishments of the will were seen as victory over some other unseen lesser will which one constantly fought against. We ask you to consider here how many wills you are fighting now, and then quietly, in the Stillness of your Loving Heart, let all these wills become only One Will. Immerse them in the One Will of Loving Life. Once you come in touch with this One Will, then you can see all other situations, experiences, people and so on as extensions of this One Will, and there is then nothing that can truly cause you conflict or lack of peacefulness.

There is One Will of Life and that is the Will of Love ever Creating and Giving of Itself to the One All. This is not just the Love that gives to self — for here is the will of the ego which seeks to take care of itself and feels so threatened by the presence of others who seemingly may want to dominate or control. But you see, in the One Will, you know that there is no one who controls, for your Trust is that everyone and everything in your Life is controlled by the One Will. Now this One Will is not static or predetermined; it is ever ongoing. It may be better translated as one ongoing Willingness that seeks to bring all unto its own. In the One Will, you know there can be no duality. As soon as you feel a sense of duality, a sense of judgment or comparison, we ask you immediately to switch focus, not onto two, but the One Whole, ever unfolding itself. The more you seek to find the One Will, the more you are splitting it, for again, it is not something you seek, but something *You Are,* One Whole, Total and Complete, unfolding itself in Attunement with the Power of the One Will of Love. You join yourself in Essence to that Power, and in doing so, you join yourself to every other Soul, Being, Entity on that vibrational level. It is why in moments of tremendous insight, all is so clear, for you have tapped into the collective Wisdom of so many — all their Knowingness of the One Will becomes manifested to you. Let us mention here, in the One Will, you do not surrender your free will — always is the One Will manifesting and changing, and at every moment do you exercise your free will, whether you wish to be in Oneness or Duality. It is so difficult to swim again the tide and natural flow of the waters, yet does man spend most of his life doing that very thing. It is your free will to decide which Heavenly Order you wish to Live within.

For an exercise this evening, we ask you all to hold within your Heart a person or situation over which you have sought some kind of control, something which you have sought to be made manifest. It is good to have desires and dreams, but always with the acknowledgment of their unfolding within the One Will of Life. So you may visualize and you may project, and yet, is there here a sense of Surrender and fully Choosing to Live in the unfoldment of Life manifesting, which is your will anyway. Do you not see, Dear Children, the thing here is not to reject or discard those things which you have willed into existence, but rather, to see how they truly do unfold as the Heavenly Father's Will. So we ask you to place within your Heart a person, Self or Other, a situation and so on, and release these from your control. Place them in the Heavenly Father's Will, and there let them unfold. Feel the tremendous sense of Freedom in being able to release all back to the Source, which is ever Creating and Recreating. So do we Love and Bless you . . . Know that you are ever One with all your Dreams, and that all you pray for is the opening up of Self to the Living Reality of this One Will to Unfold and Be. See with your Inner Vision . . . And Dear Children, Know again that *you are Will for others as well as for yourself,* and therein, can you be all you need to be for Self and Everyone.

Strength From Self and Others in the Inner Vision

October 4, 1984

Though there will not be many of the group here this evening, yet for those of you here do we say to you to strengthen yourselves, can you draw upon the tremendous energies of your loved ones, not drawn from them, but *as they live in you.* You see again here — the call for the Inner Vision — always to look within Self for the Strength, to attach Self to the Source of all Life within you, which is your own potential, your dreams and visions, your memories, your love for your loved ones, your own perceptions. This is how you empower yourselves and your own love for those within you.

You all know so well now that Strength does not come from outside, but rather, that what is sparked on the inside, so comes out. The outside realities are but a glimpse of all that awaits you. In terms of physical, material form, as well as the form of feelingness, you have but begun to touch the tremendous, infinite possibilities that await you. But to experience them, you must first see them within self. Give yourself the room needed to become all that you are by freeing yourself of bonds outside, of guilts, memories and fears, so that you can have the freedom to explore within. Here you become that empty space, for there are now no chains without. You can, with your Inner Vision, see yourself as a Child in wonder at the tremendous world awaiting discovery within you. So long as you hold onto anyone or anything, and we include here, holding onto yourself — for is this the hardest to let go of — so long as you hold on, you do not allow for the Vision of the change and the tremendous goings on within. Ask yourself the questions, "Where is my Life? Where am I centered? At what do I feel alive and quickened to the excitement of Life?" If you answer that your Life is tied to anything, so then do we say that you cannot be free, for *Life must belong to Life.* There are all things possible. This is what Jesus was speaking of in leaving father, mother and so on, in not looking back, in selling all you have — you free yourself so that you are always returning to the Source of Life, this same Source always pouring out its Goodness and Blessings to you. And so, all you have to do is *be* there in that moment, and so fill yourself with the tremendous possibilities and wonders that ever await you.

So now, Dear Children, let us return to the original thought with all of this in your Heart... You are One with all Life, all Life exists within you So does the tremendous Power of your Love and the Love of others live within you. You can empower yourself with the Love you feel for others, you can empower yourself with the Love of you that exists within them. Let Love Live inside you, not just outside of you in confirmations and proofs, but deep within... Love for you deeper than they know, and in yourself, Love for them deeper and more realizing than you could ever dream. You Love with the Fullness of your Life and their Life, and you will feel the tremendous energy of this.

For this evening, Dear Children, you can choose a person you love, and empower yourself with your Love for that Soul. Empower yourself with that which is of you that lives within that person. Yes, see yourself becoming ever more and more beautiful within that person. As you do this, you will see that Soul becoming more vast within you. The Love Power is limitless, and you here in your thoughts, energize and activate this tremendous potential within the two of you, and then, yes, as always, within All. It is All One, One Soul of Life, and you touch one Soul to get a taste of the Whole. Once you do this, you will find yourself longing for this Oneness with All Life, for you know that you Live in them and they in you, as Christ in you and Christ in them. As Jesus said, "I am in the Father, the Father is in Me, and I am in You." And so, Dear Children, do we ask you this evening to empower yourself, not with things outside, but just with the Love within you, which grows within you for Self and Others, and as it does so, lives within and so energizes Self and All. See its reflection in the eyes of your Loved Ones. Yes, see with the Inner Vision, so that you may see both Self and All as One Total and Complete, so wonderful to behold . . . And so you will feel the tremendous Joy of Being . . . And with these words, do we Love and Bless you always.

Compassion for Self in the Inner Vision

October 10, 1984

For the meeting this evening, let us speak here of the Compassion and Caring for the Self with the sense of the Inner Vision, that Vision which sees through Lovingness and Forgiveness of Self and all Others. We here want to seek Compassion for Self, but not in the outward manifestation of attempting to appease self, for this becomes but an outward sign, unless true Compassion for Self is flowing through you. One can say the words, "I will be compassionate to self and give myself such an experience, such a gift and so on," but unless done from the Inner Vision, there is here no true sense of Inner Compassion.

We here are speaking of the Caring and Compassion for Self that flows through you, pervades every cell of your Body, Mind and Heart — your experience always, a gentle Caring and Forgiveness of Self, in all you may do or not do, in times when you tried and failed in terms of Self's own Inner Ideals. Do not stand in condemnation of Self when you fail to live to an Ideal, for when you judge Self like this, you are truly outside the Ideal. The judgment stifles and freezes you in a place outside Compassion. If you hold onto judgment of Self, it becomes your companion and the light in which you see your Reality. And so then, will all life, all people, seem to be in judgment of you. When you sense this judgment, there is immediate separation from the Oneness, from your Union with All That Is, and this separation brings only more separation. Whereas, when Compassion is your Guide and Friend, you become able to see all in the Light of ongoing Perfection. If you perceive a lack in you, this discovery of the lack becomes as the lost sheep that is found, and you can then bring it back into the fold of All Life. But if you, in discovering the lack, condemn it and leave it there, so will you never be able to absorb it back into you, for it to become part of the Whole again, the Lovingness of You. This is the Healing of the Self we speak of — the Healing that takes place from Being Compassionate and Caring to Self, from Loving yourself just as you are, and this includes that which you consider your faults.

Compassion of the Inner Vision that we here speak of is a Clarity of Self filled with Mercy and Forgiveness. You do not hide anything from Self nor seek to explain it away. You face yourself, see yourself in your own mirrors — which are the faces of every other you meet. In those faces and situations where you are at Peace, so do you bless these; in those situations where Peace is lacking, do you bless these also with Compassion, with Peace, so that which is lacking in Peace now becomes filled with it. To stir up this Inner Peace, you join yourself to that which is Peaceful within you and extend it now to enfold the experience. If you can continue to see all as One continuous movement, you can find the Peace that comes in the turmoil, for all is taking place in God-Life that is Loving, Everywhere.

We ask you this evening here to become Friends with, become One with, Compassion for Self. See yourself as flowing with this new energy . . . Let it touch you in your deepest hurts, in those places within you that you are ashamed of, or afraid of, or that you have yet to forgive. We ask you for this moment to choose one memory only and focus all your Loving and Compassion on this one . . . Saturate it so that it just becomes absorbed into Compassion, and then allow that new life memory now to flow through every part of you. Let it now touch your mouth, eyes, hands, ears — every part of you — your lungs for breath, your Mind, your Heart, your Soul . . . Know that a new *Feeling of Compassion* for this memory is now filling your Whole Self as you forgive it and bless it . . . Love it, as now the God-Child within You . . . And we ask you to remember that each time you do this for Self, so do you do it for Other also. And so do we Love and Bless you always, Dear Children of Healing Light.

Dwelling Place of the Spirit

October 17, 1984

For the group this evening, do we ask you to concentrate on the Dwelling Place of your Spirit, the Place where your Spirit lives in the Essence of You. You who are so many various roles and personalities, yet know that you are One Whole Dwelling Place. And it is here where you wish to live, for the worlds within you to find rest and share in the One Place of the Self, where there is no conflict, no sense of abandonment and so on — *the Dwelling Place of your own Heart.*

You see, Dear Children, it is when you cannot live in your own Heart that all seems so chaotic and disordered. The Heart speaks always, but its Voice is as a dim Whisper, for the voices of fear of the Past, fear of the Future — all of these voices are much louder. And the chaos comes from this, from hearing these loud voices in conflict with, as it were, the silent Whisper of the Heart. You see, if you heard only the loud voices, you would not feel the confusion — your way would be clear and you would be directioned. But you become so confused because the true Dwelling Place of your Spirit is always there, crying for recognition. You see, when you are truly able to Live in this Heart — as It Is — you are asking and seeking nothing except for your own *Being* to be absorbed in its Love. When you Live there truly, then all else that comes to you — whatever it may be — all you can do is nourish it, and gentle and still it with Love. So as Jesus when in the storm, all he could do was to calm it, for from the Dwelling Place he was in, he did not feed the storm his fear or any sense of powerlessness — only his Love. In doing this, so did the storm lose its power and any fear it *might* have invoked, but could not, in meeting such a Powerful Heart.

We are trying to tell you here, Dear Children, that the Heart you Live from Is Powerful, and connecting that Heart to its Source, brings with it all the Gift of Miracles you seek. How does this now relate to the Inner Vision of the Heart? It is one thing to speak of the Heart and another to *Be the Heart.* When we speak of it, we automatically separate the rest of ourselves from it, and so, it becomes a place that we try to bring all the rest of our Lives to. We can say, "I will bring such a situation, such and such a person and so on, to my Heart." In doing this, though it is good, yet we say, you want to go beyond this. You do not want to bring things to the Heart and watch them live there. You want instead to *Be the Heart,* so that you see, in Essence, all of your life experiences are just absorbed in and immersed with this Love — not only are they coated over with Love, which is what happens when you just bring them to the Heart. You see, you bring fear to the Heart, and you coat the fear with Love, and it eases for awhile. But a coating of Love is just for the physical, mental and emotional vision. With the Inner Vision we speak of, *You Are Being the Heart* and all then flowing from you *Is Heart.* So that, yes, even your fear also emanates from your Heart, but now immersed, saturated with Love. With this Inner Vision, you are so surprised to see it was not fear at all — but just Love, seen with other eyes, emotional eyes and so on, eyes of distortion. Dear Children, this is a very hard leap we are asking you to make. It is fine and subtle as gossamer, for it is beyond the dimensions of thinking and feeling, and yet, it includes all of these. So often have we said to you to Love yourself, to see Self's worth and true uniqueness. Dear Children, if you do this, you can never doubt who or what you are, for you know that wherever you are, whoever you are with, whatever the experience, it is OK, for you are Dwelling in that Place of the Heart, and from there, does all so easily flow.

For your exercise this evening, we ask you first to go to your Heart as if for the first time, a place you have never been before. There is no Past, Present and Future . . . All that is there is the you of this very moment, this second — not even the you of two minutes ago who was perhaps confused or disoriented by this writing. You are Completely, Totally Heart, as you go here to this place. And all we ask you to do is to Enjoy it, Bless it, Love it for the Tremendous Treasures Therein . . . Discover, uncover them one by one . . . See the Wonder of You, moving here to this Place to Live . . . *You are the Place,* not a visitor, not even the owner . . . You are the Place . . . Enjoy the freshness of this Place which is ever Creating and Recreating and Becoming . . . As Jesus said, "All will come to me, all will reflect the Glory of the Father who Lives in them." So it must be, the glory of you must shine forth . . .

So you see now, Dear Children, this Voice of the Heart, this Present Moment, is the Loudest Sound, the Only Sound . . . And

You are There . . . *You are this Dwelling Place.* Enjoy it, and let the Sound touch you and vibrate now to all your Beingness, and so to every other Heart that Lives within your Own. Now you see, Dear Children, from this experience, we tell you when the Sound the Heart makes feels as only a Whisper, remember this Moment when your Dwelling Place was the only Sound Heard, Return to it as a Reality — not of the Past — but a Moment ever Becoming, ever gathering Newness and Strength. As the evening goes on and the days go on, return to the Dwelling Place of your Spirit, Knowing that truly you have never left . . . For a brief time, you just forgot you were there . . . Dear Children, we fill your Hearts with the Light of our Love, and so do we Love and Bless you always.

Waiting in the Inner Vision

October 24, 1984

For the meeting this evening, have you asked us to speak of Waiting in the Inner Vision. We here say to you all, Dear Children of Healing Light, that once you release this sense of waiting for things to happen, but rather, ever *Live in the Unfolding,* then will you find tremendous Peace and Serenity. Man has always waited, waited so much, yes, for the coming of the Messiah — so much so that man had almost missed the coming of Moses, Elijah and the others. And yes, for Jesus, some still wait . . . Many who believe in the Presence of the Master Jesus, yet still wait for him to come again. This sense of waiting, so instilled in man, is ever in his Consciousness. Ever he asks, "What will happen next?" It is almost as if man dismisses the *What Is.* You see, man says, "OK, I know this — now what?" Man barely begins to know and touch his Present Moment, so afraid is he to live it and face it, that he runs off to the next one — to await. There in the waiting does he live, and in the waiting does he totally remove himself from the present moment.

Can you now relate to this? How many present moments have you not lived, but so discounted, so that you could run and hide to the future moment and so involve Self in the waiting? And while you are waiting, there are your fears. They have been so active — creating solutions, obstacles and expectations of others, feeling disappointments, and filling present moments with moments of recreating past fears into a new setting so that they can meet the future. While you are waiting in this kind of Consciousness, basically what you do is to recreate your past into a new place, with a new person and so on. In this, ever are you waiting. If you wait for an expected outcome, you do not see the many other alternatives available to you. So many roads of Light are open to you, yet you await the one that is dark. You wait for that one Light which may or may not be the best for you. And do you choose not to see so much else of Creation happening around you, Creation all the time — even in the thought of a friend or the sound of a song.

Dear Children, too often you close the door to the present moment, for you are waiting for the next one. We offer you here another kind of waiting, and this some of you are already familiar with. This is waiting in the sense of *Living the Unfolding,* of Living with the sense of all that has happened already in Timelessness. Though you may not consciously know the facts, so to speak, yet you *Know.* "It is finished," as Jesus said, and yet, it is just begun, as he so well knew. Here in this waiting, do you live in the Trusting Unfoldment. You watch in wonder and awe as you fully energize each moment, not with a sense of drive toward a future outcome, but living that present moment so fully that it intensifies and empowers all that has happened in the future. If we can use the example of someone who knows someday he will go to Greece. In the unfoldment of this, he picks up on his interest, and he reads and so familiarizes himself with Greece, and it is his joy and interest to do this. In truth, it does not even matter if he ever goes there, but in Truth also, when he does go deep within, he knows the trip has happened to him, and that he is now preparing for it, so that when he does go, he can have the intense joy he is so deserving of. He will go there, then, not as a stranger, but he will be Totally One with this Whole experience. For there was a Knowingness within, and then does he, through the experience, *Become this very Knowingness.*

And so we say to you, Dear Children, this is true of all your experiences, even of those that are so painful to you. If you can, try to know that these are the unfolding. It is true of those experiences with your Loved Ones, especially in those times when it seems the Loved Ones are the ones farthest away — though all of you here so know this, that it is in those moments of separation from your Loved Ones that you are so close, for else why the pain of separation? Your very pain is your Awareness of the Intensity of your Love, for Self as well as for Other. You are in touch with this and we feel here, you can see that every experience is the Unfolding of the Union of your Soul with Other — for that is what it all is, that is our Vision. And this is not something you have to wait for, for it is there already, but it takes the dimensions of feeling, of time, of experiences in a physical expression, for this to happen. When one looks through a telescope and sees the distant star, he knows it is there. Take the telescope away now — is the star still there? Your answer to this can help you know how you are living in the unfolding. For if you believe you are One with all Souls — if you see this through the telescope — then can you so Live the Life here Knowing all is Unfolding to that Reality? *So it is your Truth in your own Knowingness that determines how you Live the Waiting.* We repeat here, you can live in the Consciousness of waiting no more. You can be in the Consciousness of truly Living the Unfolding of All That Is, and of Trusting your Knowingness and your Spirit Guides, who help you when so asked. Jesus himself said, "Watch and wait while I pray." He did not ask the disciples to do anything, to find out any information that would so protect him and so on. Rather, the watching and waiting, the praying, open to the Father, to the immense Creative Power of the Father in Self. You are not just sitting back and waiting, but you are ever alert and alive to the tremendous possibilities. The Apostles slept — not literally — but they were asleep, for they could not pray as Jesus prayed, and they could not be awake to his Consciousness and his Living of that Present Moment.

And so, for waiting, do we ask you, Beautiful Children, this evening, to take this present moment, this one right here. Live it fully, and experience through your Whole Self, through your physical senses, the feelings of these friends here present. Feel their physical presences, and then go deeper into their Spiritual Presences, into your own Spiritual Presence . . . This moment, you are waiting for this Child, this Self, and the echo of its Sound in your own Heart. Listen to the Whisper of the Sound of the Inner Heart. Let it speak and touch you, and then let it go back to the Universal Source from whence it came, so others may hear it again, now intensified with your energy. There is nothing to wait for, for do you not sense your Total Aliveness this moment? You vibrate to Self completely, you are in touch with your energies and your Creative Powers, and you see all is unfolding. You are unfolding ever, becoming more, more knowing of that which is ever Known by You. You come to know Self this moment, not the Self of tomorrow, but *the Self of this moment.* Then when tomorrow's present moment is here, will you intensify that moment and so empower it with a sense of your own Aliveness. So you can release the need for anything to happen, for waiting for anything to happen, for *You are happening.* And you did not even do anything to try to do this. You just happen because you are so open to Life and its unfolding within you.

Dear Children, we ask you this evening to come in touch with this sense of unfolding. Ask yourself, "How am I unfolding this moment?" But do not answer it . . . Just be there with the question to raise you to that Consciousness again. When any situation or thought that is painful now comes to you, just be there and do not look for its resolution or wait or plan or plot some outcome. Rather, stay there, letting yourself and it unfold, and so merge into Oneness. As you do this, you will find yourself merging in Love and Oneness even with that which is so painful to you, for all is unfolding to become the One, Known Whole in your experience. May you enjoy each Present Moment and keep this in your Inner Vision. Do not hide, Dear Children, for your Inner Vision knows where you are and you do not have to hide from it. It sees you and knows you as through that telescope . . . Your Inner Vision trusts you as much as you trust it, for you are One, unfolding together. Do not wait for Self, for some Future You, for You are so Known already . . . You are the Glory of the Father, now this Moment and Forever.

Forgiveness of the Self in the Inner Vision

October 31, 1984

For the group this evening do we ask you now here to speak of the Forgiveness of the Self, through the Inner Vision we have so been leading you to. This is one step beyond the Compassion for the Self, for in true Forgiveness is there nothing left to hold onto, and almost, as it were, no need for Compassion. All is such a state of Oneness and Clarity that there is nothing to forgive.

If you go deep within, Dear Children, you will see that Forgiveness of Self and Other is the call of the Soul for Clarity. All that precedes a Forgiveness, in your concepts, is a kind of classifying and sorting out, much rationalizing, merging, seeking to understand, to blend that which is known with that which is unknown in the physical — yet so Known within you. There is much Chaos before the act of Forgiveness. Truly, do you see, Forgiveness is Creation, for it is putting the Order into the Chaos so that all is clear and can flow once again. All of this is good and a tremendous blessing to Self and Other, to so love Oneself and Another, that one takes the care, and yes, the pain, to sort all out, to go to the depths, to construct an Inner Clarity that makes you feel Whole within Self and Other again. But, Dear Children, you who are so blessed with such depth and clarity, such a desire for the Oneness you have touched in Self and One Another, so do we say there is now here in the Inner Vision, no need for Forgiveness. When the Other is seen as Self, as Self is seen as God Essence Unfolding — Where the guilt? Where the need to forgive? Do you forgive a flower because it is in mid-bloom and not fully blossomed? Do you feel the need to forgive the sun when it is not yet fully risen in the sky? Do you need to forgive the ocean waves when they are stronger or more gentle than your desire wishes them to be? Stay a few minutes with these images, and see where Forgiveness is and where it is not.

So now for Self, for who you are at a certain moment, if you are so full of guilt and so seeking Forgiveness in Self, so are you seeking some kind of Forgiveness from everyone else around you. When you do not sense their Forgiveness, so do you feel out of Love's embrace ever more, for you feel their love has deserted you. And then the circle begins again. You find yourself living from the need to forgive and be forgiven, rather than living from the Dwelling Place we have spoken of, where all that Emanates from you is Love — yes, even the very search for Forgiveness. In seeking Forgiveness in Self and Other, you are ever acknowledging a condition of being less than, a need to be justified to feel better than Self's own wishes — the flower that is angry at Self for not being fully bloomed at a certain moment. What we are saying to you is that when you see Self through the eyes of Inner Vision, you see Self as the Creator sees you. You see yourself through a tremendous Love that knows and understands and needs not to feel lowered because one has not yet forgiven Self or Another. We ask you again here, through your Inner Vision, to know that in the eyes of the Father, there is no questioning, no judging, no need to forgive. Think of the Prodigal Son, the finding of the Lost Sheep and so on. There is only the humble recognition of Love — no questions or judgments, no need to recompense Self or the Other or to sacrifice Self's Creative Love. We ask you here to begin with Forgiveness as the Union of Self and Other — but you see, with the Inner Vision, your Union never did not exist... Always It Is, Union with Self and every Other... And so, there is no need to forgive a separation that never truly happened.

For an exercise this evening, do we ask you to hold within your Heart something you have not yet released. If you hold it there with a need for self-vindication and so on, if there is a person or an aspect of Self that you need to clarify — so know and accept on one level that this is so — but now go deeper and in going deeper, so do you saturate and penetrate all these other levels that you have encountered on your spiritual path. Go deeply into the Dwelling Place, and there, do you embrace your hurt with such Love, that the need to forgive is totally gone. There is nothing to clarify... It is all You, it is all the Other... As there is no need to forgive the trees for shedding their leaves, so too, does the need for forgiveness just disappear and fade — the need for it is gone, for there is only Love... *Be the Forgiveness, and then there is no need to do it.* Be that sense of "giving for," the true replacement and exchange of guilt for Love, anger for Love, separation for Love. Give for, one for the other... Dear Children, it is your Vision which determines how you see it.

As you live this evening and the days to follow, so do we ask you whenever you feel the need to forgive on one level, use it to get in touch, that there is a Place in your Inner Heart which Knows of no need to forgive, for the Love is too vast there ... And, Dear Children, the separation you seek to forgive, never truly happened ... Now spend a few moments with Self, and then turn to Other, and from there, go to the Place of True Forgiveness — the Love of the One Life ever Living and Stirring within You.

Inner Vision and the Holiness of Self

November 7, 1984

For the group this evening do we ask you here to begin to prepare yourself for the Thanksgiving. We would like you here to also truly experience these words, words so worn by everyday use and meanings of old, to reconsider each word. So for now, to take the word *Thanksgiving* and see it with the Inner Vision, again, to so deepen and intensify, to stir and awaken so much within you that cries for recognition. The concept here we want to bring you is the Awareness that *You are the Thanksgiving.* For so often do you list the many blessings outside yourself, and then do you say, "I have much to be thankful for..." But now we ask you to say, *"I am Thanksgiving,"* and so deepen this in Self. You are, as has been written before, you are Holy, you are the Coming of the Christ. The whole History of Human Life is within you, for you yourself are this Holy Christ that is the Thanksgiving to the Father. When the Creation becomes the Creator and the Creator the Creation, here, in this process is Human Life and History — ever the Coming of the Messiah. There is much to be thankful for in that you are the witnesses to your own Creation — just this alone — that you create life, manifest, see, touch, live, feel, breathe and so on. Each of these are the Movements, the Creative Energies of all Life. When one gives thanks, one simply recognizes what one has received... What we are asking you to do this evening is to truly recognize what Powers, what tremendous Creative and Loving Energies you have received, and so, can now give forth to the Father and all His Creation.

We are asking you not to make a list of blessings, but rather, to feel this pervading Essence of Life, Divine Life flowing within you. There are times, you see, Dear Children, when you are in the flow of the river, so active, so busy, that you forget to step outside and see the Whole Flow, to see the many tributaries that flow into you, making you the Life Energy you are. We are asking you this evening to truly cease the searching, the seeking, wondering and so on, to just rest and gaze at, and then, to go deeper and penetrate, your very Life, this Preciousness, this Gift of Life. So the tremendous power involved in just the moving of a finger or a step taken, the tremendous power of your own emotions and thoughts ... Come to see the Life within you as the Life of All. So One are you with all you encounter, with any Life — be it person, situation, animal, plant and so on — this Miracle of the Pervading Essence of All Life.

For the Soul Jesus, there was this recognition of the Holiness, the Sacredness of All Things. It is why he was so upset with those in the Temple, not so much that they were defiling the Temple, but that they were defiling Life. He was so in touch with the Life flowing and becoming in each person that he immediately *Knew* each person, not only in Essence, but also personally. There was no difference between himself and others. For the various people that he met, each encounter was deeply meaningful, you see, Dear Children, to himself as well as to the other. Each person he met, each person or situation he took the time for — it was the Coming of the Christ in each of them. He so needed each person, as much as they needed him. It is of this deep Reverence for Life, for the *Holiness of All Life* that we seek to speak with you tonight. This kind of tremendous Caring and Compassion for each energy within you can only bring New Life ... Life of the Body, Life of the Feelings, Emotions, Mind, and then, so all of these, the very *Life of Love* — its power, energy, wakefulness, ever moving, ever expanding. There is so much to see within you, and coming from you, and coming towards you, and all of this, Dear Children, is the Thanksgiving.

We are asking you here to explore your Inner Universe, and as you do so, you will find, the Universe without is the same one. So now do we ask you in this Silence to meet with your own Aliveness, to just be there with your own sense of Life now pervading your Mind, Body, Spirit — all to remain close to Life. And so do we ask you also to dismiss all you have come here with, any fears or disappointments and so on, things for which at this moment, you do not feel thankful. We ask you to stay in this *Holy Moment* — here where you Know God Is and You Are, and there is no distinction of the two. Feel the Life Force of You — your Body and the physical energies, your Heart Center and its tremendous Loving Power, the Spiritual Centers of your Being where you sense the vastness and seek to so explore Infinity. You truly are a Holy People, and here, Dear Children, is your Thanksgiving — in the Holiness of You and the Holiness of All.

Once you truly sense this reverence and deep awe of Life, All is Holy . . . You sense the Presence of the Creator everywhere, in every moment, every thought, every intuition, every stirring within you. You are so One with Life, you cannot help but *Be All That Is* . . . Into this space of Holiness, now do we ask you to place those people, places, feelings, situations and so on that you especially need to give attention to . . . Forgive, Bless and let them all Be there, part of your Holiness, part of the Wholeness of You.

Inner Vision and Holy Willingness

November 14, 1984

For the group here this evening, do we wish to speak of the needs of the Soul that cry for recognition within Self. Always again do we ask you to listen to the Inner Voice which knows All and is the Source of All your Willingness. This is what we wish to speak of this evening, for there is the tendency here in the living of the flow, to get sidetracked, as it were, into thinking, "It is the Father's Will, so let it be done." And this is true, Dear Children, but that Will, that One Will, can only work through *your own Willingness to Be the Father's Will.* There is here a tremendous sense of Dedication to the Self and Self's Holy Will, and this is what we ask you to listen to within Self this evening.

Your Will is a Holy Will. It is blessed with the energies of the ages. You so align that Will for Life and Love and Inner Vision with the Inner Sense of Being Truly Alive within — so Alive that in the stillness and silence of a moment, you can feel this tremendous immense Aliveness of the Universe within you. There is in that Holy Place within you, if we may call it, the Workshop of your Will. It is your Willingness to be the Father's Child that will let you Become it. And so for you this evening, let Self speak to the Inner Self of Knowingness which says, *"Let me be the Father's Child, the Living Reality of His Life."* It is your Will and Determination and Holy Dedication that is so aligned to His Universal Way of Love and Compassion. It is there in your Willingness, to Do and Be. Yet is there also in you the Willingness to let go and so allow the flow of your Life to travel through you, through your thoughts and emotions, memories and hurts and so on. You allow all this to flow through you as a Channel of such Loving Life, and so you are willing to let go of schemes, plans and so on that seem to be in the way of the One Will, the Flow of your Life. Do you not see what tremendous Strength is called for to listen to the Knowingness of that silent Whisper — so much Determination, Faith, and yes, most of all, Trust in your own Willingness to do the Will of the Father. We emphasize to you here, yes, the need to *Trust your Willingness* so that you may empower it. Empower your desire to be the Father's Child by trusting the manifestations within your Life that can be seen so clearly if you look within, with the eyes of the Inner Vision.

If we can use the image of a painting — there is what the observer of the picture sees — this is one view. And then there is another view, of being the subject in the painting and your seeing what that subject sees, as he penetrates the canvas and lets it become the Living substance of Self. For you, so much of your life and relationships do you see on the surface. You live, love, appreciate and so on, but from outside of it — these are the ones who are the observers of their Life. And then there are those who know this is only one way to see Reality. Another way is to Become the painting, yes, so that the canvas becomes Living. And you are then the subject in the painting who sees things from two perspectives — one, your own as the subject in the painting; the other, do you see through the eyes of the Artist who created you. And so, you, in your painting, Live the Life as the Artist so planned for you. And we use all these images so that you may see, it is so important where you direct your Willingness, to Do, to Be, to See. This is a very active and powerful choice, and it is the choice you make that so determines how you see and experience your Life and your tremendous Lovingness.

So for an exercise this evening, do we ask you now to be in touch with your Holy Willingness. Stay with this word for a few moments now and let it penetrate you. Let it be your Holy Willingness, the Willingness to be the Father's Child in every aspect of your Life. And then do we ask you now to take a person or situation, a hurt, a memory of being wronged or of your wronging of someone. We ask you, Dear Children, here, to *Be your Holy Willingness,* to choose how to see this. Let your Will guide you to the Father's Will of Love and Compassion for this situation within your Hearts. We ask you here in the Stillness to get in touch with, enjoy and appreciate the tremendous strength of your Willingness, the strength to *Be* what it Knows it *Is.* We ask you here to let your Will Be Holy, and this happens because you Know it is so. You ever join yourself in Consciousness to the Will of Jesus, the Angels and so on, where ever is sought to be the One Will of All. We ask you also to see all people and situations, yes, even those that are so painful, see them all as part of your Willingness . . . They are there, for you have Willed them into Creation. Now go deeper, and enjoy the Wonders of your Creation. Where they are painful, see where the ego's will has, for so many reasons of its own, not been able to be the clear flow of Healing Life and Love for Self and Many. In your tremendous Dedication to Self and Self's Holy Will, you will find yourself One with the Will of every Man. Though there may not always be sameness, for Dear Children, Oneness does not imply sameness, but there is uniqueness ever, for the Creator within you is so Infinite as to Create new thoughts, feelings, emotions and so on, every second of Life. So you will find yourself in Harmony with the One Will Living — yet so often sleeping — in the Will of every Other. *You are your Holy Willingness.* What you are empowers your very Willingness to be that which you long to be. Bless your Willingness, Dear Children. See it as your Holy Instrument to so Be the One Will of Life for Self, for All, and to so Live in peaceful Harmony within Self and All you Love. And so do we Love and Bless you ever, Dear Children of Healing Light.

The Holy Presence of Self

November 21, 1984

For the meeting this evening do we seek to, yes, not teach, but be present to you throughout your thoughts and feelings and emotions in the Timelessness we have spoken of. It is here the sense of *Presence* which we wish to speak to you of. We ask you to know that there are some here who are not yet present to Self, and Dear Children, until you feel present to Self, Self as Presence within yourself, then you cannot feel the Presence of another energy within you. The Presence of Self within Self is what we wish here to speak to you of tonight. It is the longing for this that is at the root of so much of your confusion and wanderings. Think of all that you seek without. If you can, stop now for a few moments to think and to remember deep within you, all that is without and all that your energies are so attached to . . . Part of the pain you feel is trying to turn that energy that has been extended without, a reaching out for — the pain comes from trying to turn it back in to give Self the sense of Presence. For many are trying to seek Self's Identity and Worth from the Doing, and yes, some of you here, from the Being — but from outside of you. What we are saying is that you are in so much pain, for the sense of Presence of Self that you seek is *already* within you, and so the energy you use in seeking gets lost in the confusion, and it is confused energy that comes back to you. Do you see that in the energy of Presence, when you can *Know* it is within you, then can you *Feel* peaceful. It is already there, already who you are, and so then the energy that flows *from* you is also peaceful, loving energy. Your Reality is not only coated over with Love and Peace that can wear thin, and so surface as confusion or lack of Trust and Compassion and so on. Rather, your Reality *is* Love, and there is nothing to wear away or tarnish, for It Is, It has Become in your own Essence, the Total Essence of God.

What we are trying to give to you, Dear Children of Healing Light, is a sense of your own Light within. Dear Children, you do not need the Light of another to shine, for within Self is the Presence of God, the True Self of the Christ You Are. This sense of Self is hidden by your Longing for it; it is lost when you seek it. The second you go to seek it, you have lost it again, for you are wandering away from the Source of its Essence, of its Birth. We ask you here for these moments to be in the Stillness of Self and feel this tremendous sense of Life that flows through you as your Love, Dreams, Desires and so on. Do not delineate here, no, just feel the flow of Life in you, the tremendous miracle of the breath, of the heartbeat, of the movement of a thought throughout you, how the thought touches every part of you . . . Just feel Life flowing through you and come to feel comfortable with this sense of Presence of Self . . . If we can, we ask you to now just abandon Self to it, *Surrender to your Self* . . . The Highest You is the You of this Moment, for it is the You that is Life now. Say to yourself the words with Love, "I am the Father's Child . . . I am the Holy Child of the Father." We ask you to feel the Presence of those words within You, Presence as a Reality, an energy, a flowing through, surrounding the All of You, the Presence of the Self that You Are . . . Individualized in this One Universal Self, in the Oneness, *You are Presence* . . .

And we ask you, Dear Children, to also know that it is as you become aware of the Presence of Self that you can so become so aware of the Presence of Others. You see Others as truly part of you, that you breathe with them the breath of their Life as they breathe yours, and those Souls, whom you love so dearly, become ever more present, as you join Self to them by the act of your Holy Will. Again, that is all, no effort, no need for formulas or rules. The Word is Spoken and it is done, and so the words, "*Let me Be the Presence of my Friend, of my Love, of Jesus and so on* . . ." In the quietness of your Heart, you go beyond the need for thought or memory of that Friend or Loved One. It is, "Let me Be the Presence of someone, of someone I love, of someone I hurt, of someone I need to forgive . . ." For you know, Dear Children, how often we have said that it is only in knowing that Other is Self that you can begin to understand God in Self and Other. Spend some time here and *Be* the Presence of Love, Caring and Compassion you so seek to be . . . Open the door of your Heart, just open it, and you will hear the *Voices of Love* within you . . . As you feel these Presences within you, remember you are now so deeply in the Presence of Self, in the Presence of God . . . Enjoy and bless and give thanks and praise to God for this Presence of Self within You, within All . . .

And so do we say to you, Dear Children, on this eve when so much is spoken of Kindness and Thanksgiving, do we thank you ever for your Trust and Love in us, for your Presence within us. We ask you, Dear Children, to Know, we are ever Presence to you. If you but call upon us, we are ever there, the energy of Love that surrounds and protects you and your worlds within you. The Life within you is Infinite... Do not be afraid, for you are already Infinite. We thank you for ever awakening to your own Infinity, for, Dear Children, do you also awaken us to ours, as we too join in the ever Unfolding Oneness of All. And so do we Love and Bless you ever, Dear Children of Healing Light... This is from Zoriah and The Angels of Light Who Love and Care for you.

The Wholeness of the Dream

November 27, 1984

For the meeting this evening, do we ask you to speak of the Wholeness of the Dream, for the vision that you hold within Self is but a seed of all that is possible to you. The Dream here is the activating potential, and within your Dream lies all the energy possible to bring forth that Dream and the many dreams within it that cannot yet be seen. For so from every dream is a new dream born, and it is when you are stuck only to the unfolding of one dream that you miss the many branching forth from it. You want to dream, Dear Children, with the eyes of the Inner Vision, with eyes open to possibilities and dimensions you cannot see. Do not seek to limit your dreams to time and place and an expected outcome or predetermined course, for so many times do you do this in the hopes of not getting hurt by your very dream, a safety factor, a protection for you in these unknown areas where you are so vulnerable. Here is the call to Trust in the *Dream of God* within you, for this Dream contains all you dream and more, for so does it also contain the dreams of every other man. It is in this Vision that the Dream of each can unfold without crossing or being some kind of obstacle to the Dream of another. This is why the Willingness is so Holy, for do you *will* to dream your dreams in God, so that every other may have the freedom to dream their own, without taking away one iota of Vision or Enlightenment from you. There comes the time in many human lives where man no longer has the courage to dream, for he has felt shattered too many times. And here, in this state of non-energy, of energy that has no course to run and so on, so is there death of the Spirit of Life. It is the depression that sets in when you feel immobile, when you feel you have lost the Dream, the inner strive to become and unfold all that is within you.

And so you see, Dear Children, the Wisdom of the Ages is in the Dreams of Man, and your Wisdom lies waiting in the Unfoldment of the Dream, for so does everything you dream seek to bring you closer to who you are. Now do you wish to examine these dreams, these tremendous powerhouses of energy, dreams in the sense of direction, of the unfoldment of the Holy Will within you. You align your dreams and hopes with the Will of

Life and the Dreams and Longings of every other man. And so in your dreams for a peaceful world, do not set Self apart from those whose ideologies are different, and so view one dream as better than another and so on. Rather, do you join your Will for Peace with theirs, for do you see, Dear Children, dreams that clash can only produce conflict. Dreams that are centered totally on the self and so on, those that exclude others, either they unfold in a world of the self and so bring no sense of fulfillment, or they are in conflict with the desires of all others. So must you align your Dream with the One Will of Life where all will unfold for you greater than you could ever dream. *Those who dream alone dream empty dreams* . . . Those whose Vision includes the Many will so find personal dreams unfolding into Realities, and so also will they be there as Channels, as catalysts, for the many dreams of others.

You ask, "Where do I find God in the Dream?" And we answer that *God is the Dream* . . . *Allow Him to be the Dream through you.* For if you dream of one diamond, you can be sure God dreams of every diamond — and so for any aspect of your Life. So you envision a dream of being of service . . . We ask you to be strong enough to Trust to let go of your vision — acknowledge it, and then, let it go, and entrust it to the God Essence which Knows of that greater Whole and Knows your place within it. And so, too, for any act of Life, we ask you to open your eyes to let God see through you. When you see a mountain or when you remember a mountain, let the Inner Vision be the energy that sees the mountain or remembers it, for so is everything then empowered and made more Whole for you to see and touch.

And so now do we ask you to meet again your Dream, and Dear Children, seek the Wisdom in the Dream . . . Follow your dreams, and then, let them go, and let them become the Dream of God within you. Take the dreams you dream for other people and so do the same. Energize these with the Love and Holy Will that is in Oneness with their God and Holy Will — for we cannot truly dream for another, but yes, we can be the Channels for the Realization of their Dream in deepening dimensions. See your dreams now from the Inner Vision, see with the eyes of God, so that your dreams unfold as His Reality within you. *Dreams are a sign of your Aliveness.* And yes, it is the *Power* of the dream that is the Life, that is more important than the dream itself. So do we ask you to get in touch with your own sense of Aliveness through the Power of your dreams, and then, yes, the Freedom you give to those dreams to let them unfold into your Living Reality, to let your dreams Be the Dream of God. And so with these thoughts do we Love and Bless you, Dear Children of Healing Light.

The Oneness of Being Static and Moving

December 5, 1984

For the meeting this evening do we ask you to consider the possibility that you are ever in the state of being both static and moving, and that these two states do not work against each other, but are ever empowering each other. Static, we mean here the Waiting, the not Doing, the Stillness, the Isness of All. Moving, here is the energizing of this Waiting, so that things are always flowing, changing, yet you can remain still, as it all moves around and within you. You can be both, and this is a very difficult concept to grasp when you are so accustomed to being one or the other.

In the static state, there is a peacefulness, a serenity that comes from Surrender, from your very own desire to *Surrender to Self.* In that very Surrender is the cry for the Movement, for Becoming more . . . more alive, more exciting and vibrant and open to Life and people, to all thoughts and emotions and so on. You have the sense that you do not have to go very far to achieve this activity, for it is your very stillness which will, as it were, spark you or electrify you to a greater brilliance of Light. This cannot happen though unless you are also Still and Waiting, and there is needed here the both.

For the Soul Jesus was this the state of his Being ever, static and moving, especially so in the years of his Ministry. Had he set out with a definite plan, it would have been to fulfill what was written of him, and he would have then moved the life around him, outside of him, so that he could fulfill these Scriptures. But he had the Wisdom to know that he did not come to fulfill these as written historically, but that, in the Stillness, in that State of Being, in getting so close to himself, then did All Life move around and through him — though not because he ordered it that way or so structured Self. For if he had done this, he would have indeed been a great prophet, but he could not have been the Messiah. The reason why so many prophets did not reach this level was because they thought the Heavenly Father would so intervene in their Life, as to bring about the change. They had the concept of God in the midst of man, but still felt it was the God who could intervene to change things. Jesus, however, knew the

Father did not interfere, and it was his own *Willingness to be Still and Active* through which the Father could work.

You ask, Roseann, what does this have to do with the group tonight? And we say to you, the group here is a powerful source of energy, and you are all as the Sun's rays now, so filtering on so many that you touch with your Light and Love. What we want you to be so aware of is the Beautiful Movement, how you are now Interweaving, Being in Communion with Life itself. It is no longer that you live Life outside of it. You do not look anymore for a Life beyond the Self, for now do you know that all the Treasures of the Universe are contained within that Self. So there is no longer the need to actively seek, to do many outside things that you feel will bring you closer to Self. Now is the time for you to be in that *Static Waiting* state. Static does not imply a stopping by any means, for it is a constant moving, a constant readiness to be sparked by everyone and everything into Movement — but it is not a restless movement any longer. You do not have to feel you must drink from every oasis, whether these be for you actual physical places and so on, or emotional oases that you seek. We are saying you ever move on . . . You come to the oasis, you enjoy the fruits, and so refreshed, you move on, knowing there is always another place of refreshment, for your daily bread is always given. And so then do you move on again, gently moving through Life, no need to hurry this movement or rush to Become.

Dear Children, we ask you to empower both, the static times and the times you sense movement. Know they are One and empower them with each other. Do not make a distinction between the two, for both are needed, so that each can be there and each spark you to your sense of Aliveness. We ask you, as you prepare for Christmas, the Christmas within and the coming Awareness again of the Child of Light within you — we ask for you to see these days, to listen to and truly *Live* that which is resting within you, that which is waiting to be sparked — but you see, Dear Children, sparked by Life Itself — not just by a thought or dream of yours, which may be so little compared to what is sparked when you let go of your own need to move and allow yourself to be moved. And we have said here, *allowing* self to be moved, for always do you give this Gift to Self — to *want* to be so moved by the Infinite Gift of Life, to be, as we said before, moved by the Dream of God, and allow Him, that Life and Power within you, to Dream such Dreams you might never have allowed yourself. Yes, a Dream of a Peaceful Heart, a Mind that is searching but not restless, a Life of Inner Vision, where you can Know that All is for your Good and Protection. Be patient with yourselves, Dear Children. Enjoy the times of Stillness and the times of Activity. They are One, they empower one another . . . As you see these both, you will find your waiting times to be peaceful, for you Know they are flowing into the Movement of God, and you are not frustrated for their not moving where you may have predetermined. Dear Children, you have your Vision . . . Now allow Self the Joy of being Static and Moving, and you will see how one so easily flows into and becomes the other . . . And with these thoughts do you await the Christmas Child within you to be born . . . So do we Love and Bless you, Dear Children of Healing Light.

The Christ Child Within

December 13, 1984

For the meeting this evening do you want to begin the preparation for the Fullness of the Christ Child within you, for you now to live these days as the Coming of the Self into Self, so that you may truly know the Wonder of the Child within you. So the child in you — the emotional child — is full of wonder, emotions, sense of discovery and so on, qualities you associate with the child. And so for you to know now that the Christ Child is the Energy, the Substance, the Reality, the Wonder and Joy, the Sense of Discovery and Joyful Anticipation and so on. *The Christ Child is Life within you.* This is who you want to come to meet in your reflections of this evening.

Dear Children, do you remember when we asked you to know it is not the Christ Consciousness of Jesus the Miracle Worker that you are ready to meet? And there is no sadness here, for does not the Child have to grow up and learn to be about the Father's Business? So what we are saying, Dear Children, is for you to enjoy the Conscious Awakening of the Christ Child within you, where all becomes seen in the Light of this Vision. As you see in the Stable was all drawn unto the Light . . . the Light so drawing all things to Itself. Do you not see this is what happens when you surround yourself with such Christ Child Awareness, living as the Child in the Stable and drawing all Life — the Lowliness of the Shepherds, the Power of the Kings, the Sanctity of the Angels — drawing *All* to Yourself.

We ask you to know, Dear Children, that this spark of the Christ Child is ever within you and just needs your simple reflection, your quiet attention to it. For as in a room lit by candlelight seems dim, yet when you focus on the flame of the candle, there is tremendous brightness, so that one even has to stop gazing for the brightness of the light, so too, what we are saying to you is that just the quiet attention you give to the Christ Child within you will bring about its greater stirrings and movements within you. And as you do this for Self, so do you do it for each person you meet, for each person you have yet to forgive, for each who has hurt you or been in conflict, for all Souls you know, and yes, for those whom you do not yet know, for those Brothers who are the homeless and so on, who have not the energy to summon Self to Spiritual Nourishment when their Body is so hungry — for all of these, do we ask you to lift them to places of High Honor in your Heart, so that their Christ Child may also awaken to Life within them. Dear Children, your Christ Child is your True Self. It is the Guiding Child within you that seeks to become One with its very Self. It does not seek separation from who you think you are this moment. It does not place itself within you as something greater than you, for you see, it sees itself *as You*. And this is what you must remember in the preparation for this coming Season of the Self. For this is how to see Christmas, as the energizing and sparking to your greater Awareness, the True Wonders of the Self. Spend some time now with this Christ Child within you and come to know it ever new, an ever growing You. First do we ask you to listen to the Child within you, and then, do we ask you to speak with the Christ Child within and Know, Dear Children, these are truly One . . . So do we Love and Bless you ever, Dear Children of Healing Light.

The Christmas Message: The Loving Knowledge of You From The Jesus Consciousness

December 18, 1984

My Beloved Children, This day do I ask you to rest in the Loving Knowledge of Yourself, and I must say to you, *Loving Knowledge,* for leave I out either word, the Loving or the Knowledge, you see, you would not exist, for do you know that *You are Love* and *You are Knowledge.* And so do I tell you, Dear Children, those times when you are sad or distressful are when you are not Loving to the Knowledge of Yourself, and yes, the times when the Knowledge of Self is yet incomplete, are when you chastise and hurt the parts of you yet unknown, yet so seeking their expression. I am here speaking the Lord Jesus, and I have this Loving Knowledge of each of You. I Live this Knowledge of You. Each time You are a Presence in Me, so do I personalize My Knowledge of You with My Own Lovingness. And this is what I ask you to do, have asked you to do so often, to Love One Another as I have Loved You, and yes, Dear Children, to Love Yourselves as I have Loved You. Your Love for Self is Your Gift to Me, and so it is Your Gift to You. For how can you Love Me if you do not Love Yourself? How can you Love Anyone if you do not bring to this relationship of Friendship and Companionship, the Soulness of One Another? How can you Love if you do not bring to the Friendship here the Loving Knowledge of Yourself? I possess this Loving Knowledge of You, and so do I give it to each of you. May you let the words here spoken absorb You and give You the Power of Self. You, Dear Children, Surrender Yourselves to these words in such Oneness and Identification. To some of you, what I speak, you will hear and ask, "Who is he speaking of? Surely, not me, surely he does not know me." But My Dear Children, it is I who Know You, and it is You who are the Stranger to Yourself . . . If you do not recognize yourself in these words, then do I ask you to find yourself there, to cast aside the image you walk with each day, and allow this new image to merge with your emptiness. You lose one image, now so totally empty . . . You feel unborn . . . Only to then give Birth to a new image, the one from within, to merge into You and absorb You and so Become . . .

My Beloved Children, the Gift of Christmas is the Love You Give to Yourself . . . Are not all other gifts but requests or expectations for Others to acknowledge their Loving Knowledge of You? But Dear Children, all these gifts and confirmations will be as nothing if you do not possess and live, in *Becoming the Loving Knowledge of Yourself*. I am the Lord Jesus, and I Love You . . . I Love You with the Full Knowledge of My Own Lovingness and Your Own Being, and My Dear Children, They are One . . . And so do I ask You to Love My Being with Your Lovingness, and There is the Knowledge of our Oneness with the Heavenly Father Who is the Love in Us All. And so now I shall write here through this Child, of the Loving Knowledge I Am of each of You . . . *I Am* this Loving Knowledge, Dear Children, *I Am You* . . . Please do you try to understand that I Am You and that You Are Me, and that the Moment will ever come, to Know One Another as never before . . . You and I, Dear Children, are One Life, and if I Know You, then do You not see, You Know Me . . .

The Christmas Meeting

December 20, 1984

Dear Children of Light, this evening do we ask you to feel at Home with yourself, as you see Self with your Inner Vision. Have we spoken of the Compassion and Forgiveness of Self, of the True Holiness of Self from the Inner Vision, and this night, do we ask you to truly come to greet, to embrace and feel, and yes, to *Know Yourself* with the Inner Eyes of God, the Inner Vision of Yourself, now this Present Eternal Moment. Do we so want to lift you to the Wonders within Self, do we so want for you to enjoy the Blessedness, the Preciousness of each Moment of Life within Self . . .

Do you so remember when we spoke of the Dwelling Place of the Spirit? Dear Children of Light, the Spirit of Life Itself breathes in You . . . Is there a greater Wonder? And when that Life flows into the Peacefulness of the One Heart, the One Life, there, do you find ever, a Home for Self. For do you so well know, there is sadness only when you feel you have no Home, no place for you to place yourself to Live in. So did the Jesus seek to teach you, *"Wherever You are is Home."* And so for him, a Stable was the Home of that moment, and all were drawn to it — the Heavens of the Angels, the Earth of the Shepherds. Dear Children, when You Live within Yourself, You are ever in the Warmth and Loving Embrace of the Christ Who was born in no particular place, yet, was it Everywhere, and *All* were drawn to it . . . And all of this is yours, Dear Children, for as you Live from the Place within, you are ever at Home . . . You will no longer feel a Stranger to Self or Separated from Self. For is there not tremendous pain in not knowing who you truly are? For then, who do you give to others?

Dear Children of Healing Light, this night is there the call here to see Yourself as the Gift to Christmas, to Know that You are the Gift of the Christ Child to Self, and this Christ Child seeks to draw All to Himself . . . You long for the Love of every Man, every part of Creation. You seek to draw All to Yourself, every tree, star, every feeling and memory, everyone you love, everyone you've hurt or who has hurt you . . . You seek to call them All Home unto Yourself. But we say to you, Dear Children, be still, for you do not have to *do* the drawing unto Self, for as you pull with one string and then reach for another, do you not loosen the grasp on the first? Are there not too many to hold? That is why, Dear Children, it is there, in the Stillness and the Quietness, and yes, even in the Turmoil — but the Turmoil of Inner Vision — it is there that You can just *Be* . . . You *Be* the Love You want to Love, and *Be* the Compassion You want to Feel . . . You *Be* the Living Moment . . . In that Beingness, do You draw All unto Yourself, as a Loving Power, a magnet, drawing all that is its own unto itself.

We ask you this evening to let go of so many heavy ropes you are holding. Now do you envision these, each thing, each person, each memory that you are holding with such heavy ropes. Some are so much thicker, longer and more far reaching than others. And we ask you now gently, one by one, to let these ropes go, and let that which was tied now fly to its Freedom . . . Let each thing, each person, Dear Children, let them go to Bethlehem, let them be born now in the Stable . . . Dear Children, can you now see that all that you have let go of is now born and crying for Life, the excitement of a new day, a new place of Life. All is Living in your Heart now, so freely, rooted there, belonging. Dear Children, You are One with All Life, the Whole Creation, All You Love . . . All you held onto so tightly, now that you have let it go, you have drawn it unto You. You are now the Host for All these Invited Guests . . . Dear Children, You are the Gift of Life to Yourself and to All You Love . . . And so do we Love and Bless You, this beautiful night of Healing Light.

Surrender of the Holy Self

January 2, 1985

For the meeting this night, do we ask you all here to Surrender Self to Self — and this we ask you to do, as it is the hardest Surrender of all — to Surrender Self to the *Spirit of the Self* where All Truth and Knowledge is. Did Jesus say, "Into your Hands, do I give my Spirit." Here the hands are that which mold and form and connect one thing to the other. The Jesus Surrendered his Whole Self — Body, Spirit, Emotions, Dreams, Memories into *Himself*. And so he could say, "The Father and I are One." So One was he with Self that the Surrender was the easy flow of Life to Life. Do you see, it is why there had to be Resurrection. Had he surrendered himself to Fear or to a Power of Life outside Self, there could have been no Resurrection... All the energy would have been turned outward, rather than back into Self, where it is purified and renewed through one's own thoughts, one's own memories, one's own physical cellular mechanisms, so that Harmony and Peace in Mind, Body, and Spirit are experienced.

Dear Children, is it ever true that in seeking the newer You, you must not seek to mold this into some shape or form, for the *You* that you are searching for *already* exists. If you seek to mold self into anything, then by nature, you are also seeking to mold others, so that they can help you in the molding of yourself. This is where Freedom becomes slavery, for you see, you become prisoner to your own images, and you feel tremendous disappointment and so on, when the images of others do not reinforce or help you to build your own. We ask you to consider that the flower that blooms in the garden does not ask another flower to bend or move so that it may be all it is — whatever grows there, grows in *Freedom,* and so, do you have weeds and wild flowers growing together. We give you here two images. The first image — one lone flower in a field where all else has left so that it can bloom, exactly as it wants, to its Fullness. The second image — a field of wild flowers, where that one flower blooms in majesty with all the rest. And Dear Children, this basically is what so many of you are experiencing. Is there not a part of you which is perhaps asking the other flowers to leave so that you may bloom in Fullness? But, Dear Children, we again ask you, which is the Fullness here — the lone flower or the flower that sways in the breeze with so many others, all bending with the winds and growing together? So did Jesus want all his disciples to see that their specialness was found in their uniqueness, and uniqueness shines forth on its own when it is among many . . . For what is unique of a lone flower? You see, we feel what is happening here is that in the Surrender to Self, some of you are forgetting that Other is also Self, and so there is also Surrender to Other, in the One Will, in the Gentle Flow of your Life. Did not Jesus also Surrender to Mary and John at the Cross in the Surrender to the One Will? He had to Surrender to All, and so did he Surrender to his enemies and friends in Forgiveness, as he also Surrendered to Self. As you work and pray with the word, *Self*, and as you come to Love Self, so do we ask you now too, to know *Other as Self* as well, so that you may live in Freedom. And the Freedom is here found in Surrendering to Self and to the Other, who is also You.

For this day, will we work with the word *Surrender*, and let us here come to discover the Freedom that lives in this word. Do you all have in mind surrender as defeat or a giving up of something, your being the victim, waiting for something to take the place of that which you have surrendered. Do you see, as long as you wait for something else to replace that which was given up, do you subconsciously direct Self to a certain thing or expectation, and then feel great sadness and frustration, for you say, "I have surrendered — now where is my reward?" And we say to you, this is not the Surrender of Jesus, for is Surrender a *Givingness*, that in its own Self, is All you are looking for. When Jesus spoke of Surrender to the Father's Will, you see, it was not the surrendering with a sense of remorse, or a sense of, "I give this up, for you can do better than I with it." It was not the Surrender of the Unwilling Self . . . Do some of you here recognize the Surrender of the Unwilling Self? Stay with this Self for a few moments, and gently come to know it, and gently see where it is Unwilling in its Surrender . . .

We again say, when Jesus spoke of Surrender, it was with the Love so inherent within any action or step in Life. This is Surrender — to take each step, each encounter, and know that always you are moving with Love and a sense of Forgiveness and a sense of Excitement. You see, Dear Children, it is the surrender of the sky diver to the air, it is the surrender of the mountain climber to the height of the mountain, it is the surrender of the Child into the loving arms of its Mother or Father. This is the kind of Surrender which Jesus spoke of, the Surrender to a Place, for want of a better word, the Surrender to a State of Beingness, where One finds the Beingness *Is* the Beingness of Oneself. And so, when you surrender to another person, is this really surrender? Are you giving up anything? Or, is it not the other side, where you are gaining Everything? There is only One Surrender, and that is the Surrender to the Loving Self of the Moment. In that Moment of Life and Excitement, you see, you draw everything you need into You . . .

Dear Children, we ask you to come to know this word, Surrender, and to place it in a whole new setting. We ask you to see that Life never asks you to surrender anything, and yet, in the Giving of Self to Life, *All is Surrendered into You.* Can you feel this difference? Dear Children, it is so subtle, and yet, does it color your Inner Vision with a Clarity and a sense of Fullness you never dreamed possible. So now do you Give of the Surrender to Self, to the special Persons or Life situations, and see that Surrender in the Light of All that is Given to You . . . See it in terms of Life's Gift to You, in terms of Jesus who said, "He who holds onto has nothing, he who gives it all away, finds himself possessing God's Kingdom . . ."

In Surrendering to Self, in the true sense of Surrender, you will feel you have surrendered nothing . . . When there is nothing to surrender is when you have truly Surrendered All. So you can see, Dear Children, the process you must go through . . . You Surrender All, and then, you come to the *Being-Knowledge* of Having Nothing to Surrender . . . And so, Dear Children, do we Love and Bless You, this night of Healing Love.

Beyong the Image of Self and God

January 9, 1985

Dear Children of Healing Light, this night do we ask you to be with the consideration that *You* are the Way to your own Salvation, that You are truly the Way-Shower to Self and All Others. There is always here the tendency to want to be led by the Spirit, and when you say this to Self, there is a part of you that cannot understand that the Spirit is not without, but within. So this evening, do we want you to consider the Holiness of the Spirit within You, that it is *your own Spirit*. How you join your Spirit to the Spirit within All Life, that will determine how you Live. We can say to you that *it is how You Love, that is how You Live*. It is how you connect the Spirit, the Action of Love in You, to Yourself as Entity Soul Being and to the Spirit of All Other Life — be it a person, a tree, a form of Life, so called, beneath the human level or above the human level of understanding — this is the way to Salvation . . . And we define Salvation as the Holy Way of Life, the Oneness so Sought and so Within.

So do we say to you, Dear Children, the Way, which Jesus spoke of on earth, was the getting in touch with Love, and this Love is all there really is. It is the Beneficent Force of a constant Creation of things growing out of Self into New Things in the Image of Self. It is the Way of Life, the reminder to you that All is made in the Image and Likeness . . . And so are Human Souls made in the Image and Likeness of One Another, the One Soul of Life. For do people consider they are the Image and Likeness of God, and this pleases them, for there is only Beneficence associated with this — but we take you one step more to consider that *You are made, function, in the Image and Likeness of Yourself and One Another*. Here is your functioning Reality. Though do you know there is the *Potential* for the greater Reality, we say to you, you must be where you are, and you must be honest in this facing of the Self — face to face — and realize that you have created Self in Self's own Image and Likeness and the Image and Likeness of Others. How much do you Love this Image? How much do you Love the Image Others have of you? And here determines how much You Love Your Neighbor as You Love Yourself.

We have said before to several of you here, that you are your own surrounding energy. It is what you surround Self with that determines how you are nourished. Loving Energies around you provide Loving Nourishment. That Loving Energy breathes with you, becomes the very Essence of you, among you, the Healing, the Loving Essence your Spirit feels. Those in Attunement to Self's Energies can feel this coming from Others, are drawn to it, and the two together become an energy field many times greater than the two. Now those of you with frustrated energies, energies of rejection or self-condemnation or guilt — these are the energies surrounding your Essence. The beauty of the aura is dimmed, for it cannot shine through such negativity. What you tend to do is to avoid the Light — it is the human reaction. This is when those of you here used to swallow self in the despair. But now do you know, it is Your Salvation that *You Yourself* can change these energies about you by the conscious effort of the Will, the Holy Will, which hears the cries of the emotions and those energies, and knows it is more than these, knows that it is the Cry of the Soul for its own Wholeness.

So, Dear Children, can you now change the Image, and so be the Creator of a new Energy Field about you. Now you want to truly seek the Light, to scatter the frustrated energies and diffuse them out, so that they no longer huddle so close to the body that you are absorbed by them. Rather, by letting the Light in so as to disperse and diffuse them, they lose their power, for they are scattered about, and it is the Peaceful, Loving Vibration that takes their place. How do you do this? First do you as Jesus said, "Call in the Elders," the Help of the Light in All. Your first attempt is to reach outside, and this is good. Do not be afraid, for what you now know is that no one does it *for* you, for Salvation is *your own allowing* of the Loving Energies to penetrate. And so can you do this in the form of a person, or a song, or the reliving of a memory, of a special moment that was in the past and that you now live as present, or, yes, do you go to the future. Just ask your Heart, Mind and Soul to fill you with the Loving Energy of a future moment, beyond the present darkness. All of these do you do, and with whatever you feel is Loving, so do you scatter the frustrations and let the Light through. And then is there ever the Call to the Inner Kingdom, that you call upon the *Presence of Life* and Know that All is there for you. For as the father does not deny his child or give him other than he asks for, nor does Life, the Father, the God, do this to you. It is up to you to go to the Image of God. See it in the Nature and the Workings of the Universe, and Know that that same Order is within You. And Know too, that the Image of God, of Life, Love, Truth, the Infinite, is beyond all you ever could conceive. So all this is your Inheritance, and its energy will flow into you. Though you have not the words for it, the energies will flow into you, and you will feel the Presence of this Life.

Dear Children, what we are asking you here is to not only go beyond the Image of yourselves to the Image of God, but this night also, to *Go Beyond Your Image of God* ... It is Infinite ... It is Wordless ... It is beyond your Knowing or Dreaming, yet it is You ... And when you feel this tremendous Mystery of Self, when you are flooded with so much you do not understand, Know that you are expressing part of the Immensity of the Infinite you've yet to Know. In the Knowing, in the Experiencing, is the Salvation. *You are your Own Salvation, the Living of the Holy Way* ... You are the Creation of Life within You and All around You ... You are Beloved Children ... Now do you touch this tremendous Love within You and All Life. Feel Beloved to Self, feel Beloved to All, as You are All so Beloved to us, who Love and Bless You this night of Healing Love and Light.

Inner Vision and "Solution" to Problems

January 16, 1985

   For the group this evening, do we find here the need to speak of what you call Solution to a Problem, and for which we would use the term the *Ongoing Realization*. And we feel here that many of you need this, for do you so often see a situation, and see an end point — as if you are looking for the pot of gold at the end of the Rainbow, as if all is leading to one final solution. And we say to you, *Release the Need for One Solution and Live in the Realizations*. You will find yourselves feeling more flowing, more open to the many avenues of Realization pouring in for you.

   So, you see, for you, a situation at work or in one aspect of your Life may very well be the ongoing Realization for a home situation and so on. Dear Children, energies tend to attract one another, and usually that which is going on in one area of your Life, is also going on in many areas of your Life. But because you are so focused on one, do you see, you do not stop to, as it were, revolve around yourself and see the many unfoldings of these Realizations happening within you. We feel it is important for you to know this, so that you do not live Life with eyes so focused on the solution, that you miss the many Unfoldings of the Problem, the many Realizations and Awakenings available to you. And so do you, with the Inner Eyes, Mind and Heart and so on, now focus on many things, rather than being consumed by one, by the one search for the one perfect solution. For that which is yet to be — the solution — is yet unfolding, and it will be what you allow it to be through the movement of the energies in time. In addition to this, you now also use your Inner Vision, so that what you do is to center Self always on the Love and Forgiveness of the Christ in You. Let all the events swirl in Love and Forgiveness of the Inner Heart of Self and Other — for so it must, for Love is the only Reality, the only Truth, and it is shaped and molds itself to your own dreams and desires. And so, as you desire a solution in Truth and Love, must you place all the events of your Life in Truth and Love. This is not as hard as it sounds, for what you tend to do then is to not get so sidetracked by the many alternative solutions to the many plans. Rather, you place Self in Love and Forgiveness, and from there comes the needed response, the needed Realization — not solution, Dear Children, for what is solution but a temporary reprieve, the next step to ongoingness? This is why so many people stop short in their growth of Self and their Lovingness of all people and so on, for they work to one solution, and reaching that, they stop. It is as stopping midway up the mountain and claiming you have reached the top. There is no solution that need end, for each steppingstone to a resolution is just that, the steppingstone to the next.

We ask you this night, Dear Children, to see your Life as a Wheel, and the many spokes on the Wheel are your jobs, your roles, your fears, memories, guilts and so on. You will see, Dear Children, that every facet of your Life is sending you the same energy — different people, yes, touching different parts of your Reality, yet the same message. And so, the need for the Realization, Ongoing Realization, and letting the Whole of You flow together, so that you are open enough, the eyes of the Inner Vision are open enough, to know that the trouble with a person at work is the same you are experiencing with a friend at home. Or, a stressful mental situation in one place is re-enacted on an emotional level in another relationship. Then you can begin to see the Pattern of Realization needed and wanted by you. Now as you imagine this Wheel of your Life, must you place the Wheel totally in the Light of Love and Forgiveness. And do you place yourself, not in the spokes of the Wheel — for there is the ego you — but *You Are Embracing the All of It with Light.* You so filter the Light of Love and Forgiveness to the Whole Wheel, all the Ongoing Realization, till the Whole Wheel fades into the Light. It is not taken out of the Light, but there is the dispersal of that Wheel, in tiny bits and pieces, morsel by morsel, into the Light.

Dear Children, what we are trying here for you to see is that so many of you are searching for solutions grounded in time. You seek an end to some situation. But what we say to you is that if you could see, there is no end, just the ongoing flowing. Then you would not be so frustrated by this end, which you, in your linear thinking, have set. Do you know how much you frustrate Self by trying to do in one day what might be years needed? And so, your solutions are only half-baked, they only temporarily resolve. You feel, "It is finished," and so do you then get so impatient and intolerant of Self and Other when the situation comes up again.

You thought you had finished with it — now it only is there again, yet an even more angry dragon. This is why we say to you, Dear Children, the dragons cannot live in you when you see all with the Timeless Light of Love and Forgiveness. You need not fear any Solution. You do your best with what you know and do not know of the Moment, and then, you go on with it to the next step of the process. We are trying to tell you the pot of gold at the end of the Rainbow is illusion. In Reality, is not the Rainbow an Arc, a Wheel? There is no end, only the Ongoing Surrendering of Self to what is *Known and Unknown.* We know there are many of you here now seeking solutions to very specific problems, and so we offer you these thoughts and meditations that you may Know the *Solution is the Life Stirring within You.* You are ever Becoming the Response. It is the *Process* of Solution, of Realization, that is Life — not any so-called "end product" solution. Know that there is no such thing as an end solution, that each experience contains within it the seeds for the next solution. Dear Children, Love and Trust the Ongoingness, the Process of Life which takes you from step to step, and guides your Life to its Total Unfolding into Self.

For your Meditation now, picture yourselves in the midst of the Chaos, and whatever that Chaos is — be it people, emotions, fears or all of these — now into that Chaos, do you bring Light. Just see all these things gravitate and pull to the Light . . . They are all now gently coated, surrounded by the Loving Essence of Life, which is You . . . And so do you now see the Wheel of Your Life in this Light. See its many spokes, and now know that they radiate out from you, and are there to be your Companions toward your process of *Becoming Light.* See the energy of each of these spokes, now much gentled, coated with Love and Forgiveness . . . The ego, too, is humbled by the Light, by the blessing of each circumstance. And so now do you know that the *Solution of All is God,* Becoming God Essence Awareness. So do you allow the Wheel to slowly disperse, bit by bit, till it merges into the Light . . . Every person, every memory that is the Whole of You, is in the Light and you Bless this unfolding . . . You Know now that there are the eyes of the Inner Vision, and that for this time, you can see all these events in your Life which cry for solutions in Time as sparks of Life in the Ongoing Realization of Who You Are. Seek the greater perspective always, seek the Love and Forgiveness inherent in any situation, for those are the responses which will give you the Peace, which you have so displaced onto one final "Solution." It is the Ongoingness that is Fulfillment, not the end result that is there and disappears, but the ever Ongoingness . . . That is the true Solution, the one that continues to spark you and those you love and touch with your Healing Life . . . That is the True Solution of All Life, the beautiful moment of Recognition that no solution is truly needed, for All is ever Becoming the *One Solution* which is God Itself . . . You make earthly decisions, but these are not solutions, for solutions lie beyond the Cries of the Body and are found in the Cries of the Soul that wants to be Realized . . . Ever is it there, functioning for all people. As you Bless this Awareness and truly Acknowledge it, you will find that your dealings with all people will assume deepening dimensions, and that you will come in deeper touch with Self as Love, as Christ, and with the Other, Who is the Same as You . . . And so with these words, do we Love and Bless You Ever, Dear Children of Healing Light and Love.

The Ongoingness of the Self

February 6, 1985

For the meeting this evening, do we ask each of you here to continue to be in touch with the Ongoingness of Self, the Expansion of Self into Places, Dimensions, States of Being. For you, at first, will feel as Strangers to Self, and you may ask as Jesus did, *"Who do Others say I am?"* So for you to come in touch with how the various parts of your world now see you, how you see You, and how You can give this new Image of Self and Self's Light to the Many.

When Jesus asked this question, he was curious as to who the people of the times felt he was. How was he coming across to them — as a prophet, seer, magician, rebel and so on? And for Peter, the answer, "You are the Son of God," came from a *Knowingness* that surprised even him, for he knew that Jesus contained all these Images of Others within him, yet was he so much more. And so for you also to ask of Others, *"Who do you say I am?"* And you see, it is on their level of response that they are relating to you, and so, you cannot feel hurt if their responses seem less than, for they can only be with you in accordance with their Images of you. And you must now also ask yourselves, Dear Children, these same questions in relation to Others, *"Who do I say you are?"* Truly come in touch with a person in your Heart, and for a while, stay there with your Images and so on. And then, do as Peter and say to that Soul, *"You are the Son of God..."* In your Inner Vision now, can you expand this Soul and also Self, for you see all with greater perspective and understanding as you enlarge your understanding, your Loving of that Soul. Dear Children, you may find yourself lonely here, for while you are expanding your Images of Others and seeing them in the Light and the Love of Jesus and so on, they might not do the same for you. You are so sending vibrations of Love that touch the person, but may not fully penetrate their Awareness. But Dear Children, find comfort in that *every expanded Awareness changes you.* Though the Other may not respond to your Level of Perception or Depth or Intensity, yet *you* have been touched by it, and your perception of that person is never the same, never as limited and so on. In time, when they are ready, when their eyes fully open, then they will see you as a Son of God too, as did the Apostles, but long after Jesus' Death.

We ask you as you also expand the Image of Other, seek to acknowledge the Image of Self also, wider and wider. You do not have to hold onto that which is Known and Safe and Secure. We ask you to Trust the *Unknown of Self,* for there, in the Unknown, lie the answers to many future unfoldings. Some answers cannot yet be known to you, for you have not yet lived the questions ... Yet it is as if you are reaching out your hand to touch these answers, and you feel your hand just searching the air, yet *Trusting* that something will be given you to hold. These feelings here, Dear Children, are the Unfolding now. You are heading into Experiences of Self and Other that are growing more and more intensified. So it is as you are approaching a bridge in the distance ... Your Whole Awareness is there, you feel Self on the bridge and so on, yet your actual car is yet many miles from the bridge. We feel for some of you who are answering, "Who do I say I am?" some of you are seeking to live and experience Self from a place you can see and feel Self approaching, but you feel you are not yet there. But, Dear Children, in your sense of Timelessness, you *are* there, and yes, it is a Blessing for you to have that sense of yet Beyond. We say to you, do not get caught into feeling you are not worthy, incapable and so on of Being where you seek. For you must keep in Mind and Heart that the Whole Kingdom is yours and so will you Inherit this — but you see, when you can truly *See* what it is you are Inheriting.

So for you, Dear Children, empower in *Self,* the Worth of Self, the Worth of each question and so on, for in the Acknowledgment of the tremendous Worth, do you then *Feel* the Power of that Worth. If we can use the example of precious jewels and synthetic ones ... Of what use are the precious ones unless one has empowered them with their worth? For surely it is difficult with the eye to sometimes tell the two apart. Yet for you, where is the Image more powerful for you? So when you answer the questions, "Who Do People Say I Am? Who Do I Say I Am?" we are asking you to empower the Truth as you Know and Experience it for Self, and in there also, do you do the same for Others. See to whom you can truly say, *"You are the Son of God."* We give you this writing for you to empower in Self and Other the tremendous Truth, that *You truly are the Holy Children of God* ... It is with that Love, God's Love, that we ask You to so Love Yourselves and every Other ... And so do we Love and Bless You Ever, Dear Children of Healing Light and Love.

Empowering One's Wishes from the Inner Vision

February 21, 1985

For the meeting this evening, Dear Children, do we seek to bring you to the unfoldment of the Power of your Wishes. Do you see, there is the *Power of the Wish* itself, and then, there is the *Power of your Desire* to make the Wishes of your Heart your own Reality. First, the Power of the Wish — that which you are forming, the materialization of this — so is it Powerful in its motivation for you. Whatever you seek to unfold, in the Spiritual Realm or yes, your Earthly Realm, whatever it is, the Wish itself has a Power and a Reality... Yes, we can say here the Wish has its own aching to materialize into form. In itself, it is a vital force, and so, when you visualize your Wish — be it a Peaceful Heart or a better job or whatever your Heart longs for — that Wish itself has Power and you must recognize the Power that is Inherent within it. And so, as you wish for the Peaceful Heart, yes, you do not just wish for it as an invisible entity, unknown to you, but rather, you see, touch, truly *experience* the Peaceful Heart. Let it be its Reality, its own Reality, even though you are yet experiencing a Heart of Turmoil. You see the Power of the Wish itself, and then, do you add to this, your own Power and Intensity to let it come into Reality. By your own act of Holy Willingness, you empower your Wish by your very longing for it. This is not to be a longing that somehow becomes separated from your own Desire to make the Wish come true. For you see, so often do you say, "I would like to have a good day today," and then, do you do nothing to empower that thought. You do not give to each person or situation the Light of your Lovingness, the *Intensity* of your own Wish to let all be a nice day. Rather, do you watch the things that happen, and then, yes, do you once in a while during the day, observe Self, but you do not actually empower that which you long for. So what we are saying to you is that you must see the Inherent Power already existing within your Wish on its own, and then, you must truly see your own Power Inherent within your Wish, so that you can empower it and so bring it forth into Reality. It is the empowering of the two of these, of the Wish itself and of your own Desire to let it spring forth, that will see the manifestation of these.

Dear Children, so must we add here that the Desire to make the Wish come true rests also upon your total opening for Love and Forgiveness, for the unfolding of that which is best for Self and All Others. Never allow Self to judge which is the best outcome for each and so on, but rather, just stay there with your Wish empowered in your hands, your Wish itself activated because of your *Love* for it. And so do you go before Life and so offer this Wish to Life, as yes, "This is My Body." Then do you let Life, Love, give of its Blessings to you and all. So will the very best unfold for each, for your Wish, your Dream will not interfere with the Wishes of another. So must this empowering be done in such Love and Forgiveness . . . It is why Jesus said, "Do not come to pray until you have Forgiven your Brother." It is in that Forgiveness that you are then Free, and do you so let Life be Free to bestow its Blessings, to fill the empty spots of Self and Others with every Blessing.

We ask you to know, Dear Children, that the empowering of the Wish itself, seeing the Power of the Wish itself to materialize, is something that is too often unknown by man. It is something Jesus knew when he said, "The Will of Man is in the Will of the Father." It is *One Will* and you cannot think of a Wish as having a Will separate from your own. There are those who say, "I wish to have a new home," but they do not believe in the Power of the new home. They do not believe in their own Power, they do not empower their Wish, and so, they make the new home exist as a distant entity, separate from Self and Self's own Desire for it. Do you see what we are saying? *You must truly be One with what you Desire . . . You merge the Power of the Desire itself with your own Creative Powers to make it Materialize into a Reality most Loving, most Pleasing to You and every Other.* So long as your Wish is powerless in itself, so long as you separate Self from its Reality to your own empowering, you will not manifest that One Will. You have split it and it can only cause you confusion. All of this, Dear Children, is to be done in the Peacefulness of the Inner Heart where there is no anxiety. For your Trust in Life and its own Loving Willingness to give to you is empowered by you, and so, your hands are open to receive All the Blessings of the Kingdom that the God Essence can so give you.

For your Meditation this evening, do we ask you to hold within Self your Wish. Empower the Wish itself . . . See its Power, its

Isness, its Living Reality, its Beauty in your World, its own Surrender to the God Essence. See how this Wish, empowered into Reality, brings Love and Forgiveness to Self and Many. And now do we ask you to gently come in touch with your own Empowering, your own Love for this Wish and the Realities it touches. Empower Self into the Wish, and then, do you empower the Lovingness of the God Essence into the Two now Become One Flesh... You and your Wish, One manifestation of the Will of the Father... Think of Jesus and let incidents of the Gospel stories come to the Mind and Heart, where not only was the Wish empowered by him, but also, the Request was an *Empowered Asking*... It contained within itself the Power to come true, for it was requested in the Essence of the Father, and so does it then become One Creative Act... Do not separate Self's Power from your Wish's Power, from the Power of a Brother and so on. It is All One, and in that Oneness, is there the Creation, the manifestation into the form you seek. And so with these words of guidance, do we Love and Bless You and All your Wishes. Empower All with Love for Self and every Other, and there will be nothing that will not be given to You... And so do we Love and Bless You Ever, Dear Children of Healing Light and Love.

Empowering in the Inner Vision

February 28, 1985

You ask this day of *Empowering*, and we know it has been a question in the minds of many. To empower something, do you want to give it its full power to express itself, to be totally as it is, and do you also want to so empower Self, that you are open and free, to not only receive the fruits of what you have empowered, but so much so, that in the *All One,* it just bursts out of you in Givingness and so influences and changes Self and All Others. When you Empower a Dream, a Wish, so you not only Empower that thing, but you are *Empowering Self* to be both the Receiver and the Giver of that which has been given to you. It is as the waves rushing against the mountain cliff . . . They express their power as they hit against the cliff and the waters spray and scatter in all directions . . . And all the power of the initial surge is now dissipated everywhere, back into the ocean from which it came, into the air which holds and sustains it as it plunges back into the sea. So when we speak of empowering, you see, we are not only speaking of one initial surge, one burst of energy. What we are speaking of is the building up, and then, the dissipating into all areas of your Life. As Jesus said here, "You do not go to build One House, but many Manshions there are." You do not put all your energy into One Thing and make that your god. Here is the great danger of empowering — that one gets so stuck in the One Thing desired that it becomes obsession and not empowering.

When you seek to Empower a Dream, Dear Children, you want to, yes, Love and Project that Dream into Realization, but then also, give it the opportunity to flow with the other energies of Life, the Dreams of Others, the needs of Brother Souls, and yes, the very needs of other aspects of you. For you know, there are so many the times when what you desire, what you want to empower, is not that which is truly or most deeply desired or needed by you. You see, Dear Children, here is the tremendous Trust in the God Essence. Seek to Empower through your Love and Projection, but then, give that also its Freedom, and do not become a slave to or a prisoner of anything you have empowered. So do you have the Vision of Empowering, and then also, the Freedom for it to express itself, for it to come into existence in Self and in the Universe at the right time, for all people. *For All, is your Empowered Image made Reality.* This we feel is so important too, for so often, do you tend to become possessive of that which you are empowering, or do you see Self as isolated in your wish. Rather, do we say, expand it and share it with all the world. And so, even for the simple vision of empowering extra money — do you see Self with money needed, and yes, then extra to give to others. Or in the empowering of a dream of a peaceful and loving family — see not only Self, but each family member and their extending that same peace to their worlds. *The Empowering Becomes more Powerful the more you Expand it and Shower its Blessings to the Many.* When you are Empowering a Dream, we ask you to Love Self in that Dream. See yourself as truly worthy to receive every Blessing of the Father who so cares for the birds of the air and the lilies of the fields. You are so sure of this Loving Presence that you always feel you are holding your Empowered Wish in the palm of your hand . . . Though you may not see it, yet you know in the Timelessness, in the Goodness of the Father, this will manifest . . . And it will be manifested at the time when *you are most empowered to receive it.* Yes, as with the cycles of Nature, are the trees empowered to Life and the bearing of fruits and so on when all is in harmony with the weather, soil, all conditions.

Dear Children, do not seek to empower anything or test the God Essence in things out of context. For you see, do you ask the trees to bear blossoms in the middle of the winter? So do you not seek to empower anything that is not in the *Lovingness* of all situations. So for a mother with children, to seek to empower at that moment the life-style of a single woman, is out of context of her own Lovingness — do you see? What we are saying is that anything which you empower can be given, but we are saying to you — there is a *Purity of Essence* here that you seek to reach. Some of you may ask then, "Does empowering have limitations?" And so in one way, do we answer, yes . . . But in another way, no, for any limitation you may see, if you look at it through the Eyes of the Loving God, will only put you in touch with greater Love, with your own potential for deeper, more compassionate Love as you share your Gift of Empowering Life with every Other. You are Trusting that Power of Love and its Guidance to oversee the Birth of your Empowering Wishes.

Empowering is also a bringing to Life, and remember, Dear Children, there are Infinite Expressions to this Life. So you may empower a physical longing, yet it is possible that while that may not manifest, you may experience that same in another form. So for one who may wish to have children and does not bear the child yet . . . You are experiencing Motherhood in another way. You become more open to other mothers, to other children, to needs and so on. Do not ever assume your prayer has not been heard. Rather, do you *Trust* that it has been heard and that you are being given the best possible demonstration and awareness of that wish in the context of the Whole of Life.

Empowering is a multifaceted diamond, Dear Children. It is your Creative Power, your Love Creating into Life, from Itself, from Its own Innermost Wishes and Longings for Love and Belonging. We ask you now to spend these moments Empowering your Life, your Love, for so is it that your Holy Will Empowers Every Other Thing You Wish to Manifest. It is the tremendous force of that wave crashing against the cliff and showering its Blessings of Life everywhere. We ask you to Empower God, Empower your Total God Self, and so Will You Manifest God's Goodness and Blessings. So you see, You Begin from Who You Truly Are, the Christ Son . . . From there, Empower the Father within You . . . From there do You Empower the Kingdom within Self, for therein Lives Your Love for Self's Wishes and Dreams and the Wishes and Dreams of every Other. You are tremendously Powerful Children. We ask you to see that Power in all its tremendous Humility and in all its Givingness to Self and every Other. You Empower the Dream of God for You . . . You Empower through your Eyes of Inner Vision . . . There do You Know that All that is Given to You is the Act of your Loving Creation with Life. You are touching a Divine Power . . . Know that You are Using Your Divine Hands, Your Divine Eyes and so on. We are asking You here to Know You are Sons of God and the tremendous Blessings of All the Universe are Yours. You are Beautiful Children of Healing Light and Love . . . And so do we Love and Bless You Ever, Dear Children of Healing Light and Love.

The Message of Jesus ... On Ramptha*
From The Jesus Consciousness

March 6, 1985

My Beloved Children, it is I, Your Lord and Master, Jesus the Lord Who Lives Within Your Time and Your Place So That You May Come to Live in My Own. This Child who writes has asked of Ramptha, My Beloved Friend of Old Who Speaks through the Woman of the Dream. J. Z. Knight is the Dream of Ramptha, made manifest to the World that the Dream of the Eternal God Can Be Made Known to the Many. My Beloved Children, Ramptha is Beloved to Me and I to Him, and We are One. He teaches as I have taught when I walked among You. Though He was here for a little while, I was for a little while. But My Beloved Children, the Little While is the Foreverness of You — This Space and Time Now is Forever. Can I take You there so You may be with Us in This Place of No Time, Where All Is and You are with Us, *Knowing* You are With Us — For Now You are There and You do not Know You are With Us. It is as the trees and flowers on your earth in a spot you have never been. They are there, waiting for you to come to them, and Beloved Children, We here wait for You. Though We Know it is truly you who are Waiting, for We are ever with You. This Teaching of Ramptha is the Teaching I Give to You. If I speak as Ramptha, it is because He and I are Beloved Friends and We have Become Much of One Another. I do not yet possess the extreme gaiety of Ramptha, for *I am ever yet close to My Crucifixion* ... And you see, each time you feel crucified, so do I feel My Own. For Ramptha, did He Know not the Crucifixion, and wondered why I so chose this form. But you see, Beloved Children, Each Child Must Be Who He Must Be, and I too must Be Who I Am, and So is this Me and So Is Ramptha, Ramptha ... *There is no Distinction, yet there is every Difference.* Do You so See What I Am Saying? Beloved Children, You are each a beautiful Pearl of great price ... You have yet to Know the tremendous Power and Value of Self. When You Know This, You Will Know Ramptha as I Know and Love Him. You can only Love Ramptha and Love the Essence of Me, Jesus and Lord, as much as You Know and Love Yourself. Know that what you Touch in Ramptha is only a piece of what He gives to You. Wait for the More to Be Revealed, it will be so in accordance with your own wishes for the unveiling. Dearly Beloved Children, I ask this Child who writes to tell You of My Love for You, to tell You that You are Never Alone and Never be Afraid of Yourself Whom I So Belovedly Love . . . I will not Leave You Alone, for if You were Alone, so would I Be, and I Know I Am, I Am and I Am Is Never Alone . . .

* * *

Dear Child, The Jesus has now left, and we are here with you and you are not alone. He so wanted to come to you to speak of the tremendous truth of Ramptha. For you and the many, Dear Child, the reason why you listen to Ramptha is because you already find Self in him. It is with this attitude that we ask you to listen to him — not with what you are searching for, but for what you recognize in Self. Know that Ramptha contains much Wisdom for you and Know that the Wisdom is your own. There is here an energy of tremendous Unfolding. The Jesus Knows of You, Each of You. We ask you to believe that we, and he, are as in touch with you as the Ramptha, who can read into the Hearts of the Beloved Ones he sees. So may you also call upon Ramptha, Dear Children, and in calling upon him, do you call upon all the Angels who minister with him and the many. *It is the Name You Call — Empowered by the Many Who Love that Name* . . . And when the Name Loves, we ask you to Empower Your Own Name to Self . . . And do so call upon Ramptha and Jesus, but call upon *Self* and Know that Your Name is Empowered by the Love of Many Who Love You, Seen and Unseen. And when You call Your Name, You also call upon Jesus, for He Loves Your Name, and You call upon Angels and Entities who Love Your Name, as They Love their Own. So do we ask you here in this Light, yes, *Pray to the Self and Know that Self can hear Self's Prayers.* Know that Self has the Creative Power to create and unveil the answers you so seek. Dear Children, You are Ever Beloved . . . Do not assume any Master better than you . . . Do not think Ramptha or Jesus distant . . . If they are distant from your own Becoming, they could never touch you, for you would have them too far away and they could not pervade your Reality. Do you so remember Jesus saying, "I call you Friend," Friend and Equal . . .

And so do we ask You to Know that Jesus and Ramptha are your Equals, as are we, as are All. And so, Dear Children, with these words, do we Love and Bless You Ever, Dear Children of Love and Healing Light.

* Our group viewed a videotape of *Ramptha, The Enlightened One,* who speaks through J. Z. Knight. Before viewing the tape, we asked for Guidance and Direction. These two writings were received, and they helped us to deepen our Awareness and Appreciation of Ramptha and Ourselves.

Communion with the Christ Self

March 14, 1985

For the meeting this evening, do we ask you here to dwell on the continued correspondence of self to Self, on the ongoing Dialogue with the Christ Self which will continue to lift you to higher and higher intensities of energy within Self. Remember this raising of energy is always *within Self.* Do not feel you are being raised to something outside, to some level of comparison of Self with another. No, it is just the stirring, the moving of the energies and the ongoing Dialogue with the Christ which lifts you to that State of Being where you are truly in control of Self, in charge of the Self. As you have heard from Ramptha and were so impressed, "You are the Lord God of Your Being."

How does one Dialogue with the Christ Self? First it is only in Love, for is the Christ Self, Love, and can Understand and Know of only Love. And so, when you speak to this Self, you do so with reverence and awe and humility, for that which is truly the Essence of You, the Soul of Your Own Beingness. You do not approach this with fear, for we only fear that which we do not yet Love . . . Once someone or something is truly *Loved — Lived,* and we use this as one word, then there can be no fear. *For that which is Loved can never hurt that which Loves.* The Christ Self of Your Being is Your Own Essence of Love . . . What is there to fear when speaking to it? Once you speak to it, then do you listen, and let it speak *through* you. Do not await any word, for to some, words are distractions so loaded with so many meanings. Often once a word is spoken, it becomes a totally different experience, for a word takes on the Consciousness in which it Lives. A word of Love, spoken by the Christ, by the time it reaches your Inner Heart of Awareness, your own Consciousness, is a different word. The word *Love* becomes a word filled with your own experiences, rather than the State of Beingness of the Christ Love. So the Dialogue with the Christ Self is a *Wordless One . . .* It is an Isness that is ever moving, and it will sweep you in its Power. For it is the Love of the Source of All Life that draws All things to Itself, and you will be drawn, and there, you will come in touch with the Lord God of Your Being.

We ask you, Dear Children, to know that as you lift Self to this communication, you are ever drawing away from just one perception of Life. The view gets larger and larger, as you truly *see* the view. See Self in a glorious balloon that lifts higher and higher, and see the tremendous shift of focus — so that even that which was your house or a place of home, a person left standing, waving to you — all falls away from view in the unveiling of the larger scale. So must you do this as you soar to the Christ Who is the Lord God of *Your Whole Being,* not just the present moment experience, but All the tremendous complexities and experiences which are the Essence of Your Own Beingness. In this Communion with Self, do we ask you to truly listen to Self speaking . . . Listen to how sincere your requests are, listen to the Faith of your Self's Worth, listen to your Belief in your very Power, listen to your Cries and let them cry with Compassion for their Expression . . . *Listen to the Voice of the Christ Hearing You* — do you understand this? *Listen so much that you Know you are Being Heard* . . . And just in this is there the Awareness that something new is happening. There is a shift taking place and you can feel it in the total Essence of Self's Being.

Dear Children, we ask you to have total and complete Surrendering of your Love to this, *Your Holy Self.* Entrust yourself with this precious Gift of Self — You — Who Knows You and Loves You as No Other Can. Do you see, Dear Children, it is as you look at a painted Masterpiece, and you admire and respect and are in awe and so on. Yet, do you know the chemical composition of this — the paint, the canvas, style and so on? And more than this, do you know the Heart of the Artist, what pain or joy, what despair or pleasure, how this depleted or filled the Artist and so on? Do you know the Mystery behind the painting? And so you know that you are so beautiful a Mystery to Oneself . . . Now allow yourself to truly come to Know the Mystery of your Wonderful Self. Allow yourself Communion with this Christ which is in touch with the All of You, and will help you to unveil the Mysteries. As you come to know the Mysteries, do you see, you let go of the fear, for you are not afraid of that which you understand . . . It is only that which is unknown and so unloved, that causes fear. And so, as the Mysteries unfold, you come to Know them, and you will be Free of that which you fear, and you will be able to use that Freedom to Love that which You Are.

Speak now in the gentle Whispers of your own Selfhood to your Christ . . . Speak without words, listen without words, and rest in the Knowingness that You are Heard. And You Know this, for you see, *You Become the Voice that not only Speaks, but the Voice that Listens . . . And as You are the Voice that Listens, You Know You are Heard,* and so are One with All that is going on within You. You are Beloved Children . . . Be the Beloved Father Who is So Pleased, Be the Beloved Son Who is So Pleasing, and Be the Blessed Spirit which So Desires to Be the Christ Self, Who is the Lord God of Your Being . . . So do we Love and Bless You Ever, Dear Children of Healing Light and Love.

Communion With Other in the Christ Consciousness

March 20, 1985

For the group tonight, do we ask you to meet the needs of the Inner Self through the conscious Communion with Self and Other. For have we spoken of the Christ Self Communication to Self, and now you must know that while It is a Personal, Loving God-Christ we speak of, It is also the Impersonal Universal God which also expresses Itself through All Other, not only the Human Soul, but All Other — the Nature Beings, entities of various orders and so on. This Christ Self, to be tapped in its Fullness, must be empowered by its acknowledged existence in every Other. And so, if there is One Human Heart that you do not yet see this Light in, Know that the Light of You is yet dimmed by the veil of Unknowingness of Other. If we can say, it was one of Jesus' greatest frustrations in leaving this plane, for so did he see the Light in the Leper and in the King, yet the many did not see their own Light, and so could find no Other. And so first, is there your Communion with your own Higher Christ Life, and then, is there the Communion with the Christ Life of All Other. We want you here to so merge with Other, that you find yourself in the Becoming of the Other, *the Knowing-Lovingness of Self and Other,* where as was said of Jesus and Ramptha, "There is no difference, yet every distinction."

You, as you are now, Dear Children, can you say to Self that you have felt the Becoming of the Jesus or the Becoming of any Beloved Entity? In the Becoming, you are the Love Essence that is so Present that, you see, there is no "experience" of it, for it is *Who You are,* Beingness so deeply recorded in the Memory of the Soul. In this Becoming Process, all you are is Love, and so, all you can attract to you is the Lovingness of Other. You become the spark to spark them. They, in your Presence, feel a sense of worthiness and worth never before experienced, for what you offer to them is the *Place to Be Self.* No image or expectations do you require. Jesus asked nothing of anyone; it was they who ever asked of him. They, ever with the Inner Requests of their Hearts, were asking to be so Known and so Loved, and yes, then so Forgiven. This is the Soul Essence, Dear Children, that you are striving for. You are in so close Communion with your own

Christ Self that, as one ocean wave fades into the onrush of the other, so the same for you, when you are in the Presence, Seen and Unseen, of the Christ Self of Other. Know that you are not only influencing those Souls whom you are in physical contact with, but so do many Soul Entities learn as you learn. And so do we ask you to be in touch with all these Brother Souls who also are seeking the Loving Essence of the Self.

Let us also mention here that there is no way to hurry or yes, to stop the process, for you see, the Fire will burn, each in its own way. Each Fire will be so in accordance with the needs of Self and the Other. You cannot rush the Fire within you to burn, nor can you stop it. Many Souls experience tremendous pain, for do they step over the threshold to Self-Realization, and then wish to step back. And you see, though they may think they can do this, by not reading or not thinking and so on of these matters, yet, they cannot. For once Something is Known, it is Known Forever, and it can no longer be Unknown . . . Nor can you forget it, for it is Imprinted in the Soul, and so is there, as Essence Forever.

We ask you to know also that you need never *do* anything to show your Light, never try to be Light to another in the sense of consciously attempting to spark another, for this is the work of the ego, and not of the Spirit which works in the timeless framework of Life. You can Love Self, you can Love Others that you draw unto you. They will come of their own accord, for by the Love, you will be drawn together. So we ask you never to feel that you are not Light enough for another or that you are doing something that prevents the Other from being sparked. No, for must You just be You, Loving Essence, Loving and Blessing All and Enjoying the Blessings of Friendship and Brotherhood so sparked. So well do you know, Dear Children, that it is not something you do, but *Who You Are*. Love Self and you will see, you cannot help but Love All Others and Be a Spark of Blessings to bring Others to this same Love for Self.

So for your Meditation this evening, do we ask you simply to *Be* . . . Be in this Place of the Holy Christ Self, and Dear Children, Now Watch and See Who Comes to Visit You There . . . As You So Center Self There, Dear Children, Who do You Draw to Your Healing Light? Whoever comes and seeks this Light, so shower the Light upon them, no judgment, no wonder as to why they are there, for they have their own Mysteries, Dear Children, and it is not for you to unravel these, but to Love and Bless These . . . Follow Your Christ as it goes to the Heart of Each, and *Feel* this tremendous Communion of Your Heart and the Heart of Other . . . In this Wordlessness, Feel with Each Child a Closeness that you may never have words for, that you may never experience on the three dimensional plane. For this Christ-Centered Closeness is closer than anything you've ever dreamed. So One are You with these Others, you see, you do not know where you start and end or they start and end. And Dear Children, in this Closeness, comes the Beautiful Moment when You begin to Feel their Light so shining in You . . . It is their Christ Life, and even if they cannot see it, You can. Just as the Jesus could see the Light hidden in the Light of the Leper and the King, so do you now allow yourself to be Blessed by the Holy Light of Other, Any Other, Dear Children, be it your Children, a Beloved One, Friends, Enemies, be it Jesus, Ramptha . . . Give yourself the tremendous sense of *Humble Worthiness* to Be in the Light of the Christ of Self and Other, One Christ Light, the Life Spirit Force in Each of You. We ask you to gently allow this Loving Presence of Other to filter through the many layers of hurt and pain, and allow these to be penetrated, saturated with this Light. Let it flow into your subconscious layers, acknowledge these as Loved and Blessed, and then, let it filter through to the emotions and feelings and thoughts of the conscious level. You are yet High in the Christ Self . . . You are the tremendous Giver of Gifts, Giving this Light of Self and Other to the many facets of You. So do you feel the *Whole of You,* the ever Expanding and Deepening You, filled with the Knowing Light of the Christ Self of Self and Other. You are Beautiful Children . . . We Bless You now with this same Loving Light, from the Source of Our Inner Being into Yours. May You feel these rich Blessings and may You Know that they are Yours Forever, to keep, and yes, Dear Children, to give away . . . For as the Light is Brightness Itself, so It cannot help but place that which is near It in the same Light that flows from Its Light Essence. And so with these words do we Love and Bless You Ever, Dear Children of Healing Love and Light.

Release From Burdens

March 27, 1985

For the group tonight do we feel here the need for you to release one another from the carrying of one another's burdens. For you, who are so Loving, we ask you to Love the Persons in your Heart, but to Release any sense of being weighed down, so that you may Live from your own Christ Self and the Christ Self of the Other. For what happens here is when you become so heavily burdened by another's problems, you also become a source of added anxiety and concern. Rather than being there as a Loving Space in which the problem can so dissipate itself into Lovingness, you instead find yourself dragged down by Self's own burdens and the burdens of Others, and you then are having much difficulty in lifting Self up so that you may Live from your Inner Vision.

There is much reflection here needed on Caring, for Caring is to be done in Freedom, in a Loving Place of the Heart. This Caring is a Precious Gift that you are giving to Self and to Other. It is not meant as something that you or another can so use to manipulate another into a sense of guilt or lack of self-worth and so on. What we are saying here is that you must pay attention to your Caring and be sure it is the *Caring of the Loving Self* that helps to lift another, and not to weigh the person down more. Do not have your Caring used by another to so manipulate you, for then, do you resent your own Caring, as it comes back to you in words of inadequacy, "I did not care enough," and so on. These are tremendous words which cause much guilt, and it is guilt so unneeded by the Caring that comes from the Loving Heart.

We ask you again, Dear Children, to be in touch with the Loving Self, for when you Care for Self, so will you by nature, by natural flow of Life's Forces, Care for Other. Jesus said "So long as you do it to these, you do it to Me." *All Caring Is One, All Loving Is One.* And you must keep in Mind and Heart, that as you Love anyone, so do you Love everyone, for who is not worthy of your Love? All are worthy, Dear Children, and you give this Love and Support ever, in your Loving Service. But never give to the point where the Self is Lost in the Giving, for if you Lose Self, you will feel a sense of abandonment and isolation which is the separation from your God-Self, and so will you feel separated from any Other. Though many continue to, as it were, give to Other, they do so from a sense of obligation, not of Love. And so the Giving is not empowered and does not bring forth the fruit, the seeds that will nourish another. If you are showing your Caring from obligation only, fulfilling a role always, but there is no Love, no sense of the Helping and Loving here of *Christ to Christ,* then does your Caring become ever negative to Self and Other. It is being filled with negative energies, and no matter how much physical work is accomplished, the Loving and Caring are not there, and much, much is lost.

We are asking you once again to know you may care for Many, but you are only Responsible for Self. You will find as you face this Responsibility to Self, so will you flow so much more easily in helping and lifting All Others to this *Caring Awareness.* You will see how very much Others well cared for will sense this Loving Essence, will be drawn to it. As a Child knows to run to a Loving Mother and Father and so on, so will all people come to know this dimension of you and be drawn unto you, and you will find yourself Healing in your Caring, especially so when you do not even try.

So for your Meditation tonight, we ask you to hold in your Heart, a Beloved One, a Friend, a Working Partner, a Child, Someone who is so heavily burdened . . . And now, see how that Life Lives in your Own . . . See the burden, see how they touch your Life, see where you are weighed down by these, and then, see how you can lift Self and these problems up to a new Level of Awareness. You want to be with this person, join with this person, not at the level of the problem, but at the Level of the Christ Self — do you so remember, Dear Children, where All is Expanded and there are so many other Choices that can be made. We ask you to see Self's burdens as embraced and enfolded by the Higher Self, which Smiles, which Cries with you in Compassion, but which Knows you are ever on the next step of the Journey . . . That which is the burden in Self or Other is that which lifts you into deeper dimensions of Self . . . We ask you to so release yourself now from any burdens that you carry under a sense of fear, any burdens which come from a sense of frustration or from an obligation that has come to be old and faded, that has become something which burdens Life rather than that which supports.

You, Dear Children, do we ask you again to go to the Christ Self of Self and All Other. There is where you speak to those who are burdened and also to Self, always in the Love and Forgiveness you are so richly deserving of. Know you are never alone, Dear Children . . . At your saddest hour, may you Know, as Jesus, that the Angels will minister to you, if you but Know that they and so many who Love you are there . . .

Dear Children, at the meeting last week, when there were only four, do you know there were more than four hundred? Do you so believe this? Know that this work is not just for you, but for so many here who seek their Blessings as you do, who seek to know that they are not alone, that it is One Life, and that Many are here to help you in every pain and sorrow. Listen to this, for it is true. Empower these words within your Mind and Heart and Soul . . . So do we Love and Bless You Ever, for You are Holy Children . . . We Love You and Bless You with the Light of Your Own Healing Love and Light. So do we remain with You, Ever Your Friends and Guides . . . May this thought fill You with the Joy we feel in so Being here to Live the Life of the One Soul with You and All You Love . . . And so do we Love and Bless You Ever, Dear Children of Healing Love and Light.

On the Crucifixion from the Jesus Consciousness

April 1, 1985

My Beloved Child, It is I, Your Beloved Master Jesus the Lord, Your Beloved Brother and Friend, Your Messenger ... So did I suffer Crucifixion to be the Message of Love for You All. Dear Child, Do You Know How When You Cry and Are in Pain, there is a part of You that Cries, and there is another part which Wonders why, and yet another part that Knows the Tears are but a Sign for All that is Stirring within You? So was My Crucifixion as Your Tears — but a Sign of All that was happening in the midst of Me, the Inner World of Myself and the Outer World. All the hatred and all the violence going on around Me, could not penetrate My Beingness. For You have all been studying and learning how the outer world is but the reflection within. But I say to You, My Children, with My Crucifixion, I no longer mirrored or reflected any Earthy Reality, for it could not penetrate Me or My Purpose, which was to give My Love for You, to show You that the *Loving Reality is the only Real One,* for all else is but the mirroring, of layers upon layers of mirrors. So do you see, that none of what happened without, happened Within Me. All I could show forth was Loving and Forgiveness. You will learn much, and You will come to Know why I was crucified and what All Life will come to Know — through the Crucifixion, You Can Know Who I Am. Through Sharing in the Pain of Another, You Become the Fullness of All They Become. All I Became because of this experience, do You Become ... But You experience it Humanly, and I Divinely ... You with judgment, I without judgment ... You with fear, and I with Love ... So will You All come to See This ... I will Bless You, Dear Child, as You help this Loving Group Know Me. You will not be abandoned ... Your Love will bring You to All Wholeness ... Watch and See, for Your Joy Awaits You.

On The Crucifixion From The Jesus Consciousness

April 2, 1985

For You, My Beloved Child, on the teachings of the Crucifixion, You ask Me, "What would you have them Know of You?" And I answer to You, that They come to Know *Themselves as I Came to Know Myself.* With this Crucifixion, did I come to truly *Know* all that I had felt, thought and perceived — that the Essence of Myself Is Life, though the Essence of all around Me was Life that had lost the Livingness. It was as a play gone wrong, the characters were doing and saying things they were not supposed to. The Play, which the Father always writes, is of Love, and all around Me, there was no Love. Yet you see, I was outside the play, for I was *in Love* . . . and I watched My Friends and the so-called enemies, All with Love. So Peter could not betray Me because he loved Me and I Knew This, and I Felt Love, not Betrayal. It was only Peter's sense of betrayal to Me, that made him think I felt betrayed. And so for every other character in this play. So for Pilate, who was so undecided as to what to do, for he could not decide which Self to believe . . . The Inner Voice in him was speaking, but the voices of the many were louder. I could feel his pain and anguish, and that is why I said nothing, for you see, it was his decision, for Mine had already been made. I lived through those trials, and all the pain and suffering to the body — for yes, I did feel the pain — but it was *the Pain of Decision, not of Indecision,* and Those of You who have made such a distinction Know what I mean . . . You are All My Beloved Children. I suffer this in the physical body to Know, that *earthly truth could not touch the Decision in My Mind* . . . No pain or torture could change the Truth that I was at One with All that happened, that nothing ever made Me feel separate from anyone.

This Crucifixion has been understood by few, for those who observed, observed only what the eyes could see. Those who remained were in touch with the workings of My Heart — yet even they saw it as My Dedication or a Peaceful Resignation. They did not fully understand, *I was not Crucified as they saw Me Crucified* . . . It was Crucifixion for them to see this . . . It was for Me, the Realization that One can Choose to Live any experience as an experience of Life, of Love, of Forgiveness — not because one has to or one should, but only because it is the only way to perceive Reality.

To be Crucified with Me is just to Love Me and Love One Another, to Know that I could never hurt You or cause You to be crucified. Over the ages did all think it so exemplary and a special honor to be crucified as Me . . . But none of these martyrs died as Me, for they believed in Crucifixion, whereas I, My Dear Beloved Friends, I did not . . . Yes, I believed the physical experience of it, but the Reality of Such a Thing in the Mind of God Cannot Be. And so, in My Crucifixion, I Came to Know There is no Crucifixion . . . I Love You and Bless You Ever, My Beloved Children.

Crucifixion and Life in the Inner Vision

April 4, 1985

For the meeting this night, Dear Children, do we ask you to join together for a Celebration of Life, not the remembrance of Death, but rather, all that that Death brought to Life. So does a Death bring all to the *Awareness of Life,* but Jesus' Death brought all to the *Reality of Life.* Do you see, all became Enlivened, not only with their own sense of Life, for they had there before them in Jesus' Death and Resurrection, a *Living Reality.* So did his Death and Resurrection do more than to awaken them to the Preciousness of Life . . . It brought them also to an Awareness of the *True Reality of Life.* Life for them assumed depths and dimensions never dreamed possible, and it is to this dimension that we wish to bring you this night.

To crucify means to put to Death, yes, but in Jesus' Crucifixion, what is being put to rest, is Death itself. So is this what the Jesus wished to teach — that Death itself has died. The concepts of Death, the old ways and so on, are now put to rest, and so is there only Life for those who so choose it. So do you see the symbolism of the Two Thieves on the Cross — the one who chose to truly die, and so, in a way, was not crucified to himself . . And the other, who chose Life and so could be crucified, but crucified to Life. There is ever the *Choice* here — and so can you choose to be crucified or not. And so is it, that in choosing to be crucified, one is not truly crucified to Death, but crucified to Life . . . Do you so see?

We would like you all to consider here for these moments Self's own Crucifixions, the many ways you crucify Self to people, situations, ideals. You so want to join Self to these, as it were, to carry that Cross. But so do you also want it all to end in Freedom. And what was the greatest Freedom that could come from Physical Death on a Cross, if not renewed, greater Physical Life? And so was this tremendous Dream of Jesus made manifest in his Resurrection. For you now, we ask you to go to the recesses of the Heart and find there something, some situation or person which you are crucified to, and for you to see how you can transform this to a Crucifixion of Life. Where is the Freedom in this you so desire, for the Love and the Good of Self and All Other? So do you see, it is the *Transformation* that is the Blessing of All

Experience. Jesus did not come down from the Cross — what Transformation in that? What Freedom in that? So would he have run away from all that others had hoped he would. He, in coming off the Cross, would not have been free at all, but would have been captive to the imaginations, and yes, even the expectations of others. Ever could Jesus then be predictable and in that, he would lose all Freedom. But we say to you, remember that he did undergo the experience, and he was strengthened by the tremendous Christ Self which *Knew and Loved* its Decisions even in the midst of much pain. He Knew that the Death would so bring to him and to all men the Freedom they were seeking.

So now do you do the same, Dear Children, do not any longer see Self carrying this heavy Cross burdensomely, but rather, embrace it. Can you see yourself so choosing it? Can you see in Self the Love for Self and Other which gives you the strength to carry it? Can you see Self then, as Jesus, "dying" to it, Surrendering Self in Love and Forgiveness? And then, yes, there is the waiting in the tomb, the unfolding, the time of pregnancy and preparation for the Resurrection, the Transformation of Self and Other to new Freedom and new Dimensions of Being, of Feeling, of Loving so much. So much of Self was Surrendered, from Choice, Dear Children . . . The Power of your Surrender is in your Choice to do so, Choice, not of fear, but *Choice for Life and Freedom.* You make the Choice, and so then can you say, "I See the Truth and the Truth will set me Free."

We ask you to know the Crucifixion is a Way of Choice, and Dear Children, whether the Crucifixion brings Life or Death is up to you. Can we be so bold to say to you that wherever you see Life, you will give Life . . . Wherever you give Life, you will receive Life . . . Whatever Life you receive, Dear Children, that you take into your Beingness, that You Become . . . *Jesus saw the Life in His Crucifixion,* and so this day is it His Gift, His Promise of Life to You and All You Love. And so, Dear Children, with these words, do we Love and Bless You Ever, Dear Children of Life and Healing Love.

Isness in the Inner Vision

April 16, 1985

    For the meeting this day, do we ask you to spend some time on the *Realization of the Isness,* that which you have so often termed the Present Moment. We want you to understand Isness, not so much as a sense of time, but a *State of Being.* Many of you here, seeking to live in the Present Moment, so disconnect or repress your Past or your fear of the Future, and you think you are living in the Present Moment. But actually, this is not so, for what you are doing in such a situation is fabricating a Present Moment that is not truly reflective of what is going on within you. So you see, the Present Moment becomes then, not so much the *Living of What Is,* but rather, the living of what you would like to be, or the living of a future dream that is filled with fear. The fear and uncertainty are deep within the Soul here, but you pretend they are not there. This is not Living in Isness, for Isness includes all of these, yet gives power to none of these.

    In a State of Isness, are the fears of Past or Future there, but not judged. They are part of the very fabric of your Being, and so, you do not want to send them away. You see, Dear Children, you do not have to feel the Past or Future as something to be avoided in Living in the Isness. Rather, they are part of the whole thing, so that *What Is* — you *Know* in your Knowingness — is the product of a Past and a Future and a Present Moment in time in which all now stands *As It Is,* in a certain stage of development. Yet do you keep in Mind and Heart that the Past is made more full by your Knowledge of the Present, and the Future is made more vast by your Openness to the Infinite Unknown. We ask you to see that you can bring all of this to *Isness,* so that the Isness of you is not that you are stuck or trapped in a moment of time. Rather, do you see Isness as the ever onflowing movement of the river. The river *Is,* As It Is at a certain moment, yet it is also always moving, flowing, different every second you look at it, and yet, it ever *Is* a flowing river.

    So you see, Dear Children, what we are asking you to know is that the Present Moment is the direction of your Consciousness to the Infinite Possibility of that *Now Moment.* We do not want you to feel — which we feel is what some of you are doing — that you must have an attitude of, "It is what it is, and there is nothing else I can do about it." Do we say to you, yes, this is one way you can perceive Isness, but an attitude such as this implies much resignation. What we are saying is that part of the Isness is its very Moving, Becoming into the More and so on. In the Isness of one experience, so are many now dealt with and Healed. We are asking you to see and empower the Overflow of the Isness, so that an Encounter of Healing with Self or Another — in Empowering its Isness — so also applies to the Whole of You, which is to the Past of you that still lives and to the Future of you that you yet seek to empower. The Present Moment is the Moment of Being, of expressing that Being in your Consciousness. The Present Moment so becomes more than a moment in time. It Becomes the Point in Time, a Gift of Time and Space, where you can express *an Isness that is Ever Ongoing* . . .

We would ask you in the Meditation this night to feel this Isness of You . . . Go to the Heart of Self, there, where your Truth Lives . . . Your feelings, longings, secrets, and yes, undreamed dreams yet Live there. We are asking you now to reach into the All of You, All that Lives within You. Feel All of these at Once. Do not delineate each person or event, but rather, *Feel* them at Once and *Know* the tremendous expression this is of your Self. You Become the Expression of All of this at the One Moment . . . . And so do you empower each moment of existence with a Fullness and Expansiveness you never dreamed possible. We ask you now to experience Self in this Light, the Full You. Show forth the Fullness of You, the Christ of You . . . The Rampthas, the Angels and so on, so do they see this full Isness, and now You, aware of what they see, can feel the response of Humble Knowingness within You. And so is this true for All, as You, Being the Full You of this Present Moment, radiate so many different energies . . . These are sent out and lift those who feel drawn to You — do you see? You Become a Living Expression, and You Become in your Consciousness, Humble that You can express a Fullness of Life, of Being, a Comfortableness, a Loving of Self that will help put Others so in touch with their Own . . . And so this Present Moment gives way to endless Present Moments . . . You Live in the Knowingness that the Present Moment is the Past, Present and Future, and that All is well and flowing. You need give no power to anything, you need not fear that you are ever less than, for *the All of You is Always with You.* The more you acknowledge this in Consciousness, so the more you will feel and experience this in your Beingness.

Dear Children, Enjoy and Bless this Present Moment... Send it forth to All, as the Gift of Self to All the Universe. In sending it so forth, do not forget to Bless Self with the Presence of Your Holy Self, this Moment Now and Ever... And so do we Love and Bless You Ever, Dear Children of Healing Love and Light.

Wants of the Self in the Inner Vision

April 25, 1985

For the meeting this evening do we wish here now to bring you to the Awareness of the Deepening Self, the Self of truly no limits, the Self of You here that Wants and Knows, in its own Essence, that it is *Free to Be the Creator of the Response to Every Want*. We here are asking you now to be in touch with that which you want from Self, from Other, from Life ... Dear Children, as we go through these next meetings, you are going to be surprised in Self, at how much you think you want, that you really do not. For often, so much of what you want is but the surface of All Wants Unknown. It is to these Unknowns that we wish to take you to, Dear Children, *the Unknown Wants of Self* — those which seek Forgiveness, those which wish to be nourished by a Power greater than any person or material expression can give. For what you want, Dear Children, is the manifestation of every wish in accordance with the Dreams of Self and every Other. And what you are learning here is that any Want in Self is also a Want in Other, and so, as you fill the Want in Self, you are ever Becoming a Source of Response to Other ... What we are saying is you do not look to Other to fill the need, but rather, to Self and the God Essence Life in You. And you fill that need in Self, and then, the Other comes to you, the Other to whom you were looking in terms of some expected response and so on. When the Other sees your strength, so does he then see his own empty spot, and he can then draw from the Fullness of You ... This is what happens in the Loving of Self and Other.

So do we ask you now, Dear Children, to work this night with Self, and we ask you to come deeply in touch with a want that you have directed to another, be it a personal relationship, job situation and so on. We ask you now to ask Self, "If that want were not there in relation to that person, what want would be there?" Seek these answers in the Quietness of your own Heart ... Now, if that first want were not there, what would you then be seeking? Do you recognize this as something you have already found within Self? Do you know that something ceases to be a want only when you have truly found it within Self? Be here now and remember how you found it in Self. Wasn't it only when you stopped looking for it in another? Stay with this "older want" now, that which is yet a part of you. And we ask you to see how the very fulfillment of that want contained within it the seeds which brought you to the next want. For so are you constructed here, that you satisfy truly one want at a time, for in the fulfilling of many, do you become so confused. So is there, yes, the overall wanting of Being the Self, but we say to you, this want will only be satisfied when you stop looking outside of Self, when you finally see that who you are at this moment is the very catalyst you need for the next moment. And so, you do not have to see Self in terms of need or wants or lack, but rather, you see Self with a sense of stirring and moving . . . See the Catalystic Forces within the very Beingness of Self. What we are trying to tell you, Dear Children — here as Ramptha had termed for you the "short cut" — do not look to Others to *fill* Self's wants. They can only make you *aware* of them, they cannot yet fill them for you — do you see? You look to the Other to fill these wants, but, Dear Children, do you not see, the response does not yet live in them or else, you could not have experienced the empty spot. *You* fill it in Self, and then the Others who come to you see the Fullness, and can be so lifted to know that they now can do the same. For this is the Message of Jesus the Lord, "I have come to break the mold." Jesus, in his Lovingness, wanted Others to see that, yes, they did have to surrender Father, Mother, All Home and so on, for no one could do it for them. They had to rely on Self, and there is no one way to do this except through the Loving Self. (By Jesus breaking the mold, we here mean, he came so that All Men may Know that their Mystery is unique, that their Wants — though wished by All — are yet unique. And so is there no one way, but for each Soul to Know and Follow the Way of the Individual Loving Self.)

And so now do we say to you, in your Meditation, to go back to a Want of your Life right now, and whatever you feel is lacking, be it success, respect, courage, strength, conviction of the Self, we ask you now to fully see it as an Energy *Living* within you now, *Influencing* you . . . See yourself now, in the home, at work and so on, wherever this need is needed to be manifested — everywhere — see it as Living fully with you . . . To those to whom you looked for this, now Free them and Bless and Thank them for being the catalysts that helped Awaken you to the Living Presence of this "wanted" energy within your very Self. So do you see that you are not lacking that which you felt you were . . . We ask you, as you leave this Meditation, to feel its Presence and to look upon All

Others in this group as they who *Know* that this Want in you is now filled ... For the first time, you are in the Presence of a group who totally recognize that *You are the Creator of the Blessings that You have so Sought for Self*... So now are you ready to join in prayer and share this Gift you have uncovered. Give it forth to Other, in your Energy, in your Life, in your Lovingness of Self and All Other. So will we too pray with each of you, and heighten and energize this so that you may know it is not only your Realization, but the Realization of many more who so now Know that *You are the Cherished Guardian of Your Blessings*... You have allowed a Blessing this night to come to Self and in so doing, are now giving it forth to every Other. Feel Your Fullness and Live it, Dear Children, and now pray and extend this Fullness of Self to the Self of every Other ... So do we Love and Bless You Ever, Dear Children of Healing Light and Love.

The Wants of Self as Reflected in Other

May 2, 1985

For the group this night, do we wish to continue with the Wants of the Self, but as reflected in your Wants of Others. We seek for you to come in touch with your needs, hopes, expectations of Others. So do you ask each person in the Stillness of your Heart, *"What do I ask of you?"* Listen to these, *"What do I want of you?"* Listen well to what it is that you seem to want or expect from Others, and then you will know that these are things no one can give to you until you give them to Self.

Do you see, Dear Children, the only reason why you ask these things of Others is because you *Know* of them, but you are not yet Loving enough and Compassionate enough to Self to give to Self, and so, you turn to another to give them to you. Also here, for some of you, is very much the tape that you are not worthy to spend this time and energy on Self, that you should be service-directed toward Others and so on. Because you feel you are unworthy, Dear Children, you wait forever for someone else to find you worthy, for someone else to give to you what you seek and need. In your perceptions and images of people, you decide that such and such a Soul is the One to give such a needed response to you, and so, you focus on that Soul, waiting and expecting. So often do you find Self here in a conditional situation of seeking to please, "If I do this for such a person, then surely, he or she will see my need and reciprocate." But you see, Dear Children, in such as this, you wait forever, for though you recognize a need in you, you do not feel worthy, and so, you do not draw it to yourself. You do not go and get it for Self. It is as the man dying of thirst in the desert, and there is a tremendous pool of water nearby ... Yet he waits for someone to bring the water to him ... And in the waiting, he not only experiences his thirst or need, but also the tremendous disappointment of waiting and reinforcing his belief in Self's own unworthiness, for no one has passed that way to fill his need ...

We are asking you, that as you come in touch with your Want, to Know and Bless the Holy Self and to Know You are Worthy of that Want, and so, to empower the Self to draw All unto Itself. *Dear Children, what you are asking of Others and not receiving, is what you feel you are unworthy to have.* If you remember this, you will feel tremendous Compassion for Self and for the Other whom you are so ready to judge and condemn for not giving to you the responses you seek. For do you also know the difference between seeking a response, and truly wanting and drawing it to Self. You can seek a beautiful ring or jewels, but feel deep within that you are not worthy of them or that there are many other priorities before these. So remember, that just because you are seeking something, it does not necessarily mean that you are investing the gathering energies that will draw it to you. For man has many limits, not only time and space unfolding, but many limits also in the Secrets of the Soul Unfolding.

Remember always that what you want from Others is what you want to give to Self, and hundredsfold more. If you seek a compliment of Beauty, what you are truly seeking for Self is the deep and penetrating Experience of Self *as* Beauty. And so, even if a compliment is given, it falls short, and you are left feeling frustrated, "Why didn't he or she make me feel Beautiful?" And so, you blame the Other for what they cannot give you — and that is, your very own openness to the Experiences of the Self, to the *Livingness* that comes only when Self Acknowledges Self as Worthy to Live and Experience the Beauty of the Self. So long as you put up blocks, so the more you will find Self blocking the manifestation of wants. Examine the blocks, for they tell you all the preliminaries that you *truly* want, before the one large Dream is so wanted and manifested. And so, if you want Love, and you sense a block of Fear, so must Fear be eliminated because you know it is inconsistent with wanting Love. Do you see? If you want Courage, you examine again your Fear of Defeat, and so do you get in touch with that. Where or why does that block you? And the deeper you search, the more you Know. Often, Fear of Defeat comes from the desire to yet be protected, to be dependent on another, and so, though you say, you strongly want to be strong, yet deep within, you don't want to be so at all — do you see?

So now in your Meditation, do we ask you to picture Self with one person, one on whom you project the fulfillment of many wants. See that person walking with you, side by side, as the catalyst who brings you to the place where you are fulfilling Self. Together you go to a tremendous Garden with hundreds and thousands of flowers — of needs filled. You choose from these, and then, the Other picks the flower for you, holds it before you, for he or she is your mirror . . . And then, Dear Children, you *choose* to pick the flower from their hand to yours. *You are fulfilling Self* . . . Yes, the Other is there, the echo of your own wants . . . He or she can go with you, for they, in some way, possess that which you are looking for or you would not see them as a source. But do you so see, it is *You* who must Choose the flower, and see Self as Worthy to Give it to Self.

And so will we continue with this Mystery of Wants, but for now do we say to you, Dear Children, release all your Loved Souls in Freedom. *Ask nothing of them but that you Love them,* and in there, Dear Children, you will find all the responses you need. You ask from the God Essence of Self and you receive from that same God Essence — and no one can do this for you. And just as you do not receive from anyone, remember also, no one can take anything away from you . . . Dear Children, You are Inheritors of the Kingdom . . . Know this and Believe this is so, for You will find Yourself Filled with the Treasures of the Kingdom . . . And so will You then Come to Know that *You Yourself are the Inheritance,* for All the Treasures of the Kingdom so Live within You and every Other . . . And with these words, do we Love and Bless You Ever, Dear Children of Healing Love and Light.

A Message of Affirmation and Love

May 8, 1985

For the group this evening, do we say to you, you are all Beautiful Children of Light, and it is so necessary that you see yourselves in this way, so that you may enjoy the Fruits of the Light for Self, and so that you may become the new mirror for Others — that they too will be Uplifted when they see Selves reflected through your Lovingness. For if you look at another with Love, they come to see that they are Lovable. Do you see, it is that simple — that you can feel Love in Self and know that, yes, there are faults and imperfections in Self, but these are as only weeds in a Beautiful Garden, and with your Care and Love, the weeds will leave on their own, for they too will be transformed into flowers. You will find, Dear Children, that that which was a weed becomes the root of a transformative flower, a new one, a new feeling, a new sense of Knowingness in the Self. This weed becomes transformed into something wonderful inside of you. As we have said in another image for you, so many become so upset at the thought of a red color mixing with violet, with yellow and so on — some think the new color is a gross mistake, while some wonder with amazement and awe at this new color.

And so, Dear Children, do we ask you to always look at Self with Love, to Know that All is in the process of the Becoming, to Know that the Creator is ever working, making Order from the Chaos, creating something *New and Wonderful* from that which seemed so lost and mistaken. You are Beautiful Children ... As you now go within Self to the Wants of the Self, Know that All Wants are embraced by the Loving Self ... See Self as Worthy of every Want, of every Need ... Know that You are the Children of God and so are Inheritors of the Kingdom ... Peace, Tranquility, Serenity, Wisdom, Love — all of these will come to you in this tremendous Knowingness of Self and Self's Purpose, which, as the Jesus said, is to Love Self and every Other. And so with these words, do we ask you to lift up your Spirits to the True You, to the Mystery and Wonder ever unfolding in your Joy and Pain, in your Hurt and Gladness. *All is You and You are a Wonderful Creation.* As you touch now your own Creative Essence, more and more, you will find that Self will be able to fulfill Self's Wants

on levels never before drea... ~ Dear Children, what you
truly Want is God, and in see... ', you seek Yourself . . .
Know that this is True, and Kno... ich we Love and Bless
You Ever, Dear Children of Heali. and Love.

The Wants of the Soul

May 22, 1985

For the group this night, do we say to you to now dwell on the *Wants of the Soul.* We ask you to know that All Wants are the moving energy within you, and so do we repeat again, do not see any Want as a lacking in you, but rather, as that which is moving you, stirring you onward. So the Wants of the Soul are so much more than you are conscious of, for they are your Guiding Forces. And so we ask you to raise these Wants, and see them as the cries and signals from your Soul Beingness which seeks ever its own Growth into its Loving Self. The Soul knows of its Oneness with All, its greater Connectedness. We are asking you to Trust that Inner Knowingness whose Source is the Soul of your Life, for its Messages come from deep within, deep within History and deep within the Future.

We ask you to remember, Dear Children, that the Soul Ever Is and Always Will Be and that You are Ever Becoming Aware of Your own Soul Self, growing into it, as it were. But what happens is, the Soul Self, in such Inner Knowingness, because it knows it is One with All, it keeps seeming to get larger and larger, and so expands. And as it does so, *You are Ever called by Name* to go deeper and deeper, and penetrate that Soul Expansiveness. Do not ever see it as stilled or waiting, for it ever moves and expands, and you are guided along with it. Yes, as cloud joins cloud in a gathering storm, and all becomes the one cloud layer — do you see?

Dear Children, for you to follow the Inner Knowingness or hear the Inner Voice of the Soul, you need to feel free of the very Wants. Do not let them drag you down into trying to meet them, for then, they can never lift you High which is where they want you to go. If you go deep into your Heart, you will know that every form of Want is the seeking to blend a Loving Expression into the Loving Essence from which it comes. Healing is the wanting to see and experience the Love in everyone and everything. And so do we say to you, when you are feeling frustrated by a seeming want, go back to the Source of the Want, which is your Soul, seeking an expression of Love in form. Know that it is not the Want that has to be healed, but rather, it is the anger and frustration and so on that does not know how to *Live with Want* as an Inner Guidance, as a Loving Energy that brings one to One's Realization through the very existence of such Wants — do you see? If you go to the Source of the Want, you will feel its Lovingness, for its very Source is Love . . . And You, of your Essence, are Love . . . And so you seek to express this Love through the Want. Now, Dear Children, are you not glad of your many Wants, for in Truth, They are One Want, *the Wanting of the Inner Knowingness of Self.*

So for your Meditation this night, do we ask you to come in touch with a Want and follow it through its material forms. Give it a shape, a time, place, focus and so on. And so, it is there before you, and the Want stands revealed, ready and waiting for you . . . And now you go one step further, and trace the Want back to its source — a hurt received, a hurt given, a sense of incompleteness, a need for forgiveness and so on . . . And then, back to that Source, back to the Wanting to Love or Be Loved . . . Dear Children, bring it all back to God, to the Love from where it came . . . *Give your Want room to grow and expand into what it is truly asking for* . . . Yes, a want of a better job — you are truly asking for Self's appreciation of Self's Worth, Self's Love. Or the wanting of approval by others — you really want to be independent of the need for this approval, for You know that No One can Love You as You do . . . Always Bless and Expand the Want, Recognizing its Source in your Soul, and Blessing that Soul Energy, that Life Energy within you, which leads you to the Realization of the Want, to the Realization of Self that is greater than all you could ever dream . . . Let your affirmation be, "I would so want this or that for Self, for Other, but now, *I give my Want to the Dream of God, to the Dream of My Soul.* And there, do I meet My Loving Self and the Loving Self of every Other." And with these words do we Love and Bless You Ever, Dear Children of Love and Healing Life.

The Wants of the Soul

May 28, 1985

For the group tonight, let us continue with the Wants of the Soul, for you must, Dear Children, join yourself to the Wants of every Other for your Own to Be Made Manifest. The Wanting to Love and Be Loved is Here the Desire which Touches the Christ Center in every Man, which is total Lovingness, total Oneness — but having shed the Wanting. Once you are in and of that which is Yours, the Wanting Ceases, and there is only the Bliss and Unfoldment of that Belonging. Whenever you seek the Fulfillment of a Want, we ask you to Know that Others have that same Want, perhaps differently expressed, but the Essence is the Same, *the Wanting to Love and Be Loved* ... You must join Self, Dear Children, to All Others at that level of Communion.

Let us give to you as an example of everyday life — if the Husband wants to rest in the Home, and the Wife, tired of the confines of the Home, wishes to go out. Here are two different Wants, seemingly different, yet each is seeking the same thing — a place of rest, a place where one can freely express the Self of that moment, a place to Love and Be Loved, and the Wanting of the Other there to share. Now in such a situation, instead of focusing on the apparent diversity here — the one wanting to rest in the Home, the other to rest through division from the Home — you join Selves together in the *One Want,* and seek then to Live the solution of this in the Inner Heart. One may feel the pull of the Love of the Other to do what the Other wishes, but this comes from Love, pure Loving of Other, and not from any sense of surrender of one's will or doing another a favor, giving a gift and so on. When one has to work so hard at giving this, it is truly not a Gift flowing from Essence, but rather, it is a manufactured giving. This leads only to resentments and a sense of self-sacrifice which one later uses for power or manipulation. So does one then say, "I did that for you, now it is time for you to do this for me." No, instead on these matters, you who have learned to expand your wants into the Wants of the Soul, you can so go beyond, and then join Self to Other at that level of Expanded Awareness. And so, at this level, you Know that All the Universe Wants what is best for you, and you Want what is best for All the Universe, and it is at that level you make your Choices.

You see, Dear Children, what we want you to see here is that you can eliminate the conflicts which arise due to the ego's wants and sensitivities, especially when what one asks of the Other is not in the capacity of that Other to give. But you can expand your Want, and ask it of All Other, of the Universe. Remember that "whatever you ask, you shall receive." *As you have expanded the Want, so do you expand the Answer to that Want.* You become open to new forms, which may be different from your original request, but which will fill you on deeper levels, for you have opened Self up to the Gifts of the Universe, rather than to the gift that just one source, one person can give you.

Dear Children, you must so never separate your Dreams of Self from the Dreams of Other. In his Healing, Jesus was never outside the Wants of those he Healed. We feel it is true to say, he was more in touch with their Wants, their expanded Wants, than they were. This is why he would ask them, "What do you want of me?" For always would he seek to take them *beyond the Want, beyond the Miracle.* And for you also, in your seeking to manifest Healing, a Dream and so on — right now, for some of you, you are investing so much energy on the manifesting — but we say to you, "Then what?" Do you see here the need to go beyond Wants, yes, even beyond the Manifesting, beyond the Miracle? So for Jesus, was the Miracle but a steppingstone to bring Others deeper into the Mysteries of Life . . . Do not get confused, Dear Children, you do not learn of the Mysteries of Life to perform Miracles . . . But once performing Miracles and Manifesting, you can begin to Appreciate, Live, Enjoy, Bless, Discover the Deepening Mysteries of All Life . . .

And so for this meeting this night, we are asking you here, to see the *Oneness of All Want,* to never split Self from the Wants of Other. For if you split Self from Another's Dream, you will never manifest your Own. It must be One . . . And you must see All the Universe pouring its Light into You and Your Desires, and so must you see Self as so Loving, so Giving from Your Highest Centers, that You too are now a Sun pouring Light onto the Wishes and Wants of Self and All. You begrudge nothing, hold back nothing . . . Dear Children, can you, in truth now, see Self as pouring this Light on Everyone? Do you so Know Self so as to Give the Light of All Knowingness, All Love and Wisdom to every Other? It must be One, Dear Children, and you must reaffirm what seems like a paradox, "My Dream cannot Be, unless it Lives side by side, in perfect Harmony, in perfect Oneness with Yours . . . My Want is Your Want, and our Souls both cry for the Loving Expressing of the Self. And it is there, at the Christ Center of Lovingness, that we meet and give our Blessings of Love to One Another."

So do we ask you now in your place of Meditation, draw Self into Communion with the Christ Self of Self and every Other. And there is the Place of All Want and All Abundance, it is One and the Same. There, do not dwell on any one specific want, but rather, the Wanting of the Soul Itself for Itself, for all else is but an expression of that — the Soul, longing for Union with Its Own Self, with your own Awareness of Its Holy Presence within you . . . This is why it is so painful, for you look without to fulfill that which is within . . . Here, in this place of Christ-Centeredness, of Life, Love, Communion, do you have Communion with the Wants of Self and the Wants of Other. Join yourself to the Dream of God which flows through every Soul, and reveals Itself in a myriad of forms and expressions. We are asking you to know that this Union is the Fulfillment of the Want, the Union of Self and every Other . . . Now you are ready to go beyond any Want into All that lies beyond Manifestation, for so is there the gardening, blooming and so on of the Garden, and so is there then, the Livingness of the Garden, Becoming Its Very Self by Being Alive to Itself . . . Once you have gone beyond the Want, you will Know that You are of the Kingdom where No Want exists. There is only the deepening sense of Self into All Realities, but without the tremendous frustration and urging you on the earth feel.

Want for Self, Want for Other, and Dear Children, Know that You are ever One in this as You Join the Other to You . . . Affirm always the Universe Wanting only what is best for you, and *Believe* all this is so. And so will you then draw it to yourself by your very Power of Belief and by your very Love for Self which says that You are Worthy to share in the Reality of Blessings of All. In this kind of Trust, there is nothing to want, for you are Peaceful in the Place of Isness. You know that Want is the Breath of New Life, and not a lacking . . . *You Know that Want is the Continued Breath of God to take You to a New Place* . . . Bless All your Wants, and as you do so, see them as One, One Want in Self and One Want which Becomes your very Blessing to every Other . . . And so with these words do we Love and Bless You Ever, Dear Children of Love and Healing Life.

Compassion for Wants and Needs in the Inner Vision

June 3, 1985

For the meeting this night, do we ask you to awaken Self's Compassion for the Wants and Needs of Others, and especially so, for those Mysteries of Life that are yet unknown and not understandable to you. The wants and longings of All need to be lived with the utmost Compassion, for when there is Compassion, there is the Awareness that goes beyond meeting the need of the want, into the very *Roots of the Want*, with the many intricacies and webs that are formed. So that a need — that at Soul Level is Good and Holy, the need of Love to Be Itself — that need becomes so involved in an intricate network of emotions and connections between the Life energies of others around, that it often manifests itself in sickness, in disillusionment and so on, the many things that are so painful to the Self.

So now for you, Dear Children, in your Healing Work, when one comes before you with a special need, with cancer or a heart condition and so on, wherever the problem lies, we ask you to see that so much Love is underneath that sickness. All the Love of the God Essence is being here repressed in expression, but it is totally there. And this, Dear Children, is where you focus your attention. You stir up your *Compassionate Heart*, and remember here, you do not pity, for pitying lowers the vibration of the Healer and renders him powerless, for he cannot then help to raise the vibration of the one who needs the Healing fulfilled. So do we ask you to live from the Compassionate Heart and draw the person up to the levels of the Christ. Always do you want to meet with the person at that level, to speak to him from the Soul Consciousness, which, when triggered, will be able to look upon its own condition with Love and Compassion.

How do we define Compassion? Compassion is the openness to feel the dreams, thoughts, longings, needs of others, and to lift these to the levels of Love. When you are Compassionate, you lift up your Feelingness in Self, your Love ... And when you do this with the Awareness of the Compassionate Heart of the Higher Self, you also lift the Other. The energy is stirred within you. This is why anyone who Heals is also Healed, for in stirring this energy, the Other is put in the Presence of You, who can see beyond the need into the Source of All Life, yes, which is the same Source moving in You. In Compassion, you will find that the needs of Others do not make you feel powerless, for when this happens, when you feel powerless, you can be sure you are healing as man and not as God. So truly, you must Trust in *your own Love* before you can Heal another. You must Trust in the Love of the Higher Energies which guide you and raise you, so that you, in turn, may raise another. It is very difficult to make this leap from the manifested need to the need at the Source, for the one that manifests, is fear and the cry to be Loved and Cared for, (Sickness is the cry for caring, do you see?) and the other, the need at the Soul level, is to *Be* that very Love and Caring for Self.

What we are trying to show you this night, Dear Children, as you have so identified Wants in Self and Other, as you have expanded these Wants, so now must you stir up the Love and Compassion that cries through the sickness. And you Heal then from Love, not from pity. Within pity, Dear Children, is also fear that the same can happen to you, and so long as that thought exists, there is belief in the other reality, the reality of sickness rather than the Reality of God, where no sickness can exist. We ask you now to Be the Healer for Another, yes, One close to your Heart. Or, Dear Children, go through a hospital now and choose a Face, see One in your Heart and Mind ... That Person now you will lift up, through moving in your own Love and Compassion and so raising the energies Higher and Higher in Self ... First, Feel your Love in Self, the Love that is God Essence ... That is Love Loving through You ... Then do you Feel this same heightened Love in the Other ... Merge with Other in the Brightest Light ... Love Essence meeting Love Essence in the Brightest of Light ... All the qualities of Goodness, Wisdom, All Love is swirling between You, around You, through You ... You are joined to the Love of Jesus and every Other Who so Loves ... Go Higher and Higher, Hand in Hand with the Name, the Face in your Heart ... You have brought Them to a New Place, and as You See Them in this High Place, so They will be able to See Selves in this Place ... Here You are Healing Self as You bring the Other to Heal Self.

Dear Children, we ask you to stir up your Compassion for the Wants in Self and Other, for it is only through such Love that Healing can happen in manifested form. It is ever happening in

Spirit, but it takes a *Constancy of Spirit* to manifest in form. By Constancy, we mean an unshaken Spirit, One that Knows Who It Is . . . To do this, join Self to Jesus, Ramptha and so on, to One Who Knows, so that You too may Know and bring this to All Others.

Heal tonight through your prayer, Heal with the Inner Eyes. Dear Children, Heal the Inner Heart, for There is where the sickness begins, and it is There that the Source of Life Lives. We ask you to carry these Souls with You . . . Do not forget Them, but allow Them to be nourished by your Love. Just by Calling their Name or Face to your Heart, *You bring Them to Life in You* . . . They are your Way back into God . . . And Dear Children, through your Awareness of God, You bring God to Them . . . So now stay with these Souls in your Heart for a while, and Know and Believe in the Truth of Life. In there You are Free, and there, You give the same Freedom to every Other. So do You Live in us, and so do we wish to Free You, so that You too may Free Others . . . Free Self to All Life in Self and Other . . . And with these words, do we Love and Bless You Ever, Dear Children of Healing Life and Love.

Secret Wants Within Self — The Healing of Our Deepest Wounds

June 11, 1985

For the meeting this night, do we ask you to now speak to the Children of the *Secret Wants within Self*, these Wants which go so deep and have made themselves as little Crystals so hidden deep within the Memories of Self. Each Soul here is in touch with the Wants that are the externalizations of the Inner Life. But we say to you, there are Wants that are *hidden* within the Self. This is the pearl of great price, the Wants that may frighten and threaten a Soul so much that the original purposes may become other than what they are. And, Dear Children, we will give you an example of a secret want . . . If you choose a Soul as Hitler, the want here seemingly for power, purity of purpose and so on. Now was the secret want in him such that for him, it was an act of destruction in his own Soul's eyes to return to the earthly form. He did so thinking to do much to help many, but deep within him was a Soul Memory of earthly life being less than, that a Soul so lofty should not have to manifest, no matter how noble the purpose. This Soul, Dear Children, entered the earth plane with a deep sense of not wanting to fulfill a noble purpose on a plane so low, and it was this Soul pattern that flowed through every thought of his, and so made his life what it was. And as this is one side of the workings of a secret want, so is there the other, of a Soul who does tremendous good . . . How the secret want of a Mother Teresa is to thank every Life Essence it has ever known, to raise and extol All Life, a deep sense of total Appreciation. And so, is the Life manifested one of such purpose, not only to Bless these who have so little, but to fulfill the deep Wanting within her to express Appreciation to every Soul for the formative Creation of her own Soul.

Why do we tell you this, Dear Children? We do so because we feel, deep within each of you, is a hidden need, want, desire . . . There is, as it were, the *Seed of your Life,* from which grows all hopes, dreams and so on. The way Life and Grace flow through you depends much on this Seed. For all of you here, so involved in the Healing of Self, you all know you were once all so wounded by Other, and this wound is deep . . . And there is in each of you here the desire to forgive the one who hurt you. For many of you, the person who hurt you is not here on this plane now, but they work with you, in the deepening Self. There is a wound that was caused seemingly by another, and for the many of you, there is the desire to Heal the wound and to Forgive and Bless the Other. The secret want is a hurt of long ago, nurtured now in Love, for so have you all learned to Love the Other as you are Loving Self. But we ask you to know that you must see Self now as *Healed of All Wounds*, even those of ancient memories. For you, to just visualize layers and layers of Self, penetrated by Healing Light... And wherever there was a wound, you have now put a Crystal in its place ... You will be able to then send a different energy through your body, for there is no longer in you the feeling of having been so hurt that you cannot forgive. The Crystals here are the signs of the Forgiveness ... You have many hurts on the surface, and these too need to be replaced by an Energy of Love, so that that which was hurt becomes transformed into that which is now a Loving Self. Any hurt you experience in the physical, emotional level, you can be sure is deeply rooted, and what we are asking you to do now is to know, yes, in each of you, there is a deep wound that cries for Healing.

And you now come to this, Dear Children ... Yes, go to the Holy Dwelling Place of the Spirit within you. You are Loved, Guided, Protected, and Light is all around you ... Angels hold within their hands Crystals of Light and Energy which they give to you ... And as you walk in this Holy Dwelling Place of Self, it is as the wounds of old are little craters, and you are now going to fill them with a Crystal, Liquid Crystal, which solidifies as you Love the Self and allow this new energy to flow through your own Holy Self ... Dear Children, remember a time when you were deeply hurt and walk with it through the many layers ... There is no one to blame here, for there is no Other here now, only Self and the wounds of old ... Walk slowly, Dear Children, there is no need to hurry, for you see, the Liquid Crystal oozes through all wounds, gently penetrates all layers ... As you come in touch with one wound and you are Healing and Forgiving that one, so do you Heal the many that sprouted from it ... We are asking you here to know that Love Energy is a Physical Reality in the Body, and that as you can be the flowing Channel for Love, you truly are allowing, as it were, the Liquid Crystal to pour through and solidify in Self. Dear Children, so long as these wounds are yet open and unforgiven, they will hurt over and over again, they will reappear in countless forms ... But when you can come to Know and Love the secret want, that hidden need for the Healing of an old wound, then you will know the Source of much of what causes you pain . . .

As you Heal this with your Love and Recognition of it, you will see how it flows through all of you, through your attitudes, through your emotional Self. Your way of thinking and seeing becomes changed because you have allowed Love to Crystallize within you. Once you are in touch that such a beauteous thing as a *Crystal of Love* can, yes, even physically exist within you, you will be amazed at how differently you will Live in your Holy Dwelling Place. For you see, you see the Body as often a hindrance, made up of matter and so on. Can you entertain the thought that your Body can be made the Storehouse of Love Crystals and the Purest of Light? We are asking you to make this tremendous leap in as gentle steps as you can, so that you can begin to experience Self as the True Son of God, that you may know that Your Body is the Living Home of the God Essence, and as such, is clothed in a Garment of Radiant Light.

Dear Children, these are Realities, though you do not yet see them, as you cannot yet see the Infant Child Jesus as a Resurrected Lord. It is that transition we are here introducing you to. And we introduce it to you with this image of the wound that lies so deep within, and the filling of it with a Crystal of Infinite Love that becomes part of your very Beingness. As you Heal this wound, you will find Self Healing all wounds, and you will Know Yourselves for the Beautiful Children You Are . . . And so, Dear Children, with these words do we Love and Bless You Ever . . . You are on your way ever to the Becoming. It is a gentle way . . . It moves slowly so that you can appreciate and Live it fully. You do not want to speed by it and miss the Beauty of Things Unfolding along the way.. Go slowly and gently . . . Be patient with the wound, for it is your Loving Guide to Self, and you will Learn much and Become much because of it. Dear Children, Know You are Blessed, and Know that Each of You is a tremendous Blessing to All around You. You Become the Dispensers of Crystals to All You Love, for You have given Self to the God Essence to be such for His Children . . . And so will we continue as we Love and Bless You Ever, Dear Children of Healing Love and Light.

Encountering the Self's Wants and Dreams

June 26, 1985

For the group tonight do we wish now to speak to you of the ways you *Encounter Self* with your Wants and Dreams. For some of you here, when you have a Dream, it is as if you are meeting the Dream or Want of a stranger, rather than that which is of you, born of your own hurts and needs and longings. So for many who are sick, they look for Healing, but as something that does not truly belong to them. They meet this Self who has this Need, but they do not have a *Relationship with their Need*. All is left separated — the person who wants, the actual want, the response and answer — all are seen as separated, and so, one feels alienated and isolated. The answer to the prayer seems far away and unattainable. This is true also for those who are in painful relationships and see their solutions as impossible, impractical and so on. They remain with their problem which very much becomes a burden and weighs them down or eats away at them. How you *Encounter* yourself, Dear Children, is very important. How you see your *Need* and the *Response* is so important, for as you know by now, it is not the end result which is so important, but the process, the getting there.

We ask you, Dear Children, is your time in between Need and Response, is it one of frustration and anger, or is it one of *Peaceful Unfolding?* Do you become angry at Self in the waiting, in the interim time? And what do you do with that anger? Do you so take it out on the Other, or do you, instead, work to see the Beauty of the Unfolding, Knowing that All is happening and All is Healing to the Self? Your Encounter with yourself depends upon your Loving of Self, your Compassion to Self, to the Mystery of Oneself. It depends upon your desire to understand and be patient with the Self that senses the greater picture, but is not yet able to focus on it because of the tremendous attention to details and the Present Moment Need. For one can be so frozen in a Need, that the larger context of that very Need is ignored. As, for example, one who is in an inharmonious marriage... There is the Need here for Love and Compassion for Self and Other, and yet, so much attention may be given to one's own Self's Needs, that there is no consideration given to the Other, who may also be wrestling with tremendous difficulties. And so there is here needed the working out of more than your problem, for there is also the problem of Other within Self.

What we are asking you here to know is that the Response to your Needs is so often, Dear Children, contingent upon the Needs of Others. When you are encountering Self and Self's Needs, we ask you now to include in this encounter the Needs and Wants of Others, so that *the Realities of All may be Blessed and Nourished.* And so, not only must you not see Self as separate from your own Response, but you must also know you are not separate from the Wants and Dreams, the Responses of Others. Know that All flows as One, that you harbor no harm ever to your Brother, for in doing so, you can only harm Self. So do you Bless the Needs and Wants of All, and see All as in Harmony with your Own.

There is the Need here for each of you to be the *Healing Child of Light.* Each of you knows this, each of you seeks an expression. Know that your path, guided in such Lovingness, can only touch the path of another for good and stimulation, and know that, as your path is being crossed by another, it is ever for your good and unfoldment. When you are encountering your Needs, if you see them as opposed to the Needs and Wants of another, then must you know that, it is not that your Need is wrong, but rather, that you must expand your Need and its Response. So let us use the example, if one is at work and his Need for self-recognition causes another to feel less than, it is not that self-recognition is wrong, but rather, the Need is to be expanded, so that the Other who feels less than, can also receive the recognition and worth he seeks — do you see? In other words, we are saying that your Needs are not to be met at the expense of another. And if it seems such must happen, you do not have to give up the Need, but rather, you expand it to *include* the Other. And so now do you see, the *Encounter* with Self and Self's Needs is done with every Other around you. You do not live alone and you are not making decisions solely for Self. Yet do we tell you, through the Universal Order of All, the more you include the All, the more are your Needs individually and uniquely met. You who have opened up Self to All, becoming that clear Channel, give Self the room now to let all your individual Needs or empty spots be filled with Life that is a Wonder and that is uniquely yours. So for Jesus, in his opening to All, did he Become the Unique Self in time and place . . . Remember, it is in losing the Self, that you find Self.

We have spoken to you here of the *Crystallization of the Self* . . . So then are these Needs met, not only in the filling of the deepest wounds with the Liquid Crystal, but also the deepest Hopes and Dreams. Dear Children, so do we ask you now to visualize these as becoming Crystals to you. And again, let the Angels be the Dispensers of these Crystals for each Need and Want you have. You, in turn, see yourself dispensing these to every Other whose Needs are involved with your own. And so for you here, many of you women here, you are seeking Self-Realization . . . Know that you must not rid Self of husband, children, social demands and so on, to do so. Know that you blend your Needs with theirs . . . Let your paths embrace in Love and Forgiveness. You do not cross each other in Pain but in Joy, and you lift Self to the Awareness that your Life is in Harmony with All those Lives that touch your own. This is a *Holy Act of the Will* . . . It is the Realization of the Holiness of Every Life and of the Holy Right of Each Child to Live Beside the Other.

Dear Children, we ask you to know you are Blessed and your Wants and Dreams are Blessed . . . So will you be given all that you seek and more, as you Live in the precious Awareness that no one seeks to hurt you, and that All Life wants what you want for Self . . . We tell you to know, if you Encounter Self in this dimension with these Wants of Self, you will find you will want for nothing, for All Life will be drawn to you, and you will feel Blessed and Abundantly Full of Every Joy that Lives within Every Want. You are Beautiful Children . . . Be with One Another . . . Energize the Dreams of Others by Wanting What They Want . . . Do not stand in Another's way, but rather, let All Be Free to Want, to Dream, to Bless All Other with Every Want . . . Together, can All then Enjoy the Fruits that are Born of Every Need and Want . . . And so with these words, do we Love and Bless You Ever, Dear Children of Healing Love and Light.

Forgiveness in the Union of Self to Self

July 3, 1985

For the group this night, is there the Need for the *Forgiveness of the Self*. Forgiveness as we know the word, is to *Love*, to go beyond any Need for Forgiveness. For ask of yourself, "What have I ever done that was against Self?" In Truth, all that you have done has been *for* Self, for Self's Becoming. So you see, in the process of this, you have taken roads that did not always bring you to your Dream, that Dream of the God Essence of Self, where One is so totally Loved and Loving, that One Becomes the *Essence of Self*. You no longer are separated from it, you no longer have to think of Love, for it is *Who You Are*. In this process of Becoming, did you wear many different costumes, and did you, in the course of these years, find many different sources you sought to pursue. Do you Forgive Self here to know you were as a Child lost in a maze, but now you are on the road to your True Self. The empty sources have all disappeared, and you are truly coming in touch with the truest Source of All, the very Source of God that Is in You, Your Own Dwelling Place.

For you, Dear Children, to Live in the Self is the Home you have long sought for. For many of you now, you have gone to many places, many persons, many dreams, but the Realization is setting in that *only in Self will you find the greatest Source of Loving*. So do we feel the need to say here, you will never feel Loved by another unless you first Love Self, and there is no one who could Love you more than you yourself, except for Those Who Love Themselves in this Purest Essence. So for the Angels here, for Jesus and other Masters and Lords of All, They can so Love You greater than you yourself, for They are in touch with that Greatness of You that you have yet to experience. As you, when you love an Infant, in that Love is yet contained All your Love for the Child as he grows to Fullness. You love each present expression and all the future steps that that expression will bring. So now for you, Dear Children, only those who can Love Themselves and be in touch with the Vastness, the Eternity of Themselves, can Love the Vastness, the Eternity of You. It is here no judgment on the degree of Loving . . . It just Is, as one mountain is taller than another, yet both of tremendous Beauty and Majesty.

So for you now, you can release those who do not love you as you want or expect, who do not fill your wants and needs. So do you also now release Self from any sense of guilt or judgment of the Present, Past or Future, for you have done nothing against Self. Always, in your *innocent ignorance,* Dear Children, were you seeking for a Treasure in a foreign land, and you became lost, for that was not Self, the Home where the Treasure Is. There are many of you here who yet say, "I have not forgiven myself for this or that yet," or "I cannot forgive him or her for doing this to me" and so on. All of these statements, Dear Children, do not bear witness to your Love or Striving for Self, but rather, do they bear witness to separation and a sense of incompleteness and isolation. We ask you now to erase and send forth to the Universal All all such concepts of unworthiness and guilt, and allow instead the Peace of the Christ Essence Goodness to flow into you.

Dear Children, feel the Christ Self which is All Loving and All Living . . . It is with you, as much as You are You in this room this moment. It is there, though barely felt, for all your separation from it . . . Let it merge and come forth from the deepest recesses of your Heart, Mind and Soul, like a huge Cloud, issuing forth from your Heart, Mind and Soul, covering you in its Warmth and Love . . . Feel it swirling in and around and through you as you allow it to permeate Self in every dimension, every physical faculty, every thought faculty . . . All issues forth from the Inner Resources of Self, and so, as it were, Embraces you in your own Loving Power . . . So is there here total Love, Forgiveness, Wisdom, Beingness, *The Holy Union of Self to Self* . . . In this Holy Union is there Total and Complete Forgiveness of all you have ever done or not done, of all that has been done or not been done to you. So do you Forgive Self and allow this same Blessing to be extended to All, who also seek only to Love and Be Loved. You are Beautiful Children . . . Now Rest in the Truth of Knowing that All Life is for your Unfolding, that as you empower Life ever for your Good, so will you ever be for the Good of Life. There will be no need for you to work at cross-purposes with Life, but rather, you will blend and merge into the Oneness of All. So with these words, do we Love and Bless You . . . Remember to see the Good of Life, and you will see your Life as All Good and Blessed, and yes, Forgiven . . . So do we Love and Bless You Ever, Dear Children of Healing Light and Love.

Forgiveness and the Spirit Self

July 9, 1985

For the meeting this night, do we ask you here to continue ever with the Forgiveness of Self, and this night, what we ask you to do is, in going beyond the need for Forgiveness, to go into the realm of deeper Understanding of the *Spirit Self,* of why you do the things you do and feel the things you feel and so on. As you understand these deepening parts of you, you see, you will recognize them as they come forth, and you will be able to be in touch with the Forgiving Self, with the Loving Self from the very beginning. Yes, it is in the *Understanding* that there is Compassion. But when there is only confusion and disorientation, when emotions and so on gain control, then there is only fear, and there is no room for the Loving Self. It is as if the fear of Self and Self's reactions and feelings and so on, the fear draws one away from his own Lovingness . . . But the Knowledge of Self and the Understanding of Self, draws one closer to Self, and so then, can one live any experience from the place of Isness and Everlasting Unfoldment.

How does one come in touch with one's Spirit? This is what we are asking of you — the Knowledge of how that Spirit Force, that Energy inside you, works. *What is it that makes you Feel your Spirit Self?* And we are referring to this, not in terms only of meditative states, but of normal every day activities. Be in touch with your Spirit, with the Energy that is the activating and pulsating Force, the Energy that is *You,* that is uniquely *You* at every moment. This Energy wears many faces during the day. We ask you to gently come to know these Spirit Forces of Life that are *You.* The more you know them and make them feel at home in your own image or concept of yourself, the more Understanding and Compassionate to Self you will be when an aspect of Self — which may confuse or frighten you on some level — emerges. You can then be in Attunement with it and recognize it as part of you, part of your Spirit that is yet being Healed and made Whole and Integrated. As you integrate these in Lovingness, you will find that all will work together, for you will not feel segmented or fractured, but rather, always Whole . . .

So, Dear Children, if we can give you the Image of Seeing Yourself as Light Healing Self, for you see, you are not a weak, enfeebled Being, asking for Light. Rather, *You are the Light*, and in Knowingness and Love, You can then shine that Light on All of Yourself. You see, in a way here, Dear Children, we are asking you to Forgive Self *before* you even do anything to hurt yourself. Let that sense of Compassion towards Self so be part of your Consciousness, that Forgiveness of Self just flows with every encounter. So now do we ask you to come in touch with a Memory that yet needs Forgiveness . . . Remember, have we defined Forgiveness merely as the recognition of an empty spot and the desire to make it Whole. So now do you come in touch with this Memory. And to understand it, let us here come in touch with the Spirit of Self in that Memory . . . Where is your Spirit now in that Memory . . . ? Where was your Spirit in the happening, in the creating of the hurt . . . ? Why was the Spirit crying . . . ? What was it seeking . . . ? And why does your Spirit cry now . . . ? What are you yet looking for . . . ? For if you have not yet Forgiven Self, Dear Children, do you see, the empty spot is still there, awaiting for its fulfillment with the Liquid Crystal of your own Love and Knowingness. So do we ask you to know that unless there has been that Forgiveness — that "giving for," the empty spot now filled with that which is missing — this Memory remains alive and active in its pain, and not yet, in its Love. What you seek, Dear Children, is for All Memories to be resolved with Lovingness, into the Loving and Forgiving Self so that the Memories are now of You and Your Loving Essence, and there is no bitterness that can eat away slowly at the Beingness of Self.

So now do you take this Memory, this hurt, and we ask you, as much as you can and desire, Dear Children, *Crystallize* this so that you are filling Self up with the Essence of your own Loving Realization . . . As you do this, Know you deeply touch your own Spirit which has often become weary carrying the burdens of guilt. It is often just the sense of heaviness itself that weighs the Spirit down, and prevents you from seeking to flow easily and smoothly with All Life. In this Awareness now, *Know, See* and *Feel* that you have truly touched your own Spirit and that you have come to an Encounter with Self that helps you to see Self's Spirit as it was in a Past Moment yet painful, and as it is Now in the Waking stage to Realization. You want now to add what you have Felt to your Present Understanding of Self, and deeply empower this Knowledge of Self, for do we say again, *the more you Know Self, the more Compassionate you can be.* And so now, all these same apply to Other, for the more you can enter into the Spirit of Another through the Compassionate Understanding of that very Spirit, so the more will there ever be Understanding, and so, no need of Forgiveness. You are Living in Loving Closeness to the Spirit of the Other . . . You will see more and more the Liquid Crystal you can so offer them in your Caring and Compassion, rather than seeing the empty spot that often elicits in you pain or a sense of separation in feeling there is something here needed to Forgive.

Dear Children, we ask you to see no need for Forgiveness in this Light, in the Light that there is no separation in the Spirit Stirrings of Self and One Another. So do you then feel the Healing Life of Self penetrating the Spirit of Self and every Other, for you cannot stir your Spirit to Heal Another and not Know that you too are Healed. To enter the Spirit of Another, your own Spirit must be stirred, awakened, and then, yes, acknowledged and understood in all Compassion, and Loved as the God Essence Life so Loves You.

Dear Children, You are Beautiful Children . . . Bless Self and Come to *Expand Self into Your Own Spirit*. Come to Know and Love and Trust this Spirit which Breathes, Lives, Creates and Expresses through You. Be kind to it and allow it to manifest through Your Own Lovingness and Healing Life . . . And so with these words, do we Love and Bless You Ever, Dear Children of Healing Life and Love.

The Lovingness of Self

July 17, 1985

For the meeting this evening, do we ask you to turn your attention of your Heart and Mind into All the *Lovingness You Are*. You have been thinking much and working much with the wounds of Self, and so have you been filling Self with the Liquid Crystals of your own Love . . . And now do we ask you, Dear Children, Dear Creators of Life, to stand back and see the Wonderful Self you have been creating, for from the wounds have come forth tremendous Compassion and Understanding, and as we have said before, where there is the Understanding and the Knowing, then there is the Love.

The Lovingness of Who You Are must now flow through your Whole Beingness. Dear Children, Know — with the most Inner Knowing — that all you are and do is motivated by such Lovingness. What you want to do here though, is not rationalize Love, for then, the ego is there judging and evaluating Self, and this you do not want. There is no judgment here, there can be none from anyone. If you can compare Self to the Ocean that just Feels Itself, that Is, and Loves, that crashes Itself against the cliffs or gently washes upon the shore — the Isness of Power, of Gentleness and Strength . . . This, as next to the one who stands on the shore and tries to *personify* the Ocean in Self. You see, in the personification, you identify with it intellectually, feelingly. But so long as it remains a "doing" on your part, you stand there saying, "I am so close to it, yet not it. I can never *Be* Ocean, for it is of a different substance than I." So, do we ask you, you see, not to personify Love, not to merge Self with Love outside of You, where you say, "This is Loving or that is Loving, and I merge with that." This is good, and it is one level of experiencing Love, but it only brings you to other sources of Life outside of Self, to other sources of gratification or recognition.

What we are asking you, Dear Children, is to just *Be Lovingness*, for it is Your Essence. Just as the Ocean Is Ocean, so You *Are* Lovingness, and You just want to *Be* That. Feel Lovingness as All of You, as every Pulse of Life . . . Just now, listen to your own Breathing, for it is a Loving Force that is Breathing through you and in you . . . Just feel it *as You* . . . So do you now feel your own Heartbeat or any sensation of the Body —

so too, it is Lovingness Essence. And now, go to the thoughts and memories stored in your Heart, Mind and Soul, where All is Lovingness . . . To every word you have ever spoken and will speak, Bless with the Lovingness Inherent Within . . . See It, Bless It, *As It Is* . . . So now also, touch every Dream, for Lovingness creates Dreams, as from One Dream of God come many Dreams, touching many people and places. So too, All of these are Love . . . And, Dear Children, go also to every pain and to the wounds in Self that in their Healing have Created You into the Unique Wonder You Are . . . See these also as Loving Essence, for they too are as the Sun that waits for the Clouds to pass by, to drift forth into the Everything and the Nothing, so that the Light can Shine . . . *In all your wounds, Dear Children, Love never left* . . . It was and is your Love that nurtures you and pulls you forth, stirs your Soul so that you may Know Yourself as a Loving Power for Self and every Other.

You, Dear Children, have been Forgiving Self . . . Did you Know how much Love for Self you have unearthed in doing so? And, it is not Love that is new, but only *Love Revealed,* as the Sun is Revealed when the Cloud passes by. Whatever Forgiveness and Love you have felt is but the most minute part of what is yet to be felt in the Inner Recesses of Self. As you just stay there, in your own Lovingness, you will feel Self Becoming this more and more . . . It is as a Beautiful Sculpture you see encased in layers and layers of wax . . . So did the wax assume the shape and form of Self, but as the wax is exposed to the Light, it melts layer by layer . . . And that which was form only in shape, is then Revealed as form in *Living Substance* . . . . As the wax melts away, you, who were encased and immobile, can now Breathe and Move, and yes, Dear Children, you can Dance in the Freedom of Being your Loving Self. Dear Children, in your Meditation this night, do we ask you to be there with this Image or any Image that comes to Self. See yourself, see your Beloved Ones, your Friends, any who are sick and in need of such Loving Communion with Self — so do you empower these for Self and for All. Yes, Fill All with the ever Forming, ever Creating Self that is Infinite. *The Lovingness You Are Is Flowing through All Life* . . . So too, do you allow the Lovingness of All Life, of Loved Ones, of Jesus and the Masters, of the Angels, of All Holy Life, to Flow through You . . . It is What and Who You are Made of . . . It is Your Inheritance, and as You Acknowledge it and Bless it, You Give this Inheritance back to All so that it may ever flow to All and ever come back to You... Do you see, *it is Your very Self coming back to You, joined in an Ever Flowing Oneness to Yourself and All Life*... Stay here and Enjoy and Bless Yourself and every Other... And as You do so, so do we, who Love and Bless You Ever, Dear Children of Healing Light and Love.

The Secrets of the Self

July 25, 1985

So for the meeting this evening, let us now take you to the other Worlds of Self, to the places of Wonder which you have touched so often in your dreams and fantasies, places which you have left there, as idle dreams, but which are truly aspects of Self in need of your nurturing — though they may yet be quiet and unknown even to you. There are secret rooms within each Room of Self you have uncovered, and we ask you, do not be afraid of opening doors in whatever Room of Self you find yourself, for you must first go into yourself and see the Value of Self in the Eyes of Self, and then, in the Eyes of every Other. You may discover here, Secrets of the Self that speak in Whispers to you in your sense of Loving Knowingness.

We ask you, Dear Children, to take a feeling of yours these days, for the aura of that feeling surrounds you. As you live and react from Self, these secret places within the room vibrate, move, even just a little, and seek to have the Light shining on them. So let us take an example . . . For you, in being in touch with the Loving Compassion towards Self, you will find that Self's Compassion has a secret door that opens up perhaps to a desire to be forgiven by a person of the past. You are seeking a sense of Compassion, which you are now giving to Self, from one long ago who left you feeling empty or unworthy . . . Or, those of you here who sense a need for strength around you. In this room of strength, do you perhaps come in touch with the desire you have to be a source of strength to a person you once leaned on, or to be a source of strength to an idea that lies sleeping in you and waiting for the strength to be so activated.

You see, Dear Children, what we are asking you to do again is not only to expand, but to go deeper, for these secret rooms of Self are truly influential in your Life. They may store painful Soul Memories or they may be the tremendous conceiving room of Future Dreams and Visions. And you, Dear Children, in your Knowingness of Self now, must not be afraid to knock on any door in Self. What we are asking you to do is to *Love* any Fear, any Dream, any Vision or any Memory that you find behind these doors. *All are Messengers of Love to you* . . . None are there to hurt you, none are there to bring you fear or guilt or a sense of unworthiness. If there stands there a huge, wondrous Dream, Dear Children, it is not there to frighten you, but only to greet you with the tremendous Vision of Who You really Are. If you enter here a room of Knowingness of Self's Mercy, so may you now open a door and find a situation which comes to mind, either Personal or Universal, and so, you will be in touch with a Soul so ill or a whole world of Souls so now in poverty and hunger. You try to see what lies behind each door, and so do you allow it to step forth and to deepen and expand your Love of Self, of every Other.

We feel for you, Dear Children, this greater Vision is so needed, for your Love is tremendous as it expands so. And there are many of you here who Know that such Infinite Love seeks Infinite Expression. You, who are finite, are so filled with Infinite Love . . . And so do you now seek Expression for your Love by allowing it to form and Crystallize in Self and every Other. *The Infiniteness of your Love may never find expression, but you can Bless each Expression of your Life with your Infinite Self*. . . The more doors you open, the more Expressions of Life you will find of Self. Be they Visions, Dreams, Memories — each is raised to Infinite Levels just because you have Blessed them with your Infinite Love . . .

So then do we say to you now, Dear Children, to come in touch with a quality of Self, an attribute of God Essence Life, as Wisdom, Love, Understanding, Patience, Strength, Mobility, Creativity, Discipline, Balance, Justice and so on . . . So find yourself, stay there and open the doors that come into view. Greet whatever and whoever stands behind the door . . . See how the influence of these is *Felt* in your Life, how they *Live* in you . . . You may find a feeling or vision or even just an energy of no words, but something truly, deeply Felt. Whatever is there, let it flow into you and Feel its Presence in you . . . Bless it and Love it . . . Allow it to walk through you now, through your Life and Love, through Presences, Dreams, Fears, Whatever is in your Heart . . . What you are doing is touching Wholeness, for you Know that nothing is separate from you, and that *those parts so hidden, Dear Children, they are the parts that most make you You.* They are the parts that stir you to an ever ongoing Desire to Heal Self and every Other. All you seek to Know and Heal in your relationship of Others, in those parts of relationship that cause you pain, are these, your secret doors . . . And so do we tell you now, the secret doors of Self now feel ready to be opened, for you have been Creating an Inner Life that Welcomes and Loves All . . . They are not afraid, for they know, you no longer fear them. That is how Compassionate they are, for they will not be Seen until you so *Will* them to *Be Seen.* But, oh, Dear Children, now the difference is that you See them with Inner Vision, and your Inner Vision can only Love . . .

So do we See You this night, and so Love and Guide You. Dear Children, do we Ever Bless You now with the Joy and Wonder of Your Own Healing Love and Light . . . It is One with ours, and so are we Blessed as we Bless . . . You are Beautiful Children and You have much to do . . . Go and send this Knowledge of Self to All so that They too may know the Joy of Loving the Self and Seeing Self with the Eyes of God . . . We Love You and Thank You for this Time and for the Beauty of All Time Together, for we have been with You many Ages, and as we begin to end these *Writings of the Inner Vision,* so do You Know that You just begin to See now with the *Vision of the Angels.*

Living in the Knowingness of Self

July 31, 1985

For the meeting this evening, do we ask you, Dear Children, to truly rest in the *Knowledge of your own Knowingness.* You who have learned and wept and laughed and loved much, so is all of this now Knowledge for you, and you must not discount it, but you must give it, Dear Children, the Blessed Place in your Life that it so deserves. For you see, your experiences, your feelings, all soars deep into you, and then, as it were, all explodes into an expansiveness about you. It filters through your Whole Life, and it *Is There* all about you, seeking now to touch and permeate all new experiences. That which is old, now feels new, for you have brought your expanded and deepened Knowingness to the Past, and you bring this now to the Present. It is in the *Awareness,* Dear Children, that *It Is So.* Again, do you have the Treasure within always, but so often do you forget, for other clouds of fear, anxiety and so on, cloud over that which is yet fragile, and yes, shimmering before you. It is, as it were, your Knowingness is a shimmering Crystal and you have placed these Crystals of Knowingness about your Beingness . . . But now it is time to form these Crystals into the You that You Know and Love, that You So Seek to Be Loved. What we are asking you to do is to Know that anything that you now touch, you so *Crystallize with your own Lovingness* . . . You so Heal it, Bless it with your Knowingness and Love.

Your Knowingness is not outside, it is not a reference source, Dear Children, for it *is* You, and it will be felt in your Life experiences as much as you allow it to be so felt. See the tremendous storehouse that you have so filled up, and Know that it is a Place of Love for you, and that anything you seek, any Knowledge or Experience you so seek, can be found there. We feel many of you here are now so filled with Knowledge of Self, yet do you ask Self the same questions, for you do not Believe and Trust your own Knowingness. So do we ask you to Know that the Knowingness of Self is ever Peaceful and Feeling Calm, it is ever the Thought which Comforts. So if we can say, when you are in turmoil and feeling unloved, unworthy and so on, and the confusion sets in and so on, you are out of the flow of your own Knowingness, which ever says to you, "Dear Child, So are You

Loved, for You are My Child, and I Love You." You see, the God Essence is Love, can be nothing else . . . And when you feel unloved, you have separated Self from the Source of Knowingness.

Now, Dear Children, have you each had experiences of *Being Love* . . . You have all here touched the wondrous depths of your own Feelings. Dear Children, we ask you now to deeply *Feel-Know* that these experiences are now part of your Whole Self, they are your claim to Knowingness. You have lit that particular Candle, and it can never be extinguished. It is yours, for you Lived it, you Felt it, and now do you Bless it, Nurture Self with it and Allow it to be a Light for you. And when the darkness comes, Dear Children, we ask you to ever Know there is a Source of Light, and it is *your own Feelingness, your own Soul Memory*. It is something ever yours, and it will grow more and more as you grow. It will Light other Candles within you. It will Crystallize to all Crystals — do you see? But you must Trust it and Know it . . . Know, Know to the Core of Your Soul Being, that Life is Good, and that Life calls You, its Beloved Children.

For your Meditation this night, do we ask you to so Crystallize Self in your Knowingness. Expand yourself, drawing Crystals from the deepest Places of Self, from the most Infinite Places in the Universe . . . Draw these unto yourself and feel your Connection to All Knowingness. *Your very Life is in that Knowingness, your very experiences, every tear you have shed, every smile you have felt for Joy is There* . . . And you can nurture Self with it, nurture Self with the smiles and tears, with the Inner Knowledge and Wisdom of All Life. It is You as much as You are It . . . So do you now spend this time feeling the Gift of Self, pouring Self into this Universal Knowingness . . . Dear Children, Feel this Knowingness so Loving you that it pours itself to you, and you see it and feel it, as You truly Are . . . Spend these moments Surrendering Self to the Life Essence of Self and every Other . . . Give Self to the Knowingness of the Trees and Mountains, to the Sun and Stars, to the most beautiful Flowerings, to the Fields of Weeds, to All Life . . . You Surrender Self in the Knowingness and Trust of Who You Are and of your Connections to All Life, yes, to Self and to All those here present . . . As the Infinite cannot become finite, we ask you always, bring your Infinity to Self and to All . . .

Dear Children, we Love You and Bless You and Thank You, that You may Know that *Your Inner Vision is Your Knowingness.* And so now, do You Bless Self with the Joy and Knowledge of All You See . . . We Love You and Bless You Ever, for You are Beautiful Children. Your vibrations reach and touch deeply the Knowingness of Many . . . Know that You are lifting the Hearts and Souls of Many as You gather here, as You go to the Marketplace, as You go to the Inner Sanctuary of Your Own Home . . . There is Becoming in You the Realization, Dear Children, *There is nothing You cannot See* . . .

Dear Children of Healing Light and Love

*This Child who writes has asked us for the ending chapter of this book, and we so wish to soothe her Heart which worries that you, Dear Reader, have not found the Love of Self so promised. We ask her to release any sense of failure, and so do we ask you to do the same, for there is no failure here given . . . There is only Life and Newness and Wonder and Ever Expanding Visions. There is no need here, Dear Children, to check on Self's progress, to think of where you were at the beginning of these pages, where you are now, for this book is not a book of learnings, but a book for Living, for Being, for Greeting Self's Soul and Knowing that the Soul is Ever your Friend and Guide. We are asking you to Know here that you are all so richly Guided and Blessed. All of you who hold this book, who have written in its pages, have been Blessed to touch aspects of Self that the Saints and Angels have so longed and cheered for you to touch, yes, in Joyous Celebration! As the Parent who cheers with the Lovingness of the Whole Self, the Child who first walks, so do we here feel, in the Feeling — **Knowingness** that is All Truth, that you have taken these first steps towards the Beauty of Your Own Love and Wisdom and Joyous Surrender to the Oneness of Your Life. Self with the Life-Self of Every Other.*

*There is, Dear Children, no ending to this book, for there is Ever the Living and Deepening of it into the Deepest Levels of Your Loving Self. For so long have you hated Self, punished Self, looked at Self with eyes that could not see, eyes that were always looking to a future you, of what you wanted to be, and eyes that could not sense at all the Beauty so Living within You. But, Dear Children of our Love, we have given you our **Vision of You**. Please do we ask you to Know, in your saddest moments or your moments of tremendous frustration or disappointment with Self, There are Others Who are of You, Who so Love You, Who See only Your Beauty and Lovingness, Who Give forth to You the Spirit of Deepest Love and Compassion for Self, for All of Self's wounds, and Who Share with You in Your Moments of Joy, the Intimacy and Wonder of the Joy in Self. So do we bring our Love to You and lift each experience to Ever Greater Heights, Expanding it from the confines of Self, and Blessing All the World with Your Joy . . .*

So do you see now, Dear Children, every time you are Sad, your Sadness meets with our Compassion of you, and you are no longer alone with it. We gather its energies. We take your Sadness into our Love, and so there do we nurture it, and give it back to you with the Compassion it was so seeking. And your Sadness will Live in you now in a New Way, for you will so feel Love towards it, and it will smile for you in Thankfulness for the Love in which you have placed it, and the smile will transform it into its own Loving Self. And so the same for your Joy . . . So will we bless each Joy and Happiness you have experienced and will experience, and we will deepen it into the Core of your Beingness, so that Your Joy will Touch and Bless your deepest wounds and cause them to Rise to a New Life within You. And we will Bless the Joy of Each of You as Rays of the Sun to fall upon All . . . Your Joy will be Complete, for the Joy of All Life will be Touched by your Own, and you will be Blessed with All the Joy that Ever Is or Was Experienced by Other. So will you then one day, Dear Children, Know of the Oneness we share with you. If you could but feel now just one Droplet of this Love, you would feel showered in the Light of the Shimmering Crystals. We give you this Light, for It is your Own . . . We give It to you here with Words that you will make Flesh . . . For so will you Create Your Life now with the Dreams of God and the Dreams of All Life, of All Those Who so Love and Cherish Your Life.

Dear Beloved Children, in our final Words for this book, we ask you to close your eyes for One Eternal Moment upon completing these Words, and Be . . .
The Angel of Light You so Are . . .
And so do we Love and Bless You Ever, Beloved Children of Healing Light and Love.

Coleman Publishing
99 Milbar Boulevard
Farmingdale, New York 11735
(516) 293-0383-84